HOW IRELAND VOTED 1989

HOW IRELAND VOTED 1989

Edited by

Michael Gallagher
Richard Sinnott

Centre for the Study of Irish Elections
University College Galway

A paperback original
first published in 1990 by the
Centre for the Study of Irish Elections
in association with PSAI Press
University College Galway

© Centre for the Study of Irish Elections, 1990

ISBN   0-9515731-0-1

Cover design and maps by Michael Laver

Page makeup by the
Centre for the Study of Irish Elections
University College Galway

Printed by SciPrint, Shannon

CONTENTS

Introduction   1

1   The campaign   *Brian Girvin*   5

2   Campaign strategies
and media coverage   *David M.Farrell*   23

3   On the campaign trail   *Charlie McCreevy (FF)*   44
    Ivan Yates (FG)   48
    Eithne FitzGerald (Lab)   52
    Geraldine Kennedy (PD)   57
    Pat McCartan (WP)   61
    Trevor Sargent (Greens)   64

4   The election results
and the new Dáil   *Michael Gallagher*   68

5   How the voters decided   *Michael Marsh*   94
    Richard Sinnott

6   The European
Parliament election   *Patrick Keatinge*   131
    Michael Marsh

7   The Senate election   *John Coakley*   148

8   The Udarás na
Gaeltachta election   *Tony Parker*   162

9   Forming the government   *Brian Farrell*   179

10   Coalition and
Fianna Fáil   *Michael Laver*   192
    Audrey Arkins

11   The Irish party system
into the 1990s   *Peter Mair*   208

Appendix: maps and tables   221

Notes on contributors   229

List of tables

2.1	Party expenditure on advertising, 1989 election	36
2.2	Newspaper coverage of the 1989 election	39
2.3	Newspaper coverage of policy issues	40
4.1	Seats changing hands at 1989 election	69
4.2	Party votes 1989 by province, with changes since 1987	70
4.3	Party seats 1989, with changes since 1987	71
4.4	Fianna Fáil's electoral record under four leaders 1932-1989	71
4.5	Parties' best and worst performances in 1989 relative to 1987	72
4.6	Destination of terminal transfers	79
4.7	Interparty relationships 1981-1989	80
4.8	Constituencies where transfers affected the outcome	81
4.9	Occupations of deputies elected in June 1989	85
4.10	Educational backgrounds of deputies	86
4.11	Women deputies	86
4.12	Local government background of deputies	87
4.13	Electoral experience of deputies in 26th Dáil	89
4.14	Fianna Fáil marginals at the next election	90
4.15	Non-Fianna Fáil marginals at the next election	91
5.1	Stability of voting intentions 1987-1989	98
5.2	Votes retained and won in the course of the campaign	100
5.3	Is it necessary to have an election at this time, or not?	102
5.4	Views on necessity of election, by satisfaction with government and voting intention	103
5.5	Perceptions of party leaders, May 1989	107
5.6	Important issues in the election	108
5.7	Important issues, by party supported	110
5.8	The most important issue	111
5.9	Most important issues, start and end of the campaign	112
5.10	Best policy on health and voting intention	113
5.11	Party with the best policy on health, by vote	114
5.12	Voting intention by perception of economic improvement	115
5.13	Perception of economic improvement, by class & voting intention	116
5.14	Attitudes to taxation and public expenditure by voting intention	117
5.15	Preference for government during course of campaign	119
5.16	Major factor in vote 1977-89	121
5.17	Reasons for switching	122
5.18	Voting intention by social class, 1987 and 1989	125
6.1	Party shares of seats and votes at 1989 EP election	137
6.2	Gains and losses from 1984 EP election	139
6.3	Differences between EP and general election results, 1989	141
6.4	Switchers, stayers and reasons for voting	143
6.5	Party choice at EP election and reason for vote	144
6.6	Supportive attitudes to the EC by EP vote	145

7.1   Approximate political composition of the Senate
electorate in 1977, 1981 and 1989   151
7.2   Distribution of electorate and of first preference votes in
Senate panel elections 1989, by party   152
7.3   Distribution of seats by sub-panel at Senate panel
elections 1954-1989   153
7.4   Party composition of Senate after 1987 and 1989
general elections   155
7.5   Regional distribution of Senate seats, 1989   157

8.1   The 1979 and 1984 Udarás na Gaeltachta elections   165
8.2   Candidates, party allegiance and home location   167
8.3   Results of the 1989 Udarás na Gaeltachta election   169
8.4   First preferences in the 1989 Udarás na Gaeltachta election   171
8.5   Candidates' percentage share of the votes and transfer patterns
in the Cork-Kerry-Ring constituency   172
8.6   Candidates' percentage share of the votes and transfer patterns
in the Donegal constituency   173
8.7   Candidates' percentage share of the votes and transfer patterns
in the Galway-Mayo-Meath constituency   175

9.1   Composition and duration of Irish governments   180

11.1   Voting for the class left in Europe, 1945-85   211

List of figures

2.1   Social class viewership of news   38

5.1   Trends in party support 1987-1989   95
5.2   Fianna Fáil support in different social classes   96
5.3   Government's popularity rating 1987-89   101
5.4   Mr Haughey's popularity rating 1981-1989   104
5.5   Mr Haughey's lead over Fine Gael leader 1987-1989   106

7.1   The flow of Irish parliamentarians, 1987-89   158

8.1   Udarás na Gaeltachta constituencies and candidates 1989   163

10.1   Two dimensions of policy in Irish politics   197

11.1   Alignment of parties on left-right dimension   214
11.2   Alignment of parties on secular-traditional dimension   215

Introduction

The election on 15 June 1989 made Ireland one of the few democracies ever to experience five general elections within one decade, and for a short period it seemed as if there might be a sixth and even a seventh before either the parties or the voters wilted and deferred to the wishes of the other. In the event the Irish electorate was spared this fate, and Irish political scientists, to the relief of most of them, were denied yet another mound of data to chew over.

But the ingredients of the June 1989 elections, especially the general election to Dáil Eireann, are quite sufficient on their own to provide the ingredients for an intriguing story, and thus to contradict the opinion of one strategist, quoted in Chapter 2, to the effect that "it was Dullsville all the way". The election itself was a subject of controversy. At the outset, the courts were invoked to test the claim that any election would be unconstitutional because the Dáil constituencies needed to be revised. Then many voters clearly remained unconvinced that the election should have been called at all, a factor which dogged Fianna Fáil's steps all the way to 15 June. The campaign proper was short, yet it witnessed a striking shift in opinion. The first polls suggested Fianna Fáil could hardly fail to win an overall majority; the last made it clear that the party would probably not even reach its 1987 figure of 81 seats. Between 25 May and 15 June, something decisive happened.

The results themselves seemed to indicate some settling down in the party system after the upheaval caused by the PDs' dramatic electoral debut in 1987, and yet the aftermath showed that Irish politics are still in an unusually fluid state. With no obvious government in sight, and various party leaders eyeball to eyeball with each other, events seemed to be leading inexorably to a July election, until the emergence of what was in some respects the most unlikely government of all, a coalition between Fianna Fáil and the PDs. The pattern of the last twenty years was maintained: every election since 1969 has produced a change of government. The outcome was also replete with irony. The spoils went to the only two parties to have lost seats; the "winners", the parties that gained seats, remained on the opposition benches. Bearing in mind also the reasons for the PDs' formation in the first place, the backgrounds of its TDs, and the fact that Fianna Fáil had always made a virtue of its opposition to the very principle of coalition, it is clear that the coalition agreement completed on 12 July 1989 marks a significant moment in Irish political history.

The 1987 election was analysed in *How Ireland Voted: the Irish general election of 1987*, a book edited by Michael Laver, Peter Mair and Richard Sinnott and published by Poolbeg in association with the PSAI Press. It aimed to provide a rapid but careful analysis, covering every aspect of the election while still appearing in print before the election had been completely forgotten by the wider public. The success of the earlier volume led to the idea of establishing a series, in which *How Ireland Voted 1989* now takes its place. As before, the emphasis has been on producing a readable yet considered analysis in the shortest feasible time.

The chapters in this book give a comprehensive account of the 1989 general election and its aftermath. The background to the election, and the campaign itself, are covered by Brian Girvin, while David Farrell in the second chapter deals with the strategies employed by party head offices and their advertising agencies to sell their products to the public, and with the way the media covered the campaign. Michael Gallagher charts the ebb and flow of votes and seats between parties around the country, and in Chapter 5 Michael Marsh and Richard Sinnott provide a detailed analysis of the findings of the many opinion polls carried out during the campaign. The wealth of data available enables them to discuss just what went wrong for Fianna Fáil: which groups switched their support, which issues were the most important, and what role other factors played in determining the way people voted.

One of the most dramatic aspects of the general election was the formation of the coalition government, the subtle twists and turns of whose construction are detailed in Chapter 9 by Brian Farrell. Another perspective on the emergence of the Fianna Fáil-PD coalition is provided by Michael Laver and Audrey Arkins, who consider how well it fits in with the theory of coalition formation and with conventional views about what the parties stand for. In the book's final chapter, Peter Mair discusses 1989's implications for the future, and raises the possibility that Fianna Fáil may henceforth be a permanent fixture in government.

There is always the danger, of course, of academics looking for a coherence and a pattern in elections that is not there in the eyes of participants. Consequently, in Chapter 3, candidates from six different parties give an account of their own constituency campaign. What they write does not bear out the view that candidates are merely cogs in a machine run from party headquarters. On the contrary, the picture to emerge is that candidates have to fight their own fight in their own constituencies, often with little or no contact with head office throughout the campaign. The whole perspective at local level is sometimes very different from that of the national strategists. One candidate even goes so far as to say that, at bottom, all that matters on the campaign trail is whether at the end of it you get elected; who forms the next government is another day's work entirely. Candidates live, eat and breathe the campaign, and are generally too busy knocking on doors, avoiding the Rottweilers, speaking at after-mass meetings or pressing the flesh at Dart stations to be concerned with the nuances of the marketing strategies devised at headquarters. Some of the contributors to Chapter 3 were elected, some were not; they all have useful advice for would-be TDs on what to do and what not to do.

Of course, we should not forget that there were other elections too taking place in the summer of 1989. Until April, it seemed as if the major political event of the summer would be the third direct elections to the European Parliament. In the event, the EP elections were inevitably overshadowed by the Dáil election, but with the approach of 1992 and the single European market their significance should not be underrated. They are analysed by Patrick Keatinge and Michael Marsh, while in Chapter 7 John Coakley writes about the politicians' private election, the largely hidden but ruthlessly competitive battle for the Seanad seats. Another "forgotten election" was that for Udarás na Gaeltachta, covered by Tony Parker.

In putting the book together, the editors have not tried to impose a uniform perspective on authors. As readers will discover, there are different views within the academic community on such questions as whether Fianna Fáil is to the right or the left of Fine Gael, and there are also different interpretations of the significance of the coalition agreement. The book reflects just a part of the work being done by Irish political scientists, whose efforts have been aided and encouraged in recent years by the Political Studies Association of Ireland (PSAI), which was founded in 1982 to promote the study of politics in and of Ireland, north and south. The PSAI now has a membership of about 160, mainly drawn from departments of politics in third level institutions, of whom just over a half are based in Ireland, the rest being based in Britain, continental Europe, north America, Australia or Japan. The Association holds an annual conference and other meetings, and publishes an annual journal, *Irish Political Studies* (now into its fifth volume), which contains articles on Irish politics, reports, book reviews, a data section and a comprehensive bibliography of works on Irish politics. Further information on the PSAI is available from the Association's secretary at the Department of Politics, Trinity College, Dublin 2.

3

Introduction

The editors would like to express their thanks to all those who made this book possible. Pride of place must go to the contributors. The academic contributors delivered high quality typescripts fairly promptly, three of them even meeting the agreed deadline. The six politician contributors brought a note of hard-headed political experience into the book. Three TDs took time off from their important legislative work (and their clinics), and three unsuccessful candidates relived some painful moments. This book is published by the Centre for the Study of Irish Elections at University College Galway, and we would like to thank the President of UCG, Colm O hEocha, for having the enlightenment to make this possible. Finally, Michael Laver has made a major contribution throughout to the project. He was instrumental in arranging its publication, and has subsequently taken on responsibility for many aspects of the production process, and we should like to express our appreciation for his determination that this book should see the light of day, and for his strenuous efforts which have ensured that it has.

Michael Gallagher
Richard Sinnott

Dublin, January 1990

4

1. The campaign
Brian Girvin

THE OUTGOING GOVERNMENT

When Charles J. Haughey, Taoiseach and leader of the Fianna Fáil party dissolved Dáil Eireann on 25 May 1989, he brought to an end an unprecedented period in Irish politics. Between March 1987 and May 1989 Mr Haughey had led a minority Fianna Fáil administration which was dependent on the support of Fine Gael and the Progressive Democrats, its erstwhile competitors in the electoral arena, to remain in government. This was but one of the many ironies in Irish politics during the 1980s. Alone among Irish political parties, Fianna Fáil had refused to share power, and while it has previously maintained minority administrations, the experience of 1987 to 1989 differed considerably from previous tenures in office. Another irony was the extent to which the Fianna Fáil administration implemented the policies which it had opposed during the 1987 election campaign. During most of that campaign, Fianna Fáil had stressed its traditional commitment to growth, social partnership and strategies to reduce unemployment. Yet by the end of of a defensive campaign, Fianna Fáil had effectively accepted the main objectives of the parties to its right.[1]

At the February 1987 election Fianna Fáil had increased its representation from 75 to 81 seats but was still short of an overall majority. Even so, it was strongly placed to form a government, and in contrast to previous elections the balance within the Dáil favoured this outcome. In November 1982 there had been two clear alternatives: a Fianna Fáil government (unlikely in the circumstances), or a Coalition between Fine Gael and Labour (the actual outcome). By February 1987 government formation had become more complex. There was no foundation for an alternative government, as the opposition was now more fragmented than at any time since the 1950s. Even if Fine Gael, the Progressive Democrats and the Labour Party had combined they could not have formed a majority government, and could not have depended on the eight other votes of the Workers' Party and independents to achieve a stable majority. The opposition's fragmentation facilitated Fianna Fáil's formation of a government and contributed to its stability. In particular, relations between Fine Gael and the Progressive Democrats were not good, while the Labour Party was stressing its independence of the centre-right parties. In theory the government was always at risk, but in practice, adroit manoeuvring permitted Fianna Fáil to dominate the Dáil for over two years. The arithmetic in the Dáil has to be related, however, to policy. Throughout this period there were different majorities for different issues. The most clearcut consensus concerned fiscal and budgetary policy. Besides the votes of its own deputies, Fianna Fáil could attract those of Fine Gael and usually the Progressive Democrats on these issues. In addition, on questions relating to Northern Ireland or to Anglo-Irish relations, the government could command an overwhelming majority among deputies even when there were doubts among its own supporters as, for example, was the case when extradition was debated. There was also a corporatist/welfarist majority available, comprising the government, the Labour Party, the Workers' Party and some of the independents. As a consequence, privatization, which was advocated by both the Progressive Democrats and Fine Gael, was not seriously entertained during the lifetime of the Dáil.

The key to Fianna Fáil's success lay with its newfound commitment to fiscal probity and its willingness to ruthlessly cut public spending. Between 1977 and 1982 the national debt had almost trebled from £4,200m to £11,700m. Under the 1982-1987 Coalition government, which was nominally committed to restricting borrowing, the national debt had almost doubled again (to £21,600m) by the end of 1986. The exchequer borrowing requirement as a percentage of gross national product stood at 13 per cent by early 1987. Although inflation had declined to 3.8 per cent by 1987 from its double digit high of 1982, most other indicators were negative: economic growth had been slow or stagnant for most of the 1980s, real income fell in most years up to 1987, and there was little growth in gross national product for most of this time. The 1987 budget demonstrated Fianna Fáil's commitment to controlling public spending; it was considerably more deflationary than both the proposals which marked the end of the Fine Gael / Labour Coalition and the later Fine Gael budget estimates which had been criticised by Fianna Fáil during the election.

The severe cuts which were introduced had a serious effect on the public sector and resulted in a substantial rise in unemployment between 1987 and 1989. By June 1989 unemployment stood at over 240,000. This number did not include the significant exodus of young emigrants: estimates for the year ending April 1989 concluded that over 40,000 may have left the country during the previous year. Nevertheless, Fianna Fáil's economic policy was remarkably successful in other areas. Strong economic growth was in evidence after February 1987, in part a reflection of good international

6

conditions, but also due to Irish industrialists' belief that the government was following policies which contributed to growth and stability. By 1988 inflation was down to two per cent (considerably lower than that of the United Kingdom); for those in work real income and living standards improved in absolute terms and the balance of payments was in surplus. By the time the election was called the exchequer borrowing requirement as a percentage of gross national product stood at six per cent, half of what it had been in 1986, and continued to decline. A further reflection of new found confidence in Ireland's fiscal policy came when the punt was more closely aligned with the European Monetary System and interest rates were no longer linked with those of the United Kingdom. There has now been an unprecedented gap in the British and Irish interest rates for over a year, highlighting the independence of Irish fiscal policy and weakening further the historic link between the two currencies.

Fianna Fáil succeeded in implementing most of its policies because it recognised the delicate nature of its minority status, and because it accepted that on fiscal and monetary policy it could not advocate expansionary measures. Yet what is surprising is how little opposition there was in the Dáil to the policies and their consequences. The left provided the main focus for opposition but, given its size and divisions, could not hope to obstruct government legislation. Obstruction could occur only if all the opposition groups combined against the government. Two factors prevented this. One was the government's sensitivity to the possibility of defeat, as a result of which it rarely introduced legislation which would induce the opposition to combine. More important was the recognition that the government was implementing policies with which a sizeable section of the opposition concurred. After all, the 1987 and 1988 budgets had been passed comfortably with the support of Fine Gael. The consensus on economic policy was given powerful public support in September 1987 when Alan Dukes, the newly-elected leader of Fine Gael, argued that those who accepted the need for cuts had a duty to support the government and not act negatively. It appears clear that while one of Dukes's motives in formulating the so-called Tallaght Strategy was to avoid another election which Fine Gael was not in a position to fight, he was also responding to the belief that action had to be taken to reduce the national debt. With this support the government was unlikely to be defeated on a major issue.

This right wing consensus on fiscal policy was not an example of Thatcherism Irish style. The Thatcherites (Fine Gael and the Progressive Democrats) were outside the Cabinet and were not able to influence the details of government policy. This can be seen in the government's decision to return to national pay bargaining and to reach agreement with the "social partners" on the broad outlines of a social contract. *The Programme For National Recovery* was accepted by government, employers, the farming organizations and the trade unions in October 1987. It underpinned the political consensus which had been achieved on the economy by providing a framework for a similar consensus among the corporate interests. This was not a unique departure in Irish politics; there had been a series of tripartite agreements during the 1970s which had led to high levels of corporatist intermediation by 1979, when the first National Understanding had been negotiated.[2] However, in the context of the 1980s it was unusual. In the United Kingdom, and elsewhere in Europe, the corporatist structures which had been designed during the 1960s and 1970s were often dismantled or reduced to ineffectiveness. In Ireland, similarly, corporatism appeared dead by 1980 and the Coalition government in particular made no attempt to revive the earlier structures.

Fianna Fáil's decision to reactivate corporatism, which may appear surprising when contrasted with its newfound approach to economic policy, was based on a number of considerations. Most importantly, the party has a significant working class constituency, which would be seriously affected by cutbacks. Arrangements with the trade unions could deflect some of the expected criticism. It should also be recognized that Fianna Fáil has never been monetarist or neo-liberal in ideological terms. Its decision to introduce controls over expenditure was based on the fear that national sovereignty and integrity would be impaired if action was not quickly undertaken. *The Programme for National Recovery* served two purposes; it allowed the government to claim that a wide-ranging national consensus had been achieved on economic policy and it could demonstrate that Fianna Fáil retained its traditional links with working class organisations.

The social partnership involved in the programme included government, farmers, employers and trade unions, and all agreed on the need for consensus. However, the main strategic aim of the programme was to gain agreement from the trade union movement for a degree of wage restraint. The tone of the programme differed considerably from earlier exercises in corporatism. Whereas previous arrangements had assumed that economic growth and full employment were easily obtainable, a more sober mood is now detectable. While the introduction to the Programme states that all participants are 'conscious of the grave state of our economic and social life, [and] have agreed on this Programme to seek to regenerate our economy and improve the social equity of our society through their combined efforts', the main objective of the agreement is the "creation of a fiscal exchange rate and monetary climate conductive to economic growth". At the heart of the macroeconomic policy are essentially monetary and fiscal targets. These targets, once achieved, it is claimed, would contribute to generating new employment opportunities. In contrast to the 1970s when full employment was the primary objective, the policies of 1987-1989 presupposed solving debt, fiscal and monetary difficulties as a precondition for dealing with unemployment. Again, unlike the earlier phase, the agreement on wages was realistic in that the parties subscribed to a maximum increase of 2.5 per cent per annum over the years 1988 to 1990.[3]

There can be little doubt that the wage restrictions agreed between 1987 and 1989 contributed to the stabilization of the economy. The Minister for Labour stated in 1989 that the number of industrial disputes was at its lowest level for nearly thirty years and that few of the actual disputes could be attributed to the demand for wages. The rise in real income contributed to this acquiescence but so also did the recognition that in the absence of the Programme, only the best organised workers would benefit in an environment of high unemployment. By reactivating corporatist arrangements which had been absent from policy-making since the early 1980s, it gave the Irish Congress of Trade Unions (ICTU) access to and influence over government decision making for the first time since 1980. Such arrangements also meant that 'new right' policies such as privatization would not be introduced.

THE POLITICAL PARTIES 1987-1989

Fianna Fáil's considerations in most of these initiatives were essentially political. Charles Haughey had failed to achieve a majority on each of the four elections into which he had led the party. Consequently, the actions of the government have to be analysed as part of a wider search for an overall majority as well as a response to specific economic problems facing the country. The collapse of Fine Gael's vote at the 1987 election and its subsequent support for the government's budgetary strategy seemed to confirm Haughey's claim that only Fianna Fáil could achieve a stable government with sustained economic growth. This belief rested on the assumption that a marginal shift in voter preferences would provide Fianna Fáil with a parliamentary majority. Moreover, Fianna Fáil's decision to engage in corporatist politics with ICTU could be seen to undermine the importance of the left in the Dáil; there was considerable anger in the Labour Party towards ICTU, which was criticised for making Fianna Fáil's path easier than had been the case with Labour when it was in Coalition.

The reality was more complex than this, however. In February 1987 Fianna Fáil had received just over 44 per cent of the vote, after experiencing a sustained drop in its opinion poll ratings prior to the election. The most that could be said of the outcome was that a significant section of the electorate withheld support from Fianna Fáil when it came to voting. Nor did the new Fianna Fáil administration win acclaim for its newfound economic policies in the short-term. There was considerable dissatisfaction with the government throughout 1987. The consequences of its public expenditure cuts affected large numbers of people and by November 1987 only 29 per cent were satisfied with its performance. There was also a precipitous decline in the proportion of the electorate who were intending to vote for Fianna Fáil by the end of 1987, while Charles Haughey's own popularity also suffered. This loss of support can be attributed to the specific policies introduced by the new government, but it is also a consequence of Fianna Fáil's decision to implement policies which it had criticised during the election as unfair and unnecessary.

Fianna Fáil's electoral fortunes began to recover during 1988. Between February 1988 and February 1989, and as a consequence of two well received budgets, satisfaction with the governing party improved considerably; by February 1989 45 per cent of those interviewed (a majority if the undecided are excluded) indicated a preference for Fianna Fáil if an election were held at that time. In contrast, support for the other parties remained stable or declined throughout this period. The most striking feature by early 1989 was the popularity of Charles Haughey; two thirds considered that his performance as Taoiseach was satisfactory. This was the best rating that he had received during his tenure in office. It is all the more significant as hitherto Haughey had proved a liability in attracting all but the most dedicated Fianna Fáil supporters. But notwithstanding the very real success which Fianna Fáil had registered during 1988, the increased support was of recent origin and could not be guaranteed in a future election, a point explored more fully by Michael Marsh and Richard Sinnott in Chapter 5 below.

Yet Fianna Fáil had reasons to be optimistic. The real upturn in its popularity, as measured by voting intentions and satisfaction with the government, did not come until early 1989 when, for the first time, more people are satisfied than dissatisfied with the government. Three factors help to explain this outcome. The first is the relative success of Fianna Fáil's budgetary strategy both in economic terms, as outlined above, and in political terms. The three budgets introduced by the government, the consensual approach to fiscal policy, and the belief that the actions taken were in the best interests of the country, all contributed to Fianna Fáil's new-found attractiveness. What can be seen during 1988 and early 1989 is a strong current of support for the government strategy among the wealthy, the middle-class, and large farmers. The 1988 budget in February was particularly well received, with only 29 per cent believing that living standards would fall. The subsequent increase in support for the government appears to have ensued when experience showed that the cutbacks did not necessarily affect all sections of the population. This conclusion is confirmed by the further rise in support following the February 1989 budget. The most striking feature of the 1989 data is that while the proportion believing the budget was bad for the country declined so did those who considered it good. Fianna Fáil appears to have benefited in popularity from its two years of austerity.

The second factor which helps to explain this is the decision by Fine Gael in 1987 to support the government. If it had not done so the government might well have collapsed, and another election would have been necessary. Alan Dukes, the newly elected leader, wished to avoid an election and, at the same time, to consolidate his position within the party. The Tallaght Strategy fulfilled the first of these objectives, although as an act of statesmanship it did not increase the party's poll rating to any significant degree. Dukes also faced internal opposition to the leadership strategy. Austin Deasy, a leading member of the front bench, resigned early in 1988 in what was clearly a challenge to Dukes. The main consequence of this was to facilitate Dukes' consolidation; he reshuffled the front bench later in the year, removing those known to be identified with Deasy and appointing TDs close to his own position.

The third factor was the virtual collapse of the Progressive Democrats' support base following the 1987 election. The other opposition parties held their own throughout the tenure of the government, but the Progressive Democrats, who had done so well in the election and promised to radically change the direction of Irish politics, now faced the erosion of much of their support. This support in any event had been fluid, a type of urban protest vote blended with that section of Fianna Fáil which had been attracted by the former Taoiseach Jack Lynch and his commitment to economic development. However, during the 1987 election the Progressive Democrats had won most of their seats from Fine Gael rather than Fianna Fáil, although the latter was probably deprived of seats in a number of constituencies due to the presence of Progressive Democrat candidates.[4]

Once Fianna Fáil adopted a policy of fiscal constraint, the distinctiveness of the Progressive Democrats disappeared. As such, its electoral base was squeezed from the centre by Fianna Fáil and from the right by Fine Gael. Fine Gael recognised the danger to its own support base, and sought to assert itself as *the* opposition party while at the same time demonstrating its responsibility by its public support for the government. Fianna Fáil also prevented any further drift of support to the Progressive Democrats; its ability to dictate the political agenda contributed to this, as did its refusal to simply embrace the PDs' new right ideology. The Progressive Democrats could be condemned as extremist, and initiatives such as the Programme for National Development could be used to distance Fianna Fáil from their policies. Nor was their image as a radical party helped by the sequence of events that occurred when they introduced a draft constitution to replace the existing 1937 Constitution. The new document embraced an essentially secularist world view in an attempt to replace the Catholic nationalist ethos of *Bunreacht na hÉireann.* Controversy arose when the draft document left out any reference to God in the preamble; after criticism from political opponents and party members, the leadership reversed the earlier decision. A special conference was called, and the preamble was amended to restore God to his primary position.

Fianna Fáil was the main beneficiary of these developments. By the beginning of 1989 it was clearly in the political ascendancy. Haughey was at his most confident and authoritative as leader while the party's popularity continued to increase. Pressure began to build up for an election after the successful February budget. Two points of view were discernible by the end of March 1989. The first of these insisted that Fianna Fáil's popularity would not necessarily be translated into votes and seats if an election was called. This group urged Haughey to wait for at least another year and to allow the opposition to precipitate the election, thus giving the government the moral high ground. The other view maintained that Fianna Fáil should now maximize the support available to it, and that to postpone an election would mean that when the next election eventually came it would be fought under less advantageous conditions. Opinion within the party swung in favour of the optimists during April, and Haughey himself made the decision when his government suffered a Dáil defeat on 26 April over the issue of additional funding to haemophiliacs suffering from the AIDS virus.

While the opposition did not accept that the defeat would precipitate an election, opinion within Fianna Fáil had discernibly hardened. Haughey and his close advisors believed that the opposition could or should not dictate to the government on money matters, and the absence of a majority meant that the threat of defeat was always there. The government had in fact been defeated on only six occasions during the life of the Dáil, but the arithmetic indicated that the government remained dependent on the good will of the opposition, and particularly on Fine Gael, and was consequently vulnerable. This was a situation which could not last indefinitely, and both Fianna Fáil and Fine Gael activists were questioning *when* rather than *if* the consensus would end. The vote on AIDS confirmed many in Fianna Fáil in their belief that Fine Gael was taking a far more discretionary approach to the consensus than hitherto. Moreover, the unusual circumstances of the consensus rested uneasily with most Fianna Fáil members. They disliked the dependence on Fine Gael, believing that in the longer term it might erode the party's distinctiveness and independence. The consequence of these considerations was that Haughey dissolved the Dáil on 25 May, with the election to be held on 15 June.

THE DISSOLUTION

There were a number of considerations behind the decision to dissolve the Dáil. Opinion was running in favour of the party, its leader and its policies. The worst of the recession was over and the government believed it could benefit from this and from having taken hard decisions during the previous two years. It also calculated that it could stabilise its vote at or around 50 per cent and at the very least achieve a net gain of eight from among the fourteen or so marginal seats which it had identified as being within its grasp. More profoundly, Fianna Fáil intensely disliked the reality of sharing power with anyone. While this might appear irrational to continental Europeans, it has been act of faith in Fianna Fáil for over fifty years. Fianna Fáil's patience had been exhausted by April 1989, and the party was glad to discard what it regarded as an artificial arrangement. The European elections were in any event scheduled for 15 June, and this provided an ideal opportunity to twin the two elections.

The initiative lay with Fianna Fáil from the outset. Charles Haughey insisted from the moment of dissolution that a majority for Fianna Fáil would be the main issue in the campaign. This majority was required 'to enable the government to carry out its programme without interruption, and to tackle the twin problems of unemployment and emigration'. The early campaign strategy concentrated on the need for this majority; an overall majority would be in the national interest, it was claimed, as it would allow the government to complete its objectives. Haughey supplemented this approach by arguing that a minority government was unstable, and that the uncertainty this engendered would lead to defeat on financial estimates in the future. In addition, the threat of defeat should not be allowed to undermine Ireland's forthcoming Presidency of the European Community. Haughey added that the public now recognised the need for financial restraint; one of the consequences of this recognition was that the social partners in the *Programme for National Development* had "agreed to the measures and the restraint necessary to generate growth". Fianna Fáil publicity at this stage in the campaign implied that its actions over the previous two years had received widespread support, and that an electoral majority would reflect this.

The decision to call the election was criticised by sections of the media often hostile to the Fianna Fáil party. It was argued that the informal consensus provided a secure basis for government and that none of the defeats in the Dáil had been on an issue of confidence. The former Taoiseach Dr Garret FitzGerald made this explicit, and confirmed that Fine Gael had not changed its view on supporting the government on the major fiscal issues. He also claimed that "the only Fianna Fáil government which people have found in any way acceptable is one with Fine Gael support", adding that at no time was the Fianna Fáil budgetary strategy at risk. FitzGerald was once again raising the question of Haughey's competence, and he referred specifically to the one time that Haughey had an overall majority, the period from December 1979 to June 1981, when serious doubts were raised about the behaviour of Haughey and those close to him in the exercise of power.[5] Despite this, Fianna Fáil was clearly hoping to break the cycle which had existed in Irish politics since 1981. No single party had won an overall majority at any of the elections; minority or coalition government had been the norm. Indeed, the greatest degree of instability in recent Irish politics had occurred between 1981 and 1982, and not during either the formal coalition government of 1982 to 1987 or the informal consensus of 1987 to 1989.

For a short time the status of the election itself was in doubt. Its constitutionality was challenged on the grounds that some constituencies were under-represented and others over-represented, and that an election should not take place until the necessary rearrangements had taken place. The threat to the holding of the election disappeared when Mr Justice Hamilton, in the High Court, refused to grant an injunction restraining the Taoiseach from advising the President to dissolve the Dáil.

The Progressive Democrats were placed in a difficult position when it was announced that their deputy leader Michael Keating would not be standing, nor would John McCoy of Limerick West. Other well known names not standing in the election included John Kelly and Gemma Hussey, Tom Fitzpatrick and Donal Creed, all of Fine Gael. Patrick Cooney and Barry Desmond had also left the Dáil and were now running for the European Parliament. One of the early surprises was the decision by Austin Currie of the SDLP to seek and subsequently win a nomination for Fine Gael in Dublin West. This continued the party's desire, which first surfaced when John Cushnahan became a party candidate for Munster in the European Parliament election, to attract Northern politicians who wished to play a new political role in the Republic.

14

EARLY STAGES OF THE CAMPAIGN

During the first few days of campaigning Fianna Fáil seemed to have the advantage, emphasising its not inconsiderable record and suggesting that it alone could secure a majority. To counter this, Fine Gael and the Progressive Democrats formulated an "Agreed Agenda for Action" on May 27. The agreed statement by the parties attempted to capitalise on the favourable reception which the consensus on economic policy had received. Accordingly,

this election has been brought about unnecessarily by Mr. Haughey alone, who in recent months, and most particularly since April 26th, has explicitly rejected and set his face against any consensus approach to politics in the Dáil. He has turned his back on the most constructive phase in Irish politics for many decades.

Notwithstanding this criticism, the Progressive Democrats and Fine Gael accepted Fianna Fáil's challenge and agreed that the formation of a government was the key issue. The two parties recognised that each had much in common and consequently could co-operate on solving the economic and social problems which the country faced. The agreed agenda included a commitment to reduce the exchequer borrowing requirement to three per cent or less of gross national product by 1993, while the control of public expenditure would remain a high priority. Two rates of taxation (25 and 40 per cent) would be introduced, while PRSI would be reformed and the tax system would provide incentives for the use of labour as well as investment. £30 million would be allocated from the National Lottery in an emergency programme for the health sector, although it was admitted that other beneficiaries of the Lottery would lose out as a consequence.

The pact was immediately attacked by Fianna Fáil, which claimed it was a marriage of convenience to create the impression that an alternative government was possible. On the contrary, it alleged, any transfer of seats would take place between Fine Gael and the Progressive Democrats rather than between Fianna Fáil and either of these two parties. Fianna Fáil's scepticism concerning the pact carried considerable weight. Although he had agreed to the pact, Alan Dukes remained distinctly wary about the commitment involved. He refused when pressed subsequently to give a clear undertaking that Fine Gael would transfer lower preferences to the Progressive Democrats, which was in stark contrast to the position taken by his predecessor prior to the 1987 election. Dukes was calculating that a number of variables would work to his party's advan-

15

tage. The decline in Progressive Democrat support between the two elections could benefit Fine Gael if Dukes could present the party as the main opposition force, something he believed possible following the successful arrangements with Fianna Fáil. However, he also had to offer the Progressive Democrats enough support to obtain a pact which would create the possibility of an alternative government, maintain the Progressive Democrats in a weak position, and obtain the transfers necessary to increase his party's representation. The impression left at this time was that Dukes was in the dominant position, while the Progressive Democrats were experiencing considerable disarray.

This point was confirmed when the Fine Gael manifesto was published on 30 May. This document followed most of the themes contained in the agreed agenda, but its tax bands were 27 per cent and 45 per cent rather than the 25 per cent and 40 per cent promised in the former. For Fine Gael, as for the Progressive Democrats, but not for Fianna Fáil, the economic issues involved the overall reduction of state participation in the economy. Thus, in contrast to Fianna Fáil, Fine Gael proposed to privatize areas of the semi-state sector. The emphasis is on creating market conditions which would induce growth rather than to politically generate these conditions: "tax reform is a pre-requisite to the growth rates we require to put people back to work". In addition, the manifesto criticised Fianna Fáil for breaking up the consensus and reemphasised the continuation of Fine Gael's "New Politics", asserting that Fianna Fáil could not be trusted.

Nor did the Progressive Democrats' manifesto offer a radical alternative to the other parties on the centre right. There were points of difference but these were nuances rather than elements of substance. The proposals on the exchequer borrowing requirement, PRSI and tax reform had already appeared in the agreed agenda, and the manifesto did not expand on these. The Progressive Democrats did propose to privatize some sectors and to continue expenditure cuts where necessary, but these were not enough to offer a distinguishable programme. It would appear that the Progressive Democrats had been marginalised by the two other parties on the right.[6]

Tensions also existed on the left, and these increased during the campaign. During the previous Dail, a loose co-operative arrangement had been maintained between the Labour Party, the Workers' Party, Jim Kemmy of the Democratic Socialist Party, and independent deputy Tony Gregory. This arrangement had been based on common hostility to the retrenchment strategy of Fianna Fáil and what was considered to be a right wing consensus in the Dáil. Not that the left could achieve much during the lifetime of the government; its total vote was lower than at any time during the 1980s, and it could hope only to combine with Fine Gael and the

Progressive Democrats on very specific issues to influence the government. Moreover, there were very real differences between the main left-wing groups: the Labour Party and Jim Kemmy remain within the European Social Democratic tradition, with its roots in the democratic, liberal and reformist approach to politics, while the Workers' Party has its origins in one wing of the IRA, but is now closely aligned with the Marxist-Leninist Communist movement. Although the left wing parties are in agreement on a wide range of issues, there remain deep ideological divisions among them. On a practical level, Dick Spring refused to agree to a formal arrangement for the transfer of votes between the Labour Party and the Workers' Party, although he was prepared to advise his supporters to transfer to other left-wing candidates, which included not only the Workers' Party but also the DSP, the Green Party and Gregory. Despite Spring's attitude, individual Labour candidates, such as Michael D. Higgins, did enter into voting transfer arrangements with the Workers' Party.

The manifestoes and policy documents issued by both the Labour Party and the Workers' Party highlight the dilemma for the left. Both parties called for the creation of a left-wing alternative to what was described as Thatcherism, monetarism, or the New Right. The need for an independent left-wing voice was considered of vital importance to left politics; indeed, each party insisted that it would not support a minority Fianna Fáil government if that possibility occurred. Dick Spring declared that his party's aim was to achieve a balance of power between the two groups of right wing parties. This was rather fanciful unless the left increased its vote in unprecedented fashion. The electoral arithmetic dictated that the left would remain a protest bloc reflecting those sections of the voters hostile to cutbacks. The Labour Party manifesto proposed the introduction of democratic economic planning to secure full employment. To achieve this aim the public sector would play a decisive part, and the manifesto contained a commitment to allow state borrowing to rise in order that high levels of investment could be maintained. These proposals and those of the Workers' Party did not ring true as preparatory documents for government, but rather operated as symbols around which opposition to the government could be generated.[7]

The Green Party and Sinn Féin also produced manifestoes. These parties reflect much narrower interests than those on the left or the right. The Greens emphasized the need for a radical reordering of the modern economic and social structure. Their concerns go well beyond those of pollution and the environment and reflect a deep hostility to industrial society, warning that this type of social organisation is the cause of the major ills of the world and will lead to catastrophe. The Green Party offered

The campaign

the most ideological programme to the electorate and one far from the mainstream of Irish politics. If the Greens challenged the consensus on growth, Sinn Féin attempted to benefit from an appeal to an older consensus, that of nationalism. Although the party offers policies on the economy, its major interest is to reflect the aims of the Provisional IRA. Its manifesto calls for an independent Ireland, the ending of extradition and the censorship of the party, and a declaration by the British to withdraw from Northern Ireland.[8]

THE CAMPAIGN UNDER WAY

The Fianna Fáil manifesto "National Recovery: The Next Phase" reiterated in more detail what had already been published in the *Programme for National Development* and *The National·Development Plan*. The party remained strongly committed to a policy of fiscal restraint. Most of the projections were fiscal, and while the manifesto assured its readers that with inflation down and unemployment declining the economic outlook was positive, it did not offer the hope of a significant increase in public spending. An extremely comprehensive document, 116 pages long, it was published late in the campaign and was designed to promote the merits and successes of the government while dismissing the challenge of the opposition. In addition to publicising the government successes and promising progress in the future the manifesto stressed three interrelated themes. It maintained that the foundations for economic growth had been laid, that this was a consequence of social partnership, and that all this would be endangered if Fianna Fáil did not achieve its overall majority. Furthermore, "Fianna Fáil has fulfilled all the key undertakings we gave the Irish people in our 1987 Election Programme, to create conditions for growth, to control expenditure, to reduce taxation and to develop the sectors with good employment potential". The main political message was that constraints on government spending would remain tight, but that Fianna Fáil should obtain a majority because of its achievements. Consequently, "A return to weak Coalition Government divided on policy and ideology would be disastrous at this stage."[9]

Within a day of publication of the manifesto, Fianna Fáil had changed electoral tactics. Responding now to the new mood in the electorate and to the possibility of a shift to the left, both Fianna Fáil and Fine Gael warned that voting for the left would bring about instability. Mr Haughey warned that if the left wing parties achieved a balance of power in the new Dáil the achievements of the previous two years would be placed in jeopardy. The Minister for Finance Albert Reynolds believed

18

that the electorate could not welcome a return to "the chronic instability of the 1980s, with three elections in 18 months." The confidence and prosperity recently achieved by his government would be seriously impaired if the left increased its support. He also estimated that the Workers' Party proposals would cost £560 million while those of the Labour Party were costed at £220 million. In either case instability would result. The government had decided to highlight what was in fact an imaginary threat from the left. The fear that the left would hold the balance of power was unwarranted. It assumed that the lines between the government and opposition, or more particularly between Fianna Fáil and all other parties, were clearly demarcated. The Tallaght strategy had demonstrated that these lines were blurred, a point confirmed by the Fine Gael spokesman on Finance Michael Noonan, who assured the electorate that his party would not allow left wing parties to hold the government or the country to ransom.[10]

Once such a commitment had been given by Fine Gael (and one can assume that the Progressive Democrats were supportive of such an approach), then the only question which remained was the extent to which the electorate would punish the government for its policies. As a result, all the parties on the right continued to jockey for position, in the belief that each could benefit from voters' disillusionment with one or other of the parties. A joint Fine Gael/Progressive Democrat press conference held on 8 June insisted that they offered a viable alternative to Fianna Fáil and were well placed to form a government. Desmond O'Malley asserted that Fine Gael and the Progressive Democrats were "like minded parties, and there is broad compatibility between our policy priorities". He also appeared to offer a point of distinction between these two parties on the one hand and Fianna Fáil on the other, in that the former favoured "a political system that ensures high standards in high places from those who aspire to high places." Each of the party leaders reiterated his belief that there could be no compromise with the left wing parties in the event of a hung Dáil.

Left wing criticism of policy continued to concern the government. Throughout the latter stages of the campaign socialism was attacked as a failed economic dogma unsuited to Irish conditions. Mr Reynolds returned to this theme on a number of occasions; he claimed that the Workers' Party programme would lead to the demise of private employers and that the full implementation of its economic strategy would increase emigration, double the numbers unemployed, and bankrupt the country. Nor were the prospects much better, he added, if the Labour Party's proposals were implemented. For Reynolds any result other than a Fianna Fáil majority would lead to political chaos, which in turn would undermine all the achievements of the government. This criticism of the left was combined with a strategy which sought to highlight the main defects of the previous coalition government and to discredit any possibility of a future alliance. In an advertising campaign shortly before polling day the stability of a majority Fianna Fáil government was juxtaposed with what was characterised as multi-party chaos. Fianna Fáil's successes were emphasised while the failures of the 1982-1987 Coalition government were given prominence. The advertisements pointed out that on the basis of existing Dáil representation it would require an alliance of at least four parties to form an alternative government. Such an arrangement was deemed to be impossible, as the basic objectives of the left wing parties were incompatible with those of Fine Gael and the Progressive Democrats. What Fianna Fáil refused to consider was the possibility of a coalition of right wing parties, an arrangement which had been promoted by the left as the most rational outcome as there was general agreement among them on many policy issues.

By this time Fianna Fáil was clearly on the defensive, although the party would not admit defeat. Its biggest setback came when Haughey admitted on the Pat Kenny radio show that he had not been aware of the hardships caused by the health cuts. In response to a query Haughey accepted that "I have to admit that's true. We were not aware - I personally wasn't aware of the full extent of the problems and difficulties and hardships it was causing." He added that now that the government was aware of the problem it was willing to respond to it. Although Haughey promised that resources would be made available for health in the next budget he was extremely cautious about commitments.[11] The following day he promised that there would be no more expenditure cuts if Fianna Fáil won the election, as the necessary cuts had already been made. Despite this, Haughey was not prepared to offer extra financial support, and he criticised the Fine Gael proposals for increased expenditure, complaining that no proposals of this kind had been made while the previous Dáil had been in session. Throughout the campaign Fianna Fáil remained concerned to demonstrate its commitment to fiscal responsibility and argued that if Fine Gael's spending plans were realised this would involve "a very serious setback to the public finances".[12]

Haughey reiterated on a number of occasions his belief that only a return to one party government could guarantee the country the full implementation of the government's programme. In particular, the threat to government control of fiscal policy could not be accepted: "if it loses control of the public finances it is not a government at all." The search for this stability justified calling the election: "I am convinced we had no alternative for the best interests of the country, to be able to implement the economic and financial policies we want, but to look for a simple working majority." He appeared to sense that many voters were reluctant to give him this because he added: "We are not looking for a landslide, only for a working majority that will give us the capacity to implement our policies on a long term basis without insecurity or instability".[13]

This was to prove an elusive goal. Opinion polls carried out after the dissolution of the Dáil identified considerable dissatisfaction with the decision to call an election, especially among the urban middle class and large farmers, the very groups which had contributed most to Fianna Fáil's popularity during the previous twelve months. By early June this concern can be identified as the cause of a significant decline in Fianna Fáil's core support; the party was now in a weaker position than had been the case at a similar point prior to the 1987 election. It had not only lost the advantage acquired at the time of the February 1989 budget but its ratings were at their lowest level since February 1988. Subsequent polls revealed that Fianna Fáil was unable to stem the tide of defections. The health cuts proved to be the most damaging issue for the government throughout the campaign. In particular, traditional working class supporters deserted the party because of their hostility to the cut backs in health expenditure. This loss of support was compounded by the salience of the rod licence issue for regular Fianna Fáil voters in the south and west.

What appears to have occurred is that Fianna Fáil gambled on maintaining its new found support among the prosperous, while simultaneously containing the protest of its traditional working class support. The reality turned out to be quite different and both of these groups, for very different reasons, shifted their preferences prior to the election. One of the most striking findings of the opinion polls was the extent to which a majority government was considered to be the most satisfactory outcome of the election. However, a desire for a majority government was not translated into support for Fianna Fáil, and when this meshed with the loss of working class support over welfare issues the possibility of a Fianna Fáil majority became less realisable. This was not lost on the party and there was a detectable loss of momentum in its campaign during the final days before the election. Opinion polls, the main regional newspapers, and the opposition parties all believed that Fianna Fáil could not achieve an overall majority; what remained in doubt by polling day was the precise composition of the new Dáil and the arrangements required for government formation.[14]

FOOTNOTES

The author would like to thank Mr. Jack Jones of the Market Research Bureau of Ireland for supplying him with polling data taken during 1989. Unless otherwise noted all polling references are to MRBI material. The main media source used for the campaign proper and for referencing is the *Irish Times*.. Where necessary, this was supplemented by reference to the *Irish Press* and the *Irish Independent*.

1   Brian Girvin, "The Campaign", in Michael Laver, Peter Mair and Richard Sinnott (eds), *How Ireland Voted* (Swords: Poolbeg Press, 1987), pp. 9-29, for a discussion of the 1987 campaign.

2   Niamh Hardiman, *Pay, Politics and Economic Performance in Ireland, 1970-1987* (Oxford: Clarendon Press, 1988), for discussion of corporatism and pay negotiations.

3   *Programme for National Recovery* (Dublin: Stationery Office, 1987).

4   Thomas Lyne, "The Progressive Democrats" *Irish Political Studies* 2 (1987) pp. 107-114.

5   Joe Joyce and Peter Murtagh, *The Boss: Charles J. Haughey in power.* (Swords: Poolbeg Press, 1983), for a discussion of these issues.

6   Fine Gael, *Putting the Country First* (Dublin, 30 May 1989). The Progressive Democrats, *Putting the People First.*, (Dublin, June 2 1989).

7   The Labour Party, *Now More Than Ever: Labour's Policy Proposals Election '89* (Dublin, June 1989).

8   The Green Party, *Manifesto* (Dublin, June 1989). Sinn Féin, *Make Your Vote Count* (Dublin, June 1989).

9   Fianna Fáil, *National Recovery: The Next Phase,* (Dublin, 6 June 1989).

10   *Irish Times,* 8 June 1989.

11   Quoted in the *Irish Times,* 10 June 1989.

12   *Irish Times,* 13 June 1989.

13   *Irish Times,* 12 June 1989.

14   This paragraph is based on assessment of the two *Irish Times* / MRBI election polls taken during the campaign.

2. Campaign strategies and media coverage

David M. Farrell

For a number of reasons this was going to be an unusual election. It was unexpected, so preparations were necessarily hurried. It was early: the parties were still paying for the last one. It clashed with the European Parliament election, whose lower priority meant it received far less attention and expenditure. In this chapter we explore the campaigns of the parties, focusing in the first section on the preparations of the parties and on the campaigns themselves. The second section examines new developments in Irish campaign strategies in recent years. In addition, since a major part of modern election campaign strategy revolves around the mass media, the chapter concludes with a brief analysis of media coverage of the election.

THE CAMPAIGNS OF THE PARTIES

Fianna Fáil

Fianna Fáil started preparing for the European elections in October 1988, when an election committee was formed with Máire Geoghegan-Quinn as chair. Among its members were the party's general secretary, Frank Wall, the government press secretary, PJ Mara, Orla Kavanagh (printing and funding) and Martin Larkin (advertising). This committee also served as the basis for a general election committee. Once the general election was called its membership expanded and Geoghegan-Quinn was replaced as chair by Séamus Brennan, the director of elections.[1] By then, the local directors of elections had been appointed.

Quite extensive use was made of market research as the party prepared for the elections. Preparatory polls were commissioned for both the European and the general elections, carried out by the polling agency Behaviour and Attitudes. These were both quantitative polls, which indicated vote trends, and qualitative research (group discussions and detailed questionnaires), which helped to identify themes and give more insight into voter attitudes in general. Constituency polling was also carried out (by the local party organisations), particularly in the marginal constituencies, to guide both candidate selection and vote management strategies. The party ran 115 candidates, seven fewer than in 1987. Only four candidates were added to those chosen at constituency level.the party had 78 sitting TDs going into the election, and so there were few "vacancies". In the few cases where problems arose, a careful process of consultation was engaged in by the general secretary, who usually managed to find a reasonable consensus. The most difficult constituency was Roscommon, where internal feuding caused concern. The election committee identified eleven marginal constituencies targeted for electoral gains (Dun Laoghaire, Dublin South-East, Dublin South-Central, Dublin North-Central, Dublin North-East, Carlow-Kilkenny, Wexford, Limerick East, Kerry North, Cork North-West, Clare) and two constituencies for possible losses (Sligo-Leitrim and Tipperary South).

It is difficult to tell how much was spent by Fianna Fáil on the election. Newspaper estimates during the election ranged from a low of £1.5 million to a high of £4 million. When asked in a private interview, the party's general secretary would only respond: "There are only three people who know the answer to that question: me, the party's accountant, and the party leader. Anyone else suggesting a figure is only guessing". All that Wall will admit is that more was spent than in 1987 (though he attributes much of this to inflation) and that expenditure increased in the latter half of the campaign. Fianna Fáil is also not prepared to say how many posters and items of election literature it produced during this election. What is apparent is that a large number of billboard and bus-stop advertising sites were booked,[2] and that all the usual merchandising items (such as balloons and T-shirts) were produced. Like the other parties Fianna Fáil left its individual constituency organisations to print their own candidate posters and other constituency literature, with the election committee providing all the necessary artwork. Fianna Fáil used the same agencies as in 1987 for preparing its various communications activities. Saatchi and Saatchi was commissioned to handle the party's extensive advertising campaign,[3] Windmill Lane produced the election broadcasts, and Carr Communications provided exclusive television and radio training programmes for the party's spokespersons both before and during the campaign.

As the party in a government viewed as having been relatively successful, Fianna Fáil was in an ideal position to emulate the approach adopted by the British Conservatives (1983 and 1987) and the American Republicans (1984) in their respective incumbent campaigns. In each of these cases the central theme was "continuity". The parties usually attempted to take the initiative from the beginning of the campaign, spending some time stressing past successes and then presenting attractive new policies suitable for "the next stage" of a successful administration. Leader image was stressed, the respective party leaders being used to personify the "success" of the administration. At first glance the Fianna Fáil 1989 campaign fitted such a pattern quite well. The party's manifesto was entitled "the next phase", and much of its advertising centred on the same theme. The first part of the manifesto set out the achievements of the party in government and then went on to specify what "the next phase" would entail. Posters, billboards and advertisements stressed leader image, with the phrase "sound leadership, good government". Haughey appeared regularly on television and radio, gave extensive newspaper interviews, and was whisked around the marginals by helicopter, in a cavalcade of cars, or on a "DART Special" (with guest personalities and hired bands). While his constituency touring may have been less than in earlier elections, reflecting his persisting health difficulties, he still figured prominently in the party's overall campaign strategy. Nine major press conferences were held in Dublin hotels, at which the party's policy proposals were spelt out in some detail. During the campaign Fianna Fáil produced no policy documents other than its manifesto. Unlike earlier elections where detailed scripts and press releases were produced, few scripts were handed out and press releases were generally only a few lines long. The party also took advantage of special occasions to attract some extra publicity (such as hiring advertisement space at Lansdowne Road during a World Cup qualifying match).

The Fianna Fáil campaign also had some notable deficiencies. The party may have wanted to take the initiative in the campaign, but it never really succeeded. The manifesto was not prepared when the election was announced and, indeed, was not finally released (after one deferral) until almost two weeks into the three-week campaign. Frustrated journalists were given little material with which to assess the supposed "next phase". Furthermore, the posters and first advertisements were out of synch with the party's focus on policies and leader image, emphasising instead the party's candidates, using the slogan, "Home and Away the Best Team". Once the campaign started Fianna Fáil quickly found itself embroiled in the health issue, a problem compounded by Haughey's gaffe in the final week (see the previous chapter). Some effort was made to meet the issue head on. The party's qualitative research identified the specific aspects of the health issue which were giving voters the greatest concern, and the strategists attempted to come up with appropriate solutions. But with media coverage and public attention so fixed on the health issue the party had grave difficulty in shifting the focus. With support slipping in the polls, the strategists found themselves forced to spend more on advertising and posters to compensate for unfavourable media coverage. It was at this latter stage of the campaign that Fianna Fáil switched to a much more aggressive mode, raising the spectre of government instability and of "multi-party chaos".

Fine Gael

Despite both a new party leader and general secretary, the Fine Gael campaign was organised predominantly by old hands. Few detailed plans were necessary; the elaborate committee structure employed in the party's campaigns of the early 1980s was viewed as superfluous, and the effort made in 1987 to cut back on unnecessary expenditure on elaborate campaign schemes was continued. Indeed, financial control was the order of the day for the Fine Gael campaign. The new general secretary, Edward O'Reilly, is a former school principal with an MA in Administration. On his appointment in the summer of 1987 he saw as his principal task the "sorting out" of the party's finances which had been left in the red by an expensive election campaign and a series of referendums.[4]

Campaign preparations, starting a year before the election, were coordinated by an election committee of sixteen members, including O'Reilly, Peter White (press officer), Seán O'Leary (director of elections), John Bruton (director of policy) and party leader Alan Dukes. In earlier elections the election committee had resulted from an amalgamation between a strategy committee under the general secretary and a communications committee under the press officer[5]; not so in this election, where the individual strategists knew their particular responsibilities and tended to carry these out in an ad hoc, informal manner. The preparatory work of the election committee was completed well in time for the election and so its operation was considerably wound down. During the course of the campaign it met formally only on three occasions; the strategists, working always through O'Leary, operated instead in an individual capacity. By the time the election was called the party was well prepared: finances were in a good state, the marginal constituencies had been identified, and arrangements for the selection conventions had been made. A good indication of how much work had gone into straightening out the party's finances is that of the 38 constituencies in the red after the 1987 election only two remained so going into the 1989 election. The candidate selection system went so smoothly that attention had to be paid to only four constituencies: Louth, where headquarters had to add a candidate (there had been an attempt by other aspirants in the constituency to ditch the outgoing TD, Brendan McGahon); Mayo West, where it was necessary to hold two selection conventions; Dublin South, where John Kelly announced his retirement; and Dublin West. For a time the election committee considered running Austin Currie in Dublin South, where there was an obvious vacancy. But since Dublin West was more of a battle it was decided that Currie's high profile candidature would be more suitable there.

By July 1988 the election committee had drawn up elaborate lists for each constituency of such items as location of billboard sites, printer quotes, financial and printer requirements. The leader's tour was also designed long in advance of the election with a detailed itinerary set out. As in 1987 the concentration was on the marginals and on maximising media opportunities rather than on exhaustive nationwide coverage. The party identified ten key marginals where much of the national campaigning was focused: Carlow-Kilkenny, Clare, Cork East, Cork South Central, Cork North West, Wexford, Wicklow, Sligo-Leitrim, Longford-Westmeath, and Cavan-Monaghan. In its organisational preparations the party had also given attention to Dublin Central and Limerick West. There was a certain amount of constituency polling, primarily to help in candidate selection, but less than in 1987. Fine Gael also commissioned some national polls and qualitative research, but again this appears to have been less than in earlier elections. The party, of course, made full use of the polls published in the newspapers. This reduced reliance on private polling reflected the growing confidence of experienced strategists who felt able to rely more on "gut" feeling; it also, of course, reflected financial stringency. The party ran a "very economical campaign", spending at the national level about £500,000 and keeping to budget. Campaign expenditure was pared to the minimum. In this election Fine Gael spent in real terms less than in 1987 or even in 1981!

As the main opposition party, Fine Gael put great effort into producing a comprehensive set of policies as part of its preparations. On the last occasion that Fine Gael was in opposition over an extended period (1977-1981), its policy director, Peter Sutherland, had some difficulty in persuading all the party's frontbench spokespersons to provide policy material in good time[6]. This time, under John Bruton's directorship, policy production was expeditious. Between 1987 and 1989 sixteen policy documents were produced, so by the time of the election the policy committee had already discussed extensively and received feedback on a wide range of policy areas. These were then synthesised and reproduced in the election manifesto. After the 1987 election the party had purchased its own in-house printing press which allowed speedy and cheap printing. This meant that within twelve hours of the dissolution of the Dáil, copies of the party's manifesto could be prepared, printed, ratified by the parliamentary party and made available to the media. Fine Gael used a new agency for its advertising in this election, DDFH&B, which was responsible for producing artwork for the posters and campaign literature released by the party. To prepare the party's spokespersons for broadcasting ap-

27

pearances the press officer hired a television studio and made use of the services of a television producer and a communications trainer. These facilities were used primarily for campaign preparations, but they were also available during the election if individuals required them. Unlike 1987, the party did not use a distribution agency. This was because, in the words of one strategist, "Charlie did us a favour" by giving several weeks' clear warning of the election. The party had plenty of time to produce and distribute its material throughout the country. Printing requirements were less than in 1987. In all, about 60,000 leader's posters were printed. The constituencies were responsible for printing their own candidate posters, canvassing literature, and election addresses: headquarters provided the artwork. Any merchandising or gimmickry items required by the constituencies were their own concern: headquarters provided them with a contact offering favourable rates.[7]

Fine Gael's campaign had three main phases. The first of these had a negative emphasis; the party attacked both the Fianna Fáil health cuts and Haughey's "quest for power". The latter theme was an adaptation of the party's "Haughey factor" campaigns of the early eighties; this time the emphasis was not on Haughey per se, but rather on his "desire for outright power". Fine Gael also raised the issue of Haughey's health, using photo opportunities to send the subliminal message that Dukes was younger and fitter (such as pictures of Dukes jumping walls), and implying that Haughey's refusal to participate in a television debate was on grounds of ill health. In the second phase of Fine Gael's campaign there was a switch to a positive emphasis, stressing the party's record of "putting the country first" (an indirect reference to the "Tallaght Strategy"), and pushing the party's policies, particularly on tax reform. Qualitative research indicated widespread support for the Tallaght Strategy in broad terms, together with a general lack of knowledge about its details. So Fine Gael decided to promote the notion of "responsibility" implied by the Tallaght Strategy, but not to try rationalising or explaining it. The final phase of the campaign, in the closing days (and coinciding with the Today Tonight interviews with party leaders), involved a focus on leader image, with suitable pictures of Dukes and the advertising message "new leadership, new politics, new hope". Dukes did an extensive tour of the marginals by helicopter and campaign bus. Unlike Fianna Fáil, Fine Gael in this election held few formal press conferences. In the words of one strategist, press conferences are "for the birds"; it is far more important, he argued, to maximise good photo opportunities, rather than "the picture of the man standing in the green bunker" (a reference to Fianna Fáil's press conferences). Fine Gael's press briefings were, instead, informal, impromptu affairs, held wherever the party leader happened to be located. Like Fianna Fáil, Fine Gael kept its press handouts short. The strategists viewed long speeches as "from another era". Instead, statements were reduced to one sentence, much like the "sound-bites" beloved of American strategists.

Progressive Democrats

Preparations by the Progressive Democrats for this election were less extensive than in 1987. Then the party was new and it was seeking to establish itself as a credible force in the political environment. Now the party had been in operation for over three years and was inevitably a little less fresh and enthusiastic. In the period after the 1987 election the main activity of the party was the production of policy and discussion documents on such issues as youth, health, tax reform, and the environment. More policies were in the pipeline (such as one on industry), but the small size of the organisation curtailed the speed at which policy could be produced and updated. Apart from policy the party had not done much else to prepare for a general election. Plans for the European Parliament election were at an advanced stage; but for the general election, as one strategist put it, "there was a lot of ad hocery".

From mid May the organisation found itself "sorely stretched". Its general secretary, Pat Cox, had been nominated as a European Parliament candidate, and from the beginning of April his position was left vacant. This gap in the organisation was partially filled by the party's press officer, Stephen O'Byrnes, working together with some other party officers. A strategic agenda was drawn up on 24 May at a meeting where O'Byrnes produced a "shopping list" of what had been required in 1987. The manifesto was drafted by O'Byrnes in the first week. Overall, the 1989 campaign, financially and organisationally, was a slimmed down version of the 1987 one. This was primarily because of resources; according to the strategists, it was also because the climate was not right for razzamatazz. Nobody wanted this election, and therefore campaign "hoopla" would not have been welcomed. As one party strategist put it: "It was Dullsville all the way; foisted unnecessarily and uninvited on the public". An election committee was set up and played an important role during the election, meeting daily; its involvement in campaign preparations was minimal. Members included O'Byrnes, Martin O'Donoghue[8], Paul MacKay (treasurer), and Helen Keogh (election broadcasts). Once the election began MacKay was appointed director of elections.

The election committee divided up the constituencies into three categories. The seven "A" constituencies were known as the "Bankers" where eight of the party's candidates were considered quite safe. These were Cork South-Central, Cork North-Central, Limerick East, Galway West,

29

Campaign strategies

Dublin South-West, Dublin South, and Dun Laoghaire. The party's marginal constituencies - where most campaign effort was concentrated - were the "B" (Probables) and "C" (Possibles) categories. The former consisted of Dublin South-East, Dublin West, Dublin Central, Clare, Waterford and Laois-Offaly. The "C" constituencies were Carlow-Kilkenny, Limerick West, Dublin South-Central, Kildare, Louth, Sligo-Leitrim, Cork South-Central (a second seat) and Wicklow. The remaining thirteen constituencies where the party was fielding candidates were dubbed the "Also Rans". Selection conventions were called immediately after the election was announced. The party fielded fewer candidates than in 1987, just 35 in 30 constituencies. For the most part these were candidates who had run before and so there was little tension in the selection conventions. The selection convention in Dublin Central to choose a successor to retiring deputy leader Michael Keating was tied between two candidates, and it was left to the national executive to choose one of them, Geraldine Harney.

The election committee budgeted for and spent £220,000 on the headquarters' campaign, a considerable reduction on 1987 expenditure. A debt had been carried over from the previous election but the party had taken steps to clear this. No national opinion polls were commissioned to help in campaign preparations, reflecting the party's financial stringency. Some polls were carried out by the constituency organisations at the local level, but for the most part these were for the European Parliament election. The Progressive Democrats changed their advertising agency in this election, employing Arks, who had previously been used by Fine Gael. The reason for the change was that Arks had amalgamated with the agency formally used by the Progressive Democrats, Kennys Advertising, and the party simply followed its old contact. The agency Diverse Image was commissioned to produce the party's election broadcast, which was broadcast twice. The Progressive Democrats produced substantially less promotional material than in 1987. In total headquarters printed 50,000 leader's posters and 400,000 lapel stickers, and it provided artwork for election addresses and canvassing cards which the constituencies were responsible for printing themselves. The party has its own printing press which was used principally for European election literature. A small number of billboard hoardings were booked for the European Parliament election. Some of these were subsequently "cannibalised" for the general election campaign.

Central to the Progressive Democrats' campaign was a leader's tour of the marginal constituencies; the party also organised a number of press conferences. Unlike its 1987 campaign, the party did not this time release any policy documents other than its manifesto. This was simply because so much policy had already been produced over the preceding two years. The sudden resignation of the party's deputy leader, Michael Keating, was of course a major shock, and struck the Progressive Democrats' campaign a severe blow at the outset.[9] Party morale was weakened and media attention was diverted. While it would obviously be an exaggeration to blame the party's poor result entirely on Keating, his actions certainly affected the campaign; considerable effort had to be put into damage control. A second major problem faced by the strategists was Fianna Fáil's decision to start its campaign late. The Progressive Democrats had planned to let the bigger parties "fire their guns first" before introducing their own proposals under the banner of "forcing real change". Fianna Fáil's late start delayed the Progressive Democrats' own launch and contributed to the party's problems. The Fine Gael / Progressive Democrat "pact" was a natural - if unexpected - step for both parties to take. The Progressive Democrats faced electoral annihilation; both parties had to persuade voters that a real alternative to Fianna Fáil was available. In short, the pact was designed to wrong-foot Fianna Fáil, and in some senses it was successful. Its sudden announcement in the opening days of the campaign caught everybody (including some Fine Gael strategists) by surprise. It was well organised, with strategists from both parties cooperating fully and, towards the end of the campaign, organising joint press conferences.

Labour
Preparations and campaign strategies were coordinated by an election committee whose original function had been to prepare for the European Parliament election. Among the members were Dick Spring (party leader), Barry Desmond (deputy leader), Ray Kavanagh (general secretary) and Fergus Finlay (press officer). The party was aiming for a total of 17 seats (of which it ultimately won 15). The candidate selection conventions passed quite smoothly, with just a few cases requiring the attention of the election committee. These were Cork North-Central, where the constituency organisation was persuaded to run just one candidate; Dublin Central, where a candidate was added to the list; and Dublin South-Central and Dun Laoghaire, where vacancies had resulted from the death of Frank Cluskey and the departure of Barry Desmond to concentrate on the European Parliament campaign.

The Labour Party in this election was working on a smaller budget than in 1987, spending overall about £40,000 on the European Parliament campaign and £50,000 on the general election; in addition, the constituencies spent about £50,000 between them. Labour does not have the resources to commission market research, though some private polling was done by party activists in Dublin South (see the next chapter) and Dublin South-

Campaign strategies

East. Labour headquarters printed 6,000 leader's posters and also - as in its 1987 campaign - a series of issue posters (6,000 of each) on health, education, Dublin, and a general one which stated "defend your rights". The election committee also hired some billboard hoardings and bus-stop sites. The party's reduced budget meant that, with only a few exceptions, it was left to the constituencies to produce their own candidate posters. The party also printed about 300,000 canvass cards and a designer was on hand to help the constituencies with artwork for their election addresses. Labour has a small in-house printer which during the election produced about 250,000 items. The party's advertising budget was £15,000 less than in 1987 and so it could afford only one advertisement each in the two Dublin evening papers and *The Star*, all aimed primarily at working class readerships. These advertisements were produced by the agency Quinn McDonnell Pattison, which also played a role in producing the party's election broadcast.[10]

Labour fought a relatively "traditional" campaign, in the sense that it concentrated on its strongest constituencies. Anxious to avoid a repeat of Spring's embarrassingly close call in 1987, it was decided that he should confine himself largely to his own constituency. Apart from a few "quick sweeps" of Dublin and the south-east, the party leader rarely left his Kerry North constituency. At a series of press conferences, the party released policy documents on health, education, housing, jobs and the environment. Labour started its campaign in a defensive mode. The party's vote had been dropping consistently since 1969 (with the tiny exception of November 1982). In recent elections, and particularly in 1987, the Workers' Party had been eating into its support. Another result like 1987 would have been disastrous. Labour's rejection of Workers' Party overtures for an arrangement on vote transfers reflected the threat it felt. A few constituency deals were struck (notably in Galway West and Cork North-Central), but that was as far as a "united left front" went in this election. As in 1987, Labour's principal emphasis was on health. Its campaign was designed to persuade voters that "now more than ever" a strong Labour presence in the Dáil was vital. The party's campaign may have started defensively, but within a few days it was clear that things were going well for the party, as "health" emerged as the issue with most salience among voters and the media. One senior Labour strategist described the campaign as having a "buzz" he had never before experienced.

The Workers' Party

Unlike the other parties, the Workers' Party may have benefited from the coincidence of two elections. The party's leader, Proinsias De Rossa, was running as the Dublin candidate in the European Parliament election, and was in with a very good chance of winning a seat. The Workers' Party's main electoral focus for all elections is the Dublin area. The party, therefore, found itself in the advantageous position of having a general election where the focus on the party leader helped his European Parliament campaign, and also having a well-prepared marketing strategy for the European Parliament election which could now also double as a means of promoting leader image generally. For instance the party has never before produced leader's posters; Mac Giolla had not been so keen on promoting leader image. On this occasion the "candidate" posters of De Rossa, intended for the European Parliament election, proved to be highly effective as leader's posters in the Dublin Dáil constituencies, and it can be expected that leader's posters will in future be a feature of Workers' Party general election campaigns. The party's campaign plans were drawn up by an election committee chaired by Tomás Mac Giolla. The members included Peter Kane (national organiser and campaign director) and representatives from each of the regions of the party organisation. Once the election was imminent this committee was replaced by a smaller election committee which comprised De Rossa (when he was available), Kane, Des Geraghty, Seán Garland (general secretary), and Tony Heffernan (press officer). The party had already held many of its selection conventions by the time the election was called; the remainder passed without any difficulty. Rather than adding any candidates, headquarters were involved in trying to keep candidate numbers to a manageable size in order not to spread resources too thinly, and, indeed, in some areas would not sanction the fielding of candidates. The principal marginal constituencies for the Workers' Party were the three Dublin constituencies in which the party ultimately gained seats.

The strategists chose the environment as the main campaign issue and the party leader - who was viewed generally as having brought new impetus into the party - as their principal campaign focus. Linking the environment together with the new leader, the strategists came up with the slogan, "a breath of fresh air". To avoid an unnecessary clash with Labour, the underlying theme of the Workers' Party campaign was "a socialist alternative". A significant role was played by a "Dublin committee", whose preparations for De Rossa's European Parliament campaign (especially the posters and the election broadcast) formed the basis for much of the party's strategies for the unexpected general election. The election broadcast was produced by an experienced independent television producer. Modelled on Hugh Hudson's 1987 Neil Kinnock election broadcast for the British Labour Party, it focussed on De Rossa's image.[11]

The Workers' Party paid particular attention to policy, especially at the early stages of the campaign. Apart from its manifesto, it released policy documents on health, job creation, taxation, and poverty; a policy document on the environment had been released in early May. The Workers' Party does not have the funds to finance either advertising or opinion polls. It had planned to produce a set of posters and campaign literature - designed by specialists in the Dublin committee - for the European Parliament campaign. Appropriate alterations were made for the general election, but no extra literature or posters were printed above what had been originally intended. In total the party spent about £140,000 between the two elections (both nationally and locally). This was more than had been originally intended, and was quite a bit more than in 1987. Indeed, on this occasion, for the first time ever, the campaign expenditure of the Workers' Party appears to have matched that of the Labour Party. The election committee produced 70,000 posters, 1.2 million postal manifestos, and 600,000 canvass leaflets. Some billboard hoardings and billboard sites were booked and handmade billboards were erected on derelict building sites around Dublin. The canvass leaflets were printed by the party's own in-house printing press. All other printing was done by private printers in Dublin and the material was then distributed around the country. One strategist has made the point that this operation is starting to get so big that it is likely in the future that the constituency organisations will have to handle some of the printing load themselves.

DEVELOPMENTS IN CAMPAIGN STRATEGIES

As space does not allow for a systematic treatment of campaign developments in the late eighties, this section will simply touch on three themes which show the most dramatic changes: staffing and equipment, the use of agencies, and political finance.[12]

Staffing and equipment
A vital aspect of any national campaign strategy is a well staffed and well equipped headquarters. For instance, the West German Christian Democratic Union has 200 employees in its Bonn headquarters, and regional and constituency offices throughout the country, all linked up by an elaborate computer network. Obviously the Irish system is too small to necessitate such an operation and the parties do not have the finances to provide it. But Irish parties have over the last decade made efforts in such a direction. Fianna Fáil and Fine Gael now both have 18 employees, the Progressive Democrats seven, and Labour six.[13] These staff sizes are markedly higher than a decade ago.

34

Equipment has also greatly improved. In the 1989 election, for instance, all the parties made extensive use of FAX machines both for internal communications and for press relations. Fianna Fáil and Fine Gael had a FAX machine in each of their constituency offices, and Alan Dukes had access to a mobile FAX wherever he went around the country. Extensive use is now being made of computers for word processing, and for analysis of tally data after elections. Computerised mailing lists reduce the workload of addressing envelopes. Fine Gael has also started to use computer facilities for telecommunications purposes. For a small charge Telecom Eireann provides an electronic mailing system, Eirmail, where the subscriber has access to a wide range of British data bases together with computerised links. The Fine Gael press officer, for instance, is able to access the Eirmail service from his home, examine the available data bases (such as "Profile", which records the output of international news agencies and the British media), file any material he may find interesting, and send it over the computer link to party headquarters.

Agencies

Among the most dramatic changes to campaign styles generally has been the growing use of professional consultants and agencies. Such trends have also been evident in Ireland since the mid 1970s, though without approaching the position in the USA, where consultants often appear more in control than the politicians. As we have seen, in the 1989 election all parties except the Workers' Party used advertising agencies, and most used experts or agencies to prepare their election broadcasts and train their spokespersons for television appearances. Market research is also more prominent than a decade ago; however, the rush to gather data on voters which was fashionable in the campaigns of the early 1980s seems to have died down a bit, at least in the case of Fine Gael.[14] The party usually commissions about three qualitative surveys a year. Qualitative research was commissioned both for Fine Gael's campaign preparations and during the 1989 campaign. However, the party's strategists - many of whom had already been involved in four campaigns - were of the opinion that market research, in the heat of the election, has its limitations and so they made less use of such feedback than in previous elections. Fianna Fáil made extensive use of market research both in its preparations and during the campaign itself. The party also commissioned daily tracking surveys - "daily updates"- to assess the campaign's progress. These consisted of small daily samples of voters (100-200) which were aggregated after five days to produce a large running sample, a representative overview of feedback over the period. From then on the survey became a "rolling poll"; as a new sample was added to the total, a sample from the

Campaign strategies

beginning of the period was removed. With such a system Fianna Fáil was able to track voter attitudes throughout the campaign. Such a system, while new to Irish politics, has been in use for some time in other countries.

Political finance

Political finance was a major issue in this election. Several newspaper and magazine articles assessed how much the parties (especially the larger ones) were spending on their promotional activities, and queried their sources of revenue. Campaign finance remains shrouded in secrecy. Many politicians during the election were indignant about being asked where they got their money from. The more furtive the politicians were, the more the speculation grew that there had been some political payoffs. This issue is far from being unimportant. The recent scandal in Japan, the "Flick Affair" not so long ago in West Germany and the periodic instances of financial scandal in the United States all testify to the need for the introduction of some legislative controls. As we have seen, most of the parties are prepared to give a rough figure for their campaign expenditures for national promotional activities: Fine Gael £500,000; Progressive Democrats £220,000; Labour £90,000 (£140,000 on national and local campaigns); Workers' Party £140,000 (national and local). Fianna Fáil refuses to divulge its expenditure, and, of course, for the other parties we must rely on the information they supply. On advertising specifically, though, some independent expenditure statistics are available, as shown in Table 2.1.

Table 2.1: Party expenditure on advertising, 1989 election

	National Press £100	Regional Press £100	Consumer Press £100	Outdoor £100	Total £100	Percent Total %	IR£ per Vote
Fianna Fáil	7037	1618	121	1012	9788	58.8	1.34
Fine Gael	3177	823	0	787	4787	28.8	0.99
Labour	348	90	0	151	589	3.5	0.38
PDs	335	300	37	813	1485	8.9	1.63
Total	10897	2831	158	2763	16649	100.0	

Source: Advertising Statistics Ireland Ltd; official returns.

Table 2.1 confirms that Fianna Fáil spent by far the most, at least on this aspect of its promotional activities. However, while the Fianna Fáil total - at almost £1 million - was high, it was far from the £2 million estimate being suggested by some journalists.[15] The table also shows that while Fianna Fáil (at 58.8 per cent) may have spent more than all the other parties combined, when one considers expenditure on advertising relative to votes it was in fact the Progressive Democrats (at £1.63 per vote) who spent the most. Finally, it is possible to arrive at a reasonably credible estimate of how much Fianna Fáil spent overall on its promotional activities. Fine Gael expenditure on national advertising (i.e. ignoring regional press advertising) represented 79 percent of its claimed total promotional budget: for the Progressive Democrats and Labour the figures were respectively 55 percent and 54 percent. Applying these percentages to the Fianna Fáil case gives us an estimate of total Fianna Fáil expenditure which is somewhere between £1 million and £1.5 million.

MEDIA COVERAGE OF THE CAMPAIGN

Broadcasting

Broadcasting coverage of the 1989 election was intense. Throughout the day, from *Morning Ireland* to the *News at 6:30*, there was a plethora of radio news and current affairs programmes. In the evening the television coverage was just as extensive, with the *News at 6.01*, the *9.00 News*, *Today Tonight* on weekdays, and *Questions and Answers* at the weekends. An examination of the *Today Tonight* programme log gives an idea of how much attention was given to the election, and to which aspects. Of the thirteen programmes broadcast during the campaign, ten covered the election. Their subject matters were as follows: two programmes devoted to regional and constituency profiles; one programme on health; two programmes interviewing the party leaders; and the remaining five programmes a mixture of constituency profiles and analyses of the economic issues in general. The broadcasters may have put a lot of effort into providing wide-ranging coverage of the election, but to what avail; who was listening?

Figure 2.1: *Viewership of news, by social class*

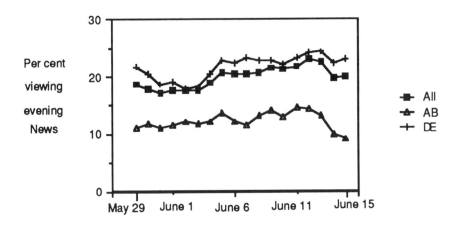

Note: The figure shows the percentage in each social group watching main evening news on RTE television. The graph is smoothed, so the figure for each day represents the average for that day and the previous four days.
Source: Irish TAM Ltd.

An examination of RTE's television viewership records - collected daily by Irish TAM Ltd. - gives a general impression of levels of interest in the election.[16]   Figure 2.1 above graphs the viewership trends of the *9.00 News* for the duration of the campaign, broken down by social class. The Figure shows what proportion of the respective social classes were watching the News. The most significant trends have been isolated for consideration here, showing the striking difference in viewership between the AB (middle and upper-middle class) viewers and the rest (particularly the working class, or DE, viewers). To avoid overcrowding the Figure, the trends for other social groupings (C1, C2, farmers) have been excluded as they do not reveal any tendencies of particular note. To a certain extent the curious viewership trend for the middle class grouping can be put down to such factors as the social activities of the AB grouping: the greater likelihood that they own video recorders, their propensity to watch 'high-brow' programmes on BBC2 and Channel 4. But such explanations do not explain the evident widening of the gap in the latter half of the campaign.[17]

Apart from the broadcasting output provided by RTE journalists, there were also sixteen election broadcasts made by the parties themselves. Time was allotted in the following proportions: Fianna Fáil got six broadcasts totalling 28.5 minutes, Fine Gael four broadcasts totalling 18 minutes, the Progressive Democrats two broadcasts totalling 7.5 minutes, Labour two broadcasts totalling 4.5 minutes, the Workers' Party one broadcast of 3 minutes and the Green Party one broadcast of two minutes. Election broadcasts are taken very seriously by the parties. According to one estimate, as much as £8,000 to £10,000 was spent per broadcast by at least some of the parties.[18] In general, the trends for the election broadcasts were similar to those for the *9.00 News* in Figure 2.1. There was, however, one significant variation. The viewership of election broadcasts actually increased at a slightly faster rate than for the *9.00 News* (the AB decline was at the same rate as in Figure 2.1). This suggests that election broadcasts have a significant role to play in increasing levels of interest (as measured by viewership) quite apart from RTE's own campaign coverage.

Table 2.2: Newspaper coverage of the 1989 election

		Irish Independent	Irish Times
Total col cms		**125,791**	**105,703**
		%	%
Game		**42.3**	**32.2**
	winning/losing	14.1	9.8
	strategies	14.2	14.3
	hoopla/appearances	14.0	8.0
Substance		**56.2**	**65.9**
	campaign issues	6.3	8.1
	personalities/traits	9.3	5.8
	policy issues	40.6	52.0
Other			
	electoral facts/laws	1.6	2.0

Note: Both newspapers were coded for each day of the campaign. The unit of measurement was the column centimetre.

Campaign strategies

Newspapers

A more thorough picture of media coverage is provided by a content analysis of the *Irish Times* and the *Irish Independent*, which reveals that total election coverage by the newspapers was extensive: 59.6 per cent of the *Irish Independent's* total column centimetres during this period were devoted to the election, while for the *Irish Times* the figure was 45.3 per cent.[19] Tables 2.2 and 2.3 provide breakdowns of what form the newspaper coverage took. In America a lot of attention has been paid to the increasingly prominent phenomenon of "game" or "horse race" coverage: in other words, that proportion of media coverage which focuses on the election as a game with winners and losers, and strategies of action. This includes coverage which examines the campaign trail of the candidates, their appearances, crowd reactions.[20] Table 2.2 gives the proportions for the two newspapers in our sample, showing - particularly for the *Irish Independent* (at 42.3 per cent) - that "game" coverage was indeed prominent.

Table 2.3: Newspaper coverage of policy issues

	Irish Independent	Irish Times
Total col cms	51,090	54,965
	%	%
health/social welfare	28.4	27.1
unemployment/emigration	8.9	8.8
government stability	12.8	7.7
taxation	6.8	6.5
state finances/debt	6.2	4.4
agriculture/fisheries	5.4	7.3
environment	2.1	5.3
inflation	0.3	0.3
industry	1.4	1.7
trade unions/corporatism	2.1	2.5
law and order	1.8	1.9
Northern Ireland	1.0	4.0
moral issues	0.8	2.3
Dáil reform	2.1	2.2
miscellaneous issues	19.8	18.1

Note: These proportions are percentages of coverage of 'policy issues'; i.e. ignoring all the other themes in Table 2.2.

40

Coverage of campaign "substance" consisted of three main categories: campaign issues, such as candidate gaffes, campaign incidents, or stories relating to possible scandals (e.g. the issue of Iraqi beef insurance); personalities and traits of candidates and their backgrounds; and policy issues. Table 2.3 shows which policy issues received most coverage in these two newspapers. As would be expected from the way the campaign went, the issue of greatest concern was the state of the health services. Other prominent issues were unemployment and emigration, taxation, state finances and the national debt, agriculture and fisheries (particularly the rod licence dispute), government stability (especially the dangers of a "hung Dáil"), and the environment.

CONCLUSION

While it might have been expected that the sudden announcement of the general election would have caught party strategists by surprise, we have seen that this was not so in all cases. Planning and preparations for the European election were at an advanced stage; few alterations were necessary to transfer these plans to the national campaign. If anything was affected detrimentally by Haughey's decision to have the two elections coincide, it was the amount of attention received by the European Parliament election rather than the ability of strategists to mount professional marketing operations. Of all the parties, in fact, it was the Progressive Democrats and, ironically, Fianna Fáil which appear to have been least prepared for the campaign. The former lacked a general secretary and had senior politicians already in the fray as candidates for the European election, while the latter apparently did not have policies or slogans ready for a national campaign and had to draw them up at the last moment.

Our examination of party finance, staffing, equipment, and the use of agencies highlighted some of the developments in recent years in the abilities of parties (including the smaller ones) to wage campaigns of a sophisticated nature, even at short notice. We also saw the extent to which the media (certainly the newspapers) are showing a distinct interest in the "game" of party campaigning. There is a linkage between these two developments: between the highly professional, marketing operations of contemporary party campaigning on the one hand, and the media focus precisely on those strategic, or "game" aspects, on the other. Both the parties and the media are moving in a similar direction: elections and the electoral process are becoming a spectator sport.

FOOTNOTES

Information on the parties' campaigns has been gathered from interviews with a wide selection of the parties' strategists in the weeks immediately following the election. As always - except with prior permission - the identity of the intervie-wees is not revealed here. I am very grateful to all the people I talked to about this election for their cooperation and their patience!

---

1   The last time Brennan had held an important position in a Fianna Fáil campaign was as the party's general secretary in 1977.

2   All parties booked billboard hoardings. One notable feature here was that whereas in most cases the party's hoardings were booked only until after the election was over on 15 June, the Fianna Fáil bookings, in contrast, were for the entire month of June. Fine Gael strategists argue that this represents another example of how much money Fianna Fáil was prepared to 'throw around' in this election.

3   Considerable media attention was given to the use made by Fianna Fáil of Saatchi and Saatchi. This was not the dramatic development it seemed. What had happened was that the Fianna Fáil advertising agency of long standing, O'Kennedy-Brindley, was bought out by Saatchis, and the name was changed. Indeed, O'Kennedy-Brindley's was already a subsidiary of Saatchis during the 1987 campaign.

4   The 1987 campaign seems to have been expensive in relative terms less because of how much was spent and more because of the difficulties faced by the party - leading an unpopular government - in attracting campaign revenue.

5   On preparations for Fine Gael's 1981 and 1987 campaigns see D. Farrell, "The Strategy to Market Fine Gael in 1981", *Irish Political Studies*, 1 (1986), and D. Farrell, "Campaign Strategies", in M. Laver et al. (eds.), *How Ireland Voted* (Swords: Poolbeg, 1987).

6   See D. Farrell, "The Strategy to Market Fine Gael in 1981".

7   The laminated "issue cards" and the "weekend leaflets" which Fine Gael used in the last election were not reproduced because canvassers did not face the difficult task this time of trying to defend government policies.

8   O'Donoghue was the principal architect of the controversial Fianna Fáil 1977 manifesto and of subsequent economic policy until 1979.

9   The retirement of McCoy in Limerick West had been expected by the strategists. The party had to persuade a reluctant Mary Harney to run for the Dáil; she was already a candidate for the European Parliament election.

10   The theme of the election broadcast - shown twice - was semi-satirical. It had a good response and according to one strategist was actually self-financing. Costing a mere £850 to produce it resulted in £1,100 of donations!

11   For an excellent account of the campaign strategies of British parties in their 1987 election, see M. Charlot, "Les elections Britanniques du 11 juin 1987", *Revue Française de Science Politique* 38:4 (1988).

12   For systematic and comparative treatments see D. Farrell and M. Wortmann, "Party strategies in the electoral market: political marketing in West Germany, Britain, and Ireland", *European Journal of Political Research* 15 (1987), and D. Farrell, "Changes in the European Electoral Process: A Trend Towards 'Americanization'?" *Manchester Papers in Politics*, No.6/89, 1989.

13   *Irish Political Studies* 4 (1989), p.161. Fine Gael actually has 17 employees at the most recent count.

14   See David Nally, "The Secret Pollsters", *Business and Finance*, 27 July 1989. More generally see Michael Laver, "Political polls, political reality and the mass media in Ireland", in T. Fahy and M. Kelly (eds.), *The role of the media in Irish society* (Dublin: Media Association of Ireland, 1988).

15   For example Gary Culliton, "FF IRL4m. splurge left purse empty", *Irish Press*, 7 July 1989.

16   This section would not have been possible without the prompting and assistance of Miriam Murphy of Irish TAM, and Shaun Bowler, University of California, Riverside. Note that the 'N of cases' varied depending on the number of homes TAM made contact with and on who was actually viewing. In general it was never lower than 1,330 individuals. TAM receives its data from 400 homes.

17   Indeed, a 'best-fit' trend-line drawn by the Harvard Graphics package shows a clear divergence between the viewership of the AB group on the one hand and everyone else on the other. Interestingly, on the night of the *Today Tonight* interviews with the two main party leaders (June 13), TAM's quarter-hour ratings show a significant increase in viewership in the second half of the programme, coinciding with Haughey's interview. This trend holds good for all classes and age groups.

18   Dermot Kelly, "The IRL4 million PR campaign to win over voters", *Irish Times* 3 June 1989.

19   These total coverage figures are considerably higher than those found by F.X. Carty in his analysis of media coverage during the elections of 1969, 1977, and 1981. See F.X. Carty, *Press Coverage of the 1981 General Election*, (Dublin: Able Press, 1981).

20   For a summary of the studies on "game" coverage see Farrell, "Changes in the European electoral process".

3. On the campaign trail

Charlie McCreevy (Fianna Fáil, Kildare)

Charlie McCreevy was elected to the Dáil in 1977 at his first general election campaign, and has held his seat ever since, heading the poll at the election of February 1982. He is an accountant, and was a member of Kildare County Council from 1979 to 1985. He has been a well-known, and indeed controversial, figure in national politics ever since he began speaking out strongly in the early 1980s against extravagant election promises by all parties.

It was 5.30 pm Monday 12th June 1989, three days to polling, and I was wet, tired and miserable. I was deep in Army territory and not looking forward to canvassing at Orchard Park, Curragh Camp, a scheme of 104 Army houses. "You are just after missing the fun", said a woman at house No. 1.

"What fun?" said I, trying to summon up interest for the umpteenth time in the campaign.

"Oh, did you not know that the Minister for Defence was in the camp this afternoon at the commissioning ceremony and there was a large protest of Army wives?"

"Oh Jesus", said I under my breath "that's all we needed" and offered up a silent prayer for one Michael Noonan.

I confess to being slightly superstitious - most gamblers have the same complaint - and in my mind the whole campaign had been one long disaster.

To some extent, I would depend on the floating vote, and my performances at elections have generally reflected the swings to and from Fianna Fáil. I needed no one to tell me at any stage of the campaign that we did not have a snowball's chance in hell of getting an overall majority.

Elections bring out selfishness in all candidates of all parties - no matter whether they are backbenchers, ministers, or party leaders. Let no one tell you anything else - when it comes to a campaign, it is everyone for himself, and irrespective of your party going up or down, all you really want to know is are you going to be elected.

The constituency of Kildare is a good microcosm of Irish society. It is no longer solely the home of cattle ranchers and stud farm owners. The population is 115,000; there are large new dormitory towns in Celbridge, Leixlip and Maynooth; a large industrial work force, small farmers, big farmers, and every possible problem that one might encounter. As the county is relatively small in area it is possible in a day's canvassing to meet every type of social class and every problem.

In particular it has a large Army influence in the middle of the county. What with the Army Headquarters at the Curragh Camp, a barracks in Kildare and another in Naas, there are few families that do not have - or did not have - an Army association. Thus, long before the general election of 1989, it was obvious to me that the Army pay issue was going to present a big problem.

I have constituency election tallies going back to 1973, and Fianna Fáil has never received less than 50 per cent of the postal vote - which breaks down as 75 per cent army and 25 per cent gardai. Apart from the postal vote analysis, the army vote is reflected in the large towns such as Kildare, Newbridge and Naas, and a myriad of smaller villages near the Curragh.

No Fianna Fáil canvasser in the constituency needed to be told that we were in serious trouble with the army vote. Things were so bad that our director of elections wrote to Fianna Fáil headquarters early in the campaign and told them in no uncertain terms that we were getting a dreadful reception and that the Army had lost all confidence in the Minister. This letter ended up in the national media and caused some embarrassment to the party nationally. How it arrived in public print is one of the lighter aspects of the Kildare campaign. Apparently, a reporter from a local newspaper called to our base in Naas and was shown the letter by a party helper - not knowing its explosive contents. Like any good reporter, he was hardly back in his office before he rang the national dailies.

There was an Army Wives candidate in the constituency, who pulled 6 per cent of the total poll, but even if there had been no such candidate we would still have taken a roasting from the army vote. The resultant election tally shows the postal vote at 12 per cent. Adjusting for the Garda voter content, it means that FF received an army vote in single figures.

It was a total disaster!

No outgoing TD ever really enjoys the campaign. He enjoys the result if he is victorious. That caveat notwithstanding, I confess that the 1989 election was the most pleasant of any previous campaign for me - excluding 1977 which was an absolute joy. Due to my "little difficulties" with Fianna Fáil over the years, I have not enjoyed a very pleasant working relationship with the Fianna Fáil organization in Kildare, and the bulk of that organization in previous elections were - to say the very least - not very enthusiastic or very helpful. However, no such problems existed in

1989 and I can only say that I received the maximum co-operation from all members of Fianna Fáil during the campaign.

Paddy Power, my party colleague since 1977, stepped down from national politics. I had been unanimously selected by the Fianna Fáil convention and was joined on the ticket by Paddy's son, Seán, and by county councillor Seán O Fearghaíl, who had unsuccessfully contested the 1987 election. Due to the retirement of Paddy Power, I was the only big name on the Fianna Fáil ticket and this was a bonus, but also a problem. For the first time in Kildare Fianna Fáil history, the candidates decided on a split of the constituency. The thought of such a division was never even mooted while Paddy and I were TDs - but with two new candidates in the field, it would have been somewhat greedy on my behalf not to agree to a split, which was also undoubtedly the overwhelming wish of the Fianna Fáil members in the county. The constituency was divided in three with yours truly taking the northern third. It was agreed that this strategy would last until the Friday night before the election, after which each candidate was free to do as he pleased. Despite the usual pressures to ignore the agreement, we abided by same. The segment allotted to me was the worst in terms of Fianna Fáil votes, going on the 1987 tallies, but I was relying on also receiving reasonable votes in the rest of the constituency, having being the TD for the previous 12 years.

Fianna Fáil gave the impression that we were going after three seats - but in truth no-one in the party really believed this. We did achieve three seats out of five in February 1982, but this was before the elevation of Alan Dukes to the Fine Gael leadership and the emergence of Emmet Stagg of Labour as a TD in 1987. It was never on - no matter how the national result was going to go.

At the outset, with Power senior retired, I was reasonably confident of being successful. However, being the front runner has its drawbacks in multi-seaters. There is the ever present danger that the party faithful would say "McCreevy is all right" and vote for the other lads. Furthermore, I had barely scraped home to the last seat in 1987. It is said that an imminent hanging wonderfully concentrates the mind, and I took no chances for 1989.

The organisation has never run a high powered razamataz effort in Kildare, and the 1989 election was no exception. Whereas the effectiveness of after mass meetings in built up areas is nil, it is still expected in rural Ireland. Each Sunday I did the usual flitting at 90 mph from church to church. It gives a fillip to the local cumann members and a boost generally to the area. Local area Directors of Election were appointed, and together with the candidates a programme of canvassing was drawn up. There is a growing tendency in Kildare for each candidate to have his own team, but

I still rely on the cumann organisation. Thus, my office, or I personally, would phone local cumann members and inform them that I would be canvassing such and such an area on a particular date. We did a few walkabouts in shopping areas but door to door canvassing occupied 90 per cent of the time. I also wrote to my personal friends asking for their support and help and would also drop a line to constituents whom I had assisted with problems over the years.

Undoubtedly door to door canvassing is very important. However, it is of greater value to a new face than to an old one like mine. As I enjoy a certain national profile, there would not be many voters in Kildare who do not have a view about me one way or the other - favourable or otherwise.

Overall, the Fianna Fáil vote dropped from 42 per cent to 36 per cent, and as I have described Kildare as a microcosm of national life, the national factors had a profound effect. Apart from the army issue, health was mentioned morning, noon and night. People of all walks of life brought it up. I said to a journalist during the campaign that I met people who were never sick for 30 years, but were going to get sick and the whole nation was going to die on hospital trolleys.

Nationally, Fianna Fáil ran an atrocious campaign. From day one we were stuck in first gear. The fundamental problem was that the Kildare electorate, like the rest of the Irish people, felt there was no valid reason for calling a general election. All the good work on the economy since 1987 was forgotten about from day one of the campaign. People voted for the status quo. The typical comment at the doorstep would be "sure there is no need for this election, is not the present arrangement very successful, should things not have been left as they were?" Thus, people effectively voted for a minority Fianna Fáil government.

The tallies in Kildare show that we gained from the middle and upper classes and lost major ground in working-class areas. To me this was so obvious even before the game started, given the type of economic measures necessarily undertaken by Fianna Fáil since 1987.

The lesson to be learned by a successful government in the future is "have a damned real excuse to call an election before you do so"!

47

Ivan Yates (Fine Gael, Wexford)

Ivan Yates became the youngest member of the 22nd Dáil when he was first elected for Wexford in 1981 at the age of 21 years and 7 months. He has held his seat at each subsequent election, and is now the only Protestant member of the Dáil. He was chairperson of the Oireachtas Committee on Small Businesses in the 1982-87 Dáil. He was promoted to the Fine Gael front bench in the last Dáil, with responsibility for Health, and was reappointed to this position after the 1989 election.

It takes a combination of a number of factors to become a TD. No single ingredient can ensure success in the complex business of electioneering. The June 1989 election was a particularly short campaign by recent standards and therefore it is vital in organisational terms to be able to swing into action immediately. In Wexford, Fine Gael knew in advance that its three candidates were to be Michael D'Arcy, Avril Doyle and myself. The three of us had been on the Fine Gael ticket at the previous two elections and maintained a high level of support for the party. Therefore our selection convention a few days after the election was called was a formality in selection terms, so much so that the election literature of canvassing cards and posters was printed as soon as the convention concluded that night.
The background to our Wexford campaign was that in the November 1982 election Fine Gael succeeded in obtaining three out of five seats in County Wexford on only 42 per cent of the vote. To achieve 60 per cent of the seats on this level of votes was miraculous. It was achieved in fact by virtue of Labour Party transfers, with the Labour candidate in effect acting as our fourth candidate pushing us in to have three candidates elected. In the subsequent election when the coalition government of Labour and Fine Gael was the outgoing government we all knew in our more honest moments that we could hold only two Fine Gael seats in Wexford. The casualty on that occasion in 1987 was Michael D'Arcy, a former Minister of State and a deputy of ten years' standing. On this occasion the same dilemma was presented to the party: we had three hardworking candidates with just two quotas. The real question therefore was who would be the two candidates elected. Therefore, as in most five-seat constituencies, there were in effect two campaigns to be waged. One to maximise the Fine Gael vote beyond its level of 30 per cent and secondly to secure enough votes to ensure my personal re-election. In this context the first preference vote was vital. In fact I had to fight a third campaign as the Fine Gael Health spokesperson. I spent more time than heretofore in Dublin for regular media programmes on what was to be one of the critical

issues of the campaign, the health service. This national campaigning factor I felt not only to be personally satisfying but also of great benefit to me in the constituency with such a high profile. The successful Labour Party candidate Brendan Howlin TD was also their party spokesperson on Health, and he too obviously found this an added advantage as he topped the poll in Wexford.

In the early days of the campaign there was tension between the three Fine Gael candidates as to an agreement on dividing up the constituency for canvassing purposes. I personally felt that I had to have access to the entire county to be re-elected. This was by virtue of the fact that the Enniscorthy electoral area had always been a Fianna Fáil stronghold, and prior to my election to the Dáil in 1981 there had never previously been a Fine Gael TD from this area. In County Wexford the political geography divides into four electoral districts. There is Gorey in the north, which is predominantly in the heartland of Fine Gael but breaks down sometimes evenly between Fianna Fáil and Fine Gael. Second, the largest populated area of Wexford town and district, which was always a Labour stronghold with Fine Gael support south of the town and consistent Fianna Fáil support across the district. Third, the New Ross district, which was the heartland of Fianna Fáil, as they currently have four out of five county councillors, and fourth the Enniscorthy district. After much negotiation it was agreed that each candidate would have two open days early in the campaign to travel outside of their own personal electoral area. In this context Michael D'Arcy's home area was Gorey, Avril Doyle's was Wexford and my own was Enniscorthy. This in fact was fully honoured by all candidates and there were no subsequent breaches of the Code of Conduct. Personalised literature was allowed by agreement subject to prior vetting by the Director of Elections.

The issues in the campaign in Wexford were microcosms of the national issues. These were unemployment and emigration, the deterioration of the health service, other cutbacks in public service such as education, the high rates of personal taxation and the constant issue of integrity in government. From the outset Fianna Fáil sought to make single-party stability of government the central issue. In the early opinion poll data that Fine Gael had it was obvious that this ranked low in terms of issues the public was concerned about. In relation to the formation of a possible alternative government, Fine Gael had seized the initiative just prior to the calling of the election by arranging a pact with the Progressive Democrat Party. This was beneficial in two ways. Firstly, it prevented attrition throughout the campaign between Fine Gael and the Progressive Democrats as to the correctness of the Tallaght Strategy or other aspects of opposition over the last two years, thereby leaving us free to put all our resources into attacking Fianna Fáil. Secondly, it provided us with an answer to the obvious suggestion in the early stages of the campaign that Fine Gael could not form a single party government on its own, which would require jumping from 50 to 84 seats. The timing and presentation of this allowed us to seize the initiative as Fianna Fáil were totally unprepared for such a development.

I believe we gained the initiative also early in the campaign by launching our manifesto which had particular attractions in the area of taxation and the health service. We were advocating the spending of £60 million of National Lottery funds over 18 months to rectify the problem of waiting lists for in-patient hospital treatment. This easily understandable remedy was saleable and popular to the electorate. Our two reduced rates of personal taxation, of 25p and 45p in the pound, were also attractive to middle income earners and single people who had felt that this issue had not got enough recognition by the previous Fianna Fáil government. The other great early boost for the non-Fianna Fáil parties, and I believe especially for Fine Gael, was the fact that the election was called at all. There was a public perception that there was no need for a general election, and therefore those precipitating the election, namely Fianna Fáil and Mr Haughey, paid some price for breaking what was perceived to be a workable and successful consensus in the national interest. The combination of all these factors allowed us in Wexford and nationally to improve on our previous position in the opinion polls. In County Wexford I found that there was far less animosity and anger on the doorsteps on this occasion compared with the previous election in 1987 when we were the outgoing government. In fact the roles were reversed; now Fianna Fáil were getting the heat on the doorsteps.

In organisational terms canvassing is absolutely vital. My personal family and relatives were invaluable to me in this regard. In a rural constituency such as Wexford, where there is a stretch of 50 by 30 miles of the constituency from end to end, it is simply impossible in two and a half weeks to personally traverse it all. The second major advantage I personally had was a very experienced core group who organised my entire canvassing arrangements, i.e. not only of myself and my family but teams of canvassers to match up with local people in the areas of Gorey, New Ross and Wexford districts. The fact that this had to be condensed into a two-day period as per the Code of Conduct made precision-type organisation absolutely critical. I was very fortunate to have again, as I have had in all my five general election campaigns, a core group of personnel who work untiringly for the period of the campaign, solely to get me and my Fine Gael colleagues re-elected. To them I owe an an enormous debt of gratitude and I have no doubt that every other TD has a similar network to which they are indebted. It is the voluntary commitment and dedication of these people that make democratic politics in Ireland work. They are unsung heroes of election campaigns and they receive little or no public credit, but they are the backbone of securing any Dáil seat. Without organisation and a certain amount of financial resources, no amount of high media profile or constituency work will ensure the election of a deputy.

One of the insidious factors in a multi-seat election campaign like Wexford is the perception of candidates being "safe" or "in trouble". I have no doubt that this can affect the result of a personal vote by one thousand or more first preference votes. In all parties voters with strong allegiance to the party will try to maximise the use of their personal vote by voting for whomever they perceive to be the weakest candidate in order to obtain the maximum number of seats for that party. Any mistaken assumptions as to who is perceived to be doing well can have lethal and fatal consequences for those candidates. Naturally, party colleagues will do all they can to create the weakest perception of their own candidature and in turn allege the safety of their running mates. To counteract this successfully is essential to being elected to the Dáil.

The final outcome in Wexford was very satisfactory from my own and Fine Gael's point of view. The party vote went up to 33 per cent, almost exactly two quotas, and my own personal vote went up in first preference terms. Michael D'Arcy was elected in place of Avril Doyle. Fianna Fáil had a similar unchanged number of seats with Hugh Byrne TD being replaced by Séamus Cullimore, an outgoing Senator. Brendan Howlin succeeded in increasing the Labour vote very substantially with over a quota of votes, thereby topping the poll. All in all the campaign was a success insofar as we prevented Fianna Fáil from gaining a third vital marginal seat in Wexford and thereby (along with other constituencies) denied them the opportunity of obtaining an overall majority to form a government. I believe our success in this regard will be a critical turning point in the history of party politics in Ireland insofar as Fianna Fáil have failed on five occasions now to obtain such an overall majority, thereby ending the days of single party government for the foreseeable future.

A general election campaign in all honesty is a time of great anxiety, trauma and exhaustion. There are no certainties and there is assuredly unlimited hard work and expense. In truth, however, a general election campaign and more especially a localised campaign is not decided in the short weeks of electioneering but rather in the continuous longer span of work as a public representative. The key work of building up an organisation, strengthening party finances, assiduous constituency work for individuals and at community development level, a public profile at national level with all the inherent research work and consultation etc - it is all of these factors that build the basis for one's re-election. In the campaign itself it is vital to bring out the vote, re-assure the faithful and make one's best attempt to obtain the maximum level of floating votes. Therefore, one's campaign for re-election to the 27th Dáil is already under way . . .

Eithne FitzGerald (Labour, Dublin South)

Eithne FitzGerald first stood for the Dáil in Dublin South in 1981, when she lost her deposit, but she improved her position to finish as runner up when she stood next in November 1982. She was unsuccessful again in 1987 and, despite an increase in her vote, in 1989. She works as a research officer for Threshold, and has been a member of Dublin County Council since 1979.

After the 1987 election which saw a landslide for the PDs in Dublin South, I muttered to friends that if Labour were ever to regain a seat in this area, I'd have to change my name to Anne Colley.

After the 1985 local elections, I'd been selected as the single Labour candidate for the general election, and my former running mate, Frank Buckley, opted to be Director of Elections. After the bruising defeat in 1987, neither of us was overly anxious to take on the role of candidate-apparent. The party only formally held the selection conference a week before the campaign opened.

From the end of April, rumours of an election began to take strong hold. Barry Desmond discounted them - wishful thinking from a Euro-candidate, I thought. He also gave us word of a Fine Gael mini-poll in the constituency - showing Labour at 11 per cent and a slump in the PD vote to their now trailing national average of 6 per cent. Was this more wishful thinking? 11 per cent, with expected transfers from candidates from the smaller parties, would give us a seat!

While a great morale-booster, I felt it was too good to be true. So did some of the other party members, who quietly organised their own mini-survey, issuing sample ballot papers at shopping centres.

Looking at the actual election result, their survey was extraordinarily accurate, except in one crucial respect. The survey showed Séamus Brennan topping the poll with a huge surplus, and correctly predicted the outcome for the other FF candidates, it gave the correct FG share of the vote though at that stage John Kelly seemed to be still in the race, and it correctly predicted a PD slide from 21 per cent to under 9 per cent. It showed Labour at 8 per cent, and a strong Green showing at 7 per cent. If the poll was accurate, the preferences from the Workers' Party and the Greens would give us a Labour seat. While we knew the Greens would do well, we felt our own strong record in the area on environmental issues and in campaigning against re-zoning scandals, as well as our broader platform on economic and social issues, would keep us ahead. We never seriously contemplated what actually happened - that Labour transfers would elect a Green TD rather than Green transfers electing a Labour TD.

Frank Buckley had said he'd run if I didn't want to, otherwise he'd be Director of Elections. I negotiated leave of absence from my job for the campaign, and was selected unanimously. Frank got stuck into the business of organising a HQ, posters, and literature.

HQ was the old Rathfarnham Credit Union building. It had no light, no water or toilets, and was full of about a hundred old storage heaters; otherwise it was grand, with plenty of parking and next door to a pub. So the campaign began with all the heavies lugging around lumps of storage heater, while a couple of us tried to discuss campaign strategy and to draft literature by the light of a candle.

We were able to recycle posters and cards from the previous election but we needed interim canvass literature until the main print order was ready. I dropped a text into my printer neighbour at two in the morning the night the election was called, and by lunchtime the next day we were ready.

John was away for the first few days of the campaign, so in addition to campaigning, I had to organise dinners, iron blouses, and find the children's socks, jobs normally the prerogative of the candidate's spouse.

Frank Buckley, a man who once won an election in a suit he bought at a sale of work for a fiver, was very insistent that the candidate be Well Turned Out. No open-toed sandals in the sweltering heat of June, respectable shoes (I went through two pairs in three weeks), always stockings, a good summer suit, and a red rose instead of the prize-cow rosette. My navy and mustard cotton suit was thought to sail dangerously close to the PD colours. Respectability paid off at one level - someone mistook me for a Fine Gael candidate - but did it jeopardise those precious Green votes?

The door to door canvass was our main method of campaigning. Every morning, my sister Barbara, myself, and any other members or supporters who were available, assembled for a cup of tea in one of our houses at ten o'clock, and headed out on the knocker at about 10.30. Then a stop of an hour for lunch, a whizz round to assemble the afternoon shift, knock off at half five to go home and make and/or eat dinner, then off again from seven to nine thirty.

At the council, I've always lobbied for interesting and varied estate layouts, geared to children, not to cars. But you curse these mazes of cul-de-sacs when you're out canvassing. You can lose half your troops, knock up and annoy half the area twice, and appear to have very little to mark off on your map when you're finished. Nothing beats a block of flats or open plan gardens for a quick and easy canvass. Provided it's Rottweiler free.

We started with the areas where we knew our support was strongest, always good for the morale, especially for newcomers to the campaign. The first week, the night canvassing started from our house and concentrated on the eastern side of the constituency, and the children loved sitting in on the gossip and political analysis from the comrades over a cup of tea afterwards. Later on, the focus of the evening canvass shifted to HQ, and the cup of tea became a pint in Rathfarnham.

For me, the campaign rarely ended at 9.30. I danced at a street ceili in Ballinteer, attended a pub quiz in Firhouse, and a race night in Templeogue. Then home, and some paperwork, following up queries or writing a script.

Saturday afternoons were spent at shopping centres. We put up sandwich boards with posters on them, offered leaflets, chatted with shoppers. I usually dislike this form of canvassing, I'm much more comfortable door to door, but the powers that be feel it offers good visibility and a chance to meet people from the rural parts of the area. Dick Spring offered us an afternoon, so we took him to my local centre, Crazy Prices, where the sun shone, my sister Barbara and her children waved balloons, and the reception was warm and friendly. Chris O'Malley appeared briefly, took a look at the massed opposition, and disappeared. Another day we did Nutgrove Shopping Centre with Barry Desmond. You feel much less of an eejit shaking hands and chatting people up when you're not the only one.

Sundays were Masses, meet the Communion trickle, then the main flood, then dive into the cars to the next church on the circuit. Again, not my favourite form of canvassing, standing like a dummy with your hand stuck out. I watched two of the real pros in action at it, Séamus Brennan and Tom Kitt. Must be the Galway blood. Finish at 2, then back again at 4.30 at Rathfarnham Church.

Changes in the election routine counted as real breaks. The visit to the Hughes's ice cream factory. Lovely people, pity half of them live in South-West, but Mervyn Taylor should do well. The party press conferences - the main one, the environment policy document launch, the health policy press conference - gave a brief chance to participate in the national campaign, and to hear the gossip from other constituencies.

It's very difficult as a candidate to really keep in touch with the campaign at national level. I heard Morning Ireland, and read the newspapers, but apart from the odd snatch on the car radio I heard and saw little or no other news or current affairs programmes. Apart from press conferences in town, I didn't venture outside the constituency for the three weeks. Just go, go, go, trying to get to as many as possible of 40,000 houses.

So it could be easy to miss some critical shift in the campaign issues, arising from a crucial radio interview or Today Tonight programme. But there was no such shift. On virtually every doorstep, the same main issue, the cutbacks in the health service, and the impact on ordinary families.

The woman who waited 24 hours for her child to get stitched after an accident. The man on the dole who borrowed £500 from the credit union because he couldn't bear to see his child in pain waiting for a tonsil operation. The elderly woman sent back home with a bandage after bleeding in the taxi home from hospital. The woman who burst into tears on the doorstep because her husband's recovery from a stroke was in jeopardy, discharged because of shortage of staff.

When I took part in Marian Finucane's programme on the health service, the phone calls from around the country confirmed the same sense of anger and despair about health care.

Everywhere I went, VHI or no VHI, there was an acceptance that health care was too fundamental to be bought and sold, and that access to health care should be the same, whatever your income.

Dublin South is characterised by the analysts as leafy suburbia, the most middle class constituency in the country. But there is also significant unemployment, hardship, poverty. We met families in Ballyogan paying £4 a week per child out of welfare incomes simply to get their children to school. A pensioner sobbed while she told me that while she could just manage on her money, she'd never again be able to afford a treat for herself - a meal, a day out, a holiday. Other homes where there clearly wasn't a thing in the house. People spoke of their sense of powerlessness, their lack of dignity, queueing for everything. "When you're down, they don't just walk on you, they fucking dance on you!" For some, all the fight was gone out of them.

Parents of teenagers were particularly concerned about emigration, about jobs, as well as the ever-present issue of health care. In outwardly prosperous areas, mothers complained about the rise in house values, as it was putting the purchase of an ordinary family home way outside the pockets of their own grown children.

By the end of three weeks, I was tanned, half a stone lighter, and exhausted. Having started with the easier areas, we were now finishing up with areas where the reception varied from politely indifferent to absolutely frosty. The electorate as well as the canvassers were suffering from battle fatigue. "Not another bloody election leaflet!"

Everyone hates polling day, the twelve-hour stint of competing canvassers jostling the voters outside polling stations, the jockeying for position with canvassers and posters. One of the advantages of being the candidate is that you escape being rooted in the one spot for twelve hours, because it is customary to drive around from one polling station to another to greet your party workers stuck on that thankless job, and to shake hands with the presiding officers and polling clerks. My sister Bríd drove me around, transferring the roofrack with the "Vote Eithne FitzGerald Labour" box on it from our beat up Renault 4 to her somewhat newer car. Our posters were doing very little jockeying, the van with them having been stolen from outside HQ the night before.

Next day, the brothers did the tallies ("A Product of Starry Plough Software"). At 12 they rang to say the result would be 2 FF, 2 FG, and an amazed Roger Garland would take the other seat, on our transfers. So close!

Could we have taken the seat? Would a better local or national campaign have made the difference?

In 1987, in spite of vigorous pre-election canvassing, and a hard fought local campaign, the Labour vote halved. Straight from an unpopular coalition government, we lost votes heavily among our traditional supporters, mainly to Fianna Fáil, while in middle class areas, the PD "Pay less tax/we're different" message went down a treat. In the 1989 election, the focus of the national campaign on a key Labour issue, the health cuts, brought our core support back. A well fought local campaign helped. But then, the Greens won a seat with a skeleton campaign.

That little extra, either locally or nationally, could have made the difference - more pre-election canvassing, more television coverage for the Party or us locally, more attention to turnout in areas of known support, more vigorous pursuit of No. 1s from tactical voters voting Green, or of 2s rather than 3s from the Workers' Party.

The Labour organisation in Dublin South is more invigorated, more experienced, and larger, than it was on May 25th. And fairly sure we'll regain John Horgan's Labour seat the next time.

Geraldine Kennedy (Progressive Democrats, Dun Laoghaire)

Geraldine Kennedy had not stood at any election before winning a seat for the PDs in Dun Laoghaire in 1987. Before entering politics she had been a political correspondent, with the Sunday Tribune and the Sunday Press, and in 1987 she won damages in court for illegal tapping of her phone in 1982. From 1987 to 1989, when she lost her seat, she was PD spokesperson on Foreign Affairs and Northern Ireland.

Dun Laoghaire has always been a unique constituency. Besides being the most middle-class in the country with a large Protestant population, it has always polled contrary to the national trend. It voted against the Pro-Life Amendment and for the divorce referendum in the mid-1980s. It was, accordingly, one of the few constituencies to swing to Fianna Fáil - by a massive 6.4 per cent - in the 1989 general election.

As a candidate and outgoing Deputy, I did not foresee this swing before or during the election campaign. The cool reception I received outside the polling stations on June 15, particularly at the Progressive Democrat strongholds of Foxrock and Dalkey - where people whom I recognised as being positive when I canvassed them did their utmost to avoid eye contact - was the first inkling I had that something could have gone terribly wrong.

Unlike two of my Dublin colleagues, Michael McDowell in Dublin South-East and Pat O'Malley in Dublin West, who anticipated going into the election that they would have serious difficulties, I was surprised that I was not re-elected. Based on opinion polls conducted by the PDs in Dun Laoghaire and reliable intelligence of the polls of other parties, I expected to have a high first preference vote. I was surprised, therefore, to lose my seat and saddened to come out with only a half quota on the first count.

I consider that I went into the campaign as well prepared as any other candidate in Dun Laoghaire, and certainly more prepared than I was in my first election in 1987. The Taoiseach, Mr Haughey, had given due warning of his intention to call the election since his return from Japan in late April. By mid May, it seemed certain to me that the die was cast. The party nationally and in Dun Laoghaire acted accordingly.

An emergency meeting of the national executive of the Progressive Democrats was held in the week preceding the calling of the election to prepare for the campaign. A national director of elections was appointed and the constituencies were asked to prepare for conventions. It was decided, because of the party's standing of 5-6 per cent in national opinion polls over the previous months, that there would be one candidate only in each Dublin constituency. On that basis, it became clear that I would be the only candidate seeking selection in Dun Laoghaire.

Thanks to the talent of my constituency chairman, Tony Keegan, a magazine publisher by profession, my canvass cards and posters were ready for distribution to members of the party immediately after the Dun Laoghaire selection convention in the Royal Marine Hotel on the morning of Saturday May 27, less than 48 hours after the election was called. We were the only party to canvass the churches in the constituency on Saturday evening and Sunday morning of the first weekend. *Southside*, the local newspaper, stated in their first issue of the campaign that the PDs had a head start on the other parties on the ground in Dun Laoghaire.

There was very little contact with PD head office during the three-week campaign. The national executive had instructed each constituency that it was responsible for the running of its own campaign. Posters of the party leader, stickers and the wording of one side of the Litir Um Thoghchán, as well as posters and canvass cards for the European election, were provided.

The slogan adopted in Dun Laoghaire, simplified by the fact that there was only one candidate compared with three in the previous general election, was "Vote No. 1, KENNEDY, Geraldine - GUARANTEE GOOD GOVERNMENT". Because of the low standing of the party in the polls going into the election and the fact that Dun Laoghaire's vote can be determined by national factors, we decided that we would have to spend some considerable time stressing the relevance of the Progressive Democrats as a parliamentary force in the 25th Dáil. A canvassers' guide was prepared for party workers spelling out the performance of the 14 TDs.

The basic message which we attempted to convey in our election literature - subsequently copied by other PD candidates - was that the PDs were the new factor that provided economic stability. Both civil war parties - Fianna Fáil and Fine Gael - had been forced to behave responsibly and to act in the national interest. This was unique in the history of the state. For the first time, Ireland had the benefit of an economic consensus. Ironically in the light of the outcome of the election nationally, the point we stressed was: "We made the last Dáil work in the interests of the country and we have to be returned in strength to do so again. We are the GUARANTORS OF GOOD GOVERNMENT. That was our role over the last two years and we want that to be our role for the next 5 years"!

Having set the "national" context, the main task of the Dun Laoghaire organisation was to cover as much of the constituency as possible, door-to-door, in three weeks. About 95 per cent was canvassed by the end of the campaign.

I had a gruelling schedule to meet this overall strategy. In the first place, Dun Laoghaire is again unique as a constituency in that it has 10 DART stations: Booterstown, Blackrock, Salthill, Seapoint, Monkstown, Dun Laoghaire, Sandycove, Killiney, Dalkey and Shankill. The DART stations provide a wonderful opportunity for the candidate to meet constituents on the way to work. My day began, therefore, at 6.30 am in order to be at the DART stations from 7.30 to 8.30 am. Up to the time the schools closed for holidays in early June I canvassed different national schools to meet parents from 8.30 to 9.00 am.

The door-to-door canvassing would start at 10.00 in the morning after a brief breakfast break. I did three door-to-door sessions a day - apart altogether from what the local PD branches would be doing in their own area. The party's best areas, in voting terms, were kept for the evening canvass because more householders would be at home. The day was broken down for me, therefore, into a door-to-door canvass from 10.00 am to 12.30 pm, 1.15 pm to 5.30 pm and 7.00 pm to 9.00 pm. There were confusing signals, in retrospect, coming from the canvass. I was generally well received personally, but the relevance of the PDs was questioned. If I had received a first preference every time a householder said "I'm giving you a vote", I would have topped the poll!!!

Each canvass, whether conducted by myself or other party groups, collected a very large number of constituency queries and detailed policy questions every day. These were collated that evening, at about 9.15 pm, with my Dáil secretary, Rosemary Dunne. They were usually answered, either by telephone or by letter, within three days.

The canvassing regime changed at the weekends when we covered all of the major shopping centres and churches. Sunday evening was the only rest period that I took, for two out of the three weekends of the campaign.

A strategy meeting was held each night at 9.30 pm at the local PD election HQ in the Victor Hotel. We reviewed developments and, sometimes, switched around manpower to canvass weak branch areas.

What then went wrong in Dun Laoghaire?

There was a combination of four factors, in my view, that contributed to my failure to be re-elected.

1. I was handicapped by the fact that the party has no local councillors in the constituency to supplement the work of the TD on the ground. No local elections have been held since the Progressive Democrats were founded. This put the TD at an immediate disadvantage against the other parties because of the absence of a local party presence in each ward. When the trend was going against the party nationally - as happened in the 1989 election - there was no local base nor traditional vote to cushion the fall for such a new party.

2. Despite the antipathy to Charles Haughey at the doors - expressed as vehemently as in 1987 - Dun Laoghaire bucked the national trend and swung 6.4 per cent to Fianna Fáil because a perception of instability was generated by the leaders of Fine Gael and the Progressive Democrats in the last couple of days of the campaign. They declared at the beginning of the last week that they would not vote for Mr Haughey as Taoiseach. This, in my view, frightened the business belt in Dun Laoghaire and allowed Charlie Haughey to claim, in his eve of poll message, that the choice was between stable government and multi-party chaos. It was then known from the opinion polls that the parties of the left were going to do well in the election.

3. The accidental choice of Senator Brian Hillery turned out to be the right candidate to win the elusive second seat for Fianna Fáil in the constituency. He was nominated a full week after the campaign had started because the local Fianna Fáil organisation revolted over the proposed imposition of Kieran Mulvey, general secretary of the Association of Secondary Teachers in Ireland and former Workers' Party activist. Mr Hillery, in contrast, was a Fianna Fáil "nice guy", he had lived in Foxrock for years and sent his children to St. Brigid's School, and both he and his wife were well known in the community. His candidature damaged me in the PD heartland of Foxrock where the PD vote in some boxes at one of the biggest polling station, St. Brigid's, dropped from 50 per cent in 1987 to about 20 per cent in 1989.

4. The national campaign run by the PDs was another factor. It was not sufficiently responsive to the climate emerging from the opinion polls and the canvass. In my view, the negative, anti-government issues were over-emphasised to the detriment of the positive contribution of the PDs to the creation of consensus politics. The national campaign was affected by the fact that the newer party deputies were not included or involved in fronting the campaign.

Despite my defeat, however, I have no recriminations. I don't believe that I could, or would, have done anything any differently at constituency or national level during my time in the Dáil in order to get re-elected. I held clinics. I received a volume of constituency work, mainly by post or phone, on a par with Bobby Molloy. I attended most functions to which I was invited in Dun Laoghaire.

If I had known that I would have come out of the campaign with half-a-quota, would I have run a different campaign?

With hindsight, I don't believe that a different campaign would have got me re-elected. However, some members of the PD organisation in Dun Laoghaire do think so. They consider that, strategically, we should have saturated Foxrock, Brian Hillery's base; that we should have paced ourselves better to peak at the end of the campaign; that we should have done leaflet drops in the constituency saying that I was in deep trouble; and that we should have plastered the place with more posters.

Pat McCartan (Workers' Party, Dublin North-East)

Pat McCartan first stood for the Dáil in Dublin North-East in 1981, losing his deposit, but by the time of his third campaign in November 1982, he had strengthened his position and finished as runner-up, less than 900 votes short of a seat. He was elected narrowly for the first time in 1987, just 235 votes ahead of Seán Haughey (the son of the Taoiseach), and his seat was widely regarded as marginal at the start of the 1989 campaign. He is a solicitor and has been a member of Dublin Corporation since 1985.

The June election in Dublin North-East presented a huge challenge to the Workers' Party. It was a snap election, a manoeuvre which favours parties of big financial resources - money at hand to spend quickly. It was an election interposed in a slowly building European campaign. But it was also the election and opportunity for the Haughey dynasty to settle the score of an impudent defeat of the youngest scion in the February 1987 campaign. We were facing into defending a seat won by a very narrow majority. Those hunting believed that the hare was an easy target and blood was in the air for the earliest stages of the chase. The Workers' Party seat was a seat to be targeted; if Pat McCartan could be knocked from the race then the fourth seat could settle the score for Haughey and Fianna Fáil, providing them with a valuable addition to their aspiration of an overall majority. For Fine Gael it could herald the return to the Dáil of Maurice Manning, and even the Labour Party had hopes of staying ahead of the Workers' Party in a scramble for the last seat.

This was the first election the Party fought to defend and so retain a seat. Obviously this required a different tactic and approach on the canvass. The big question the Party had to answer was whether the voters in the constituency perceived us as a political presence worth keeping. We would get a clear verdict on the previous two years' performance. It is a question often feared to be asked - what do people really think? A question most people can avoid if they want, for a political party it is the unavoidable question posed at each election. The anguish is all the more marked for those who are seeking out, or being presented with, the answer for the first time. All of these factors produced the inevitable panic once it was declared that June 15th would be a general and European poll day.

Panic was thankfully short lived. The organisation was in motion for the previous two weeks dealing with the EEC campaign. It was soon realised that having both elections together was a boost. The campaigning would take place for Europe anyway and the calling of the general election to coincide gave a huge lift to the EEC campaign. This decision was the second greatest mistake of Fianna Fáil in the campaign. The other of course being their miscalculation of popular resentment at their policy sellouts and swingeing cutbacks.

The response to the calling of the election on Thursday 25th May in our constituency augured well for the campaign. That same night our posters appeared on the poles of Raheny, Kilbarrack and Coolock. We had our canvass leaflet on the doorsteps the very next day. We were determined to let it be known that we intended to fight tooth and nail to retain the seat for the Party and lay the basis for a good assault on the next local government elections, due for 1990. By the weekend our convention was held, one candidate chosen and the election management team put in place. Now all we had to do - on a shoestring - was to get out to every door and speak to as many voters in the three weeks remaining. It was June, good weather, a short campaign and spirits were high.

However, there were some unknown factors in the race for the four seats. Would Liam Fitzgerald hold top of the poll having got there on a scare campaign the last time? Would Michael Woods hold his vote in the face of a poor performance as Minister for Social Welfare, forced to introduce another cut in entitlements on the very day the election was called? Would the PDs put in a big name having gone so close to gaining a seat at the height of their political existence the last time out? Would Maurice Manning pick up the PD disaffected and get ahead of Michael Joe Cosgrave, who was caught off-side by an early and snap election? Would the Labour Party run Seán Kenny yet again or find an acceptable outsider? The contest seemed wide open. There were also a few new faces in the contest. Máire Mullarney, who had stood for the Greens in Dublin South-East, came north this time. This suggested that the Greens had a particular strategy or were lured by the belief that North-East was a marginal. Her move over sent a message to our campaigners and a leaflet on the environment and the issues pursued over the two years was prepared for canvassers and voters alike.

The other big unknown factor was how the Haughey faction would settle into the campaign alongside two nervous running mates. Despite the untimely death of their fourth partner, Ned Brennan, the early feeling was that Haughey was still not welcomed by the organisation. The three candidates developed separate teams of workers and campaigns. For the Workers' Party the big question, then, was how the Haughey team would set about acquiring what they presumed was theirs for the taking. What emerged over the next three weeks could not have been envisaged in the early days of postering, leafletting and canvassing. Dublin North-East was entertained to a jamboree of free drink, gilt-edged invitations, helicopter rides and an array of personalities including Michelle Rocca, Barney McKenna, Dickie Rock, Miss Ireland and Brendan Grace. The party countered these with a leaflet distributed to the same areas that invitations were sent, entitled, "Bottler Backs the Cuts". Despite the lavishness and waste of the Americanised campaign, Haughey succeeded in gaining only 350 extra votes and lost heavily in the count. In fact, only the order of election changed. The same four TDs were returned but this time the Workers' Party took the first seat against the odds. The remaining three were obliged to wait till the last count to be elected together, Fitzgerald, the previous poll topper, being elected without reaching the quota.

"Against the odds", because all commentators and pundits at the outset had identified Dublin North-East as a marginal. The party challenged this view from the beginning, claiming the one sure seat to be the Workers' Party. The questions would hang over who would fill the other three. It was interesting to see how quickly the predictions altered and how early into the race Dublin North-East was demarginalised. The sheer force of anti-Fianna Fáil feelings on the doorsteps quickly put an end to the suggestion that they could or might take a third seat in the constituency. The presence of our Party President, Proinsias De Rossa, through the European campaign also helped our cause. The fact that it was a snap and short election meant that local groups were caught unawares and localised issues were not presented to voters as a means of deciding a vote. There was a noticeable absence of letters of promise, undertakings and support for all local demands, which fell like confetti on voters during the '87 campaign. The main issues of national concern, health services, education, jobs and emigration were those discussed and debated on the doorsteps right across Dublin North-East. Discussed, that is to the extent that canvassers went on the doors looking for votes. The Party targeted all doors and just about succeeded; apologies to the Baily area of Howth and Strand Road in Sutton - but we will be back! The impression we gained was that the main parties were reluctant to go onto the doors and into direct contact with the voters. Morale amongst their members was low, while feelings amongst the voters were high and they were acutely aware of words and slogans abandoned from previous campaigns. Haughey and others in turn abandoned the doorsteps for the relative comfort of coffee mornings and the pub jamboree.

On the campaign trail

This election also introduced, in Dublin at least, a new dimension - a campaign of press conferences. This involved two and sometimes more visits a week to a city centre hotel and the presentation of a policy document or reaction to the issues of the past week's campaign. No doubt these conferences will be a permanent feature of future campaigns. They proved a useful contact with an otherwise remote head office team. The presence of the Party President in all our campaigns also drew head office organisers closer to the general election contest. As much as North-East was a marginal for the pundits, it was a crucial seat to retain for the Workers' Party. Nothing was left to chance or fortune.

The eventual result was very gratifying and has proved a major boost to party morale and expectations for the future of north Dublin. There is no doubt that with continued effort from our party members and continued tactical efforts from Fianna Fáil, the Workers' Party can only go forward in Dublin North-East. 1989 has been a good year so far - thanks Charlie (and Seán)!

Trevor Sargent (Green Party / Comhaontas Glas, Dublin North)

Trevor Sargent first stood for the Dáil in 1987, when he lost his deposit. He had also lost his deposit when standing at the Dublin County Council elections in 1985. In 1989 he again stood for the Dáil (in Dublin North) and simultaneously ran for the Greens in the European Parliament election campaign, doing considerably better than expected in both contests. He is a school headmaster in Balbriggan.

Looking back over my candidature in the European and later on in the general election campaigns, I can recall six months of late nights, rushed meals, an accumulating overdraft and torn loyalties between the demands of my job on the one hand and the campaign trail on the other.

Back in December 1988, three Greens were being proposed as Dublin candidates, Máire Mullarney of Dublin South-East Greens, Roger Garland of Dublin South Greens and myself from the Fingal Greens. Other good people such as John Gormley were being mentioned, but in the end the selection decision was made by consensus at an open meeting of Dublin Greens in Buswell's Hotel.

Many Greens at that time expected we might double our last Euro vote to something over 10,000. The actual first preference result of 37,317 was certainly not foreseen. Of all the independent analysts, *Alpha* (27 April 1989) was closest in predicting a growth in Green support in Ireland, drawing a comparison with France where April elections had increased the strength of "les Verts" from 300 council seats to 1,400.

From January to May, Green party groups throughout the country were preoccupied with Euro campaigns. Seán English was working hard for Leinster, and Greens in Munster were campaigning for Independent Joe Noonan. In Dublin, the announcement of a general election scuttled many Euro-election plans. Finance (always on a wing and a prayer anyway) was now diverted to general election campaigns. However, the groundwork done from January to May was not wasted. Seven Green constituency groups had held public meetings at which I had been a guest speaker. These meetings were intended to be launch pads for the Euro-campaigns in these areas, especially in areas where Greens had not been politically active. As these groups were already campaigning when the general election was called, they immediately took to the second campaign like ducks to water. As a result, all Dublin constituencies (except for Dublin North-Central whose Green group opted to concentrate on the Euro-campaign) stood Green Party candidates in the general election.

Meanwhile, in Dublin North, the Fingal Greens' selection of a candidate for the Dáil was not easy. I was asked to stand, but objected to having to contest two elections. A number of members, including myself, proposed Eithne O'Connell, group secretary, as a potentially excellent candidate, but she declined. The nomination kept coming back to me. No alternative could be found and we had no money to print new leaflets. We knew that the Euro-campaign was bound to lose media attention as a result of the more "newsworthy" general election campaigns. Therefore, to keep up the Green Party/Comhaontas Glas profile in Dublin North, I had no choice but to straddle the two campaigns. No one at any stage expected me to take one seat, never mind two, so accusations of a dual mandate were always slightly tongue in cheek. Anyway, I had pledged in writing that if elected, I would only accept from my income a national average wage, the surplus to be spent protecting the environment.

On the question of campaigning technique, very little premeditated planning was involved really. Once I had been publicly announced as Dublin Euro-candidate on 19 January, invitations and letters began to arrive at my home. The letters were often in the form of questionnaires asking where the Greens stood in relation to issues such as travellers' halting sites, Nicaragua, Nuclear Free Zone, a new road being built, development aid, "the Birmingham six", hare coursing, bull fighting, the National Plan and community enterprise projects... to name but a few of the concerns about which people wrote. The invitations, however, set the agenda, by and large, for the way I spent my evenings in the following months. Various groups were requesting me as a candidate to attend various meetings to hear Green Party/Comhaontas Glas views on whatever the group was most concerned with.

The invitations varied greatly. One asked me to sing and play the guitar. Another asked me to take part in a public demonstration. Meetings scheduled for Dublin city centre were fine as I could get there easily by train. The most problematic venues were those in the suburbs which required a combination of train and one or more buses to reach and get home from a destination.

Fuair mé go leor litreacha as Gaeilge, cupla cuireadh ina measc, agus dheineas mo dhicheall freastal ar aon ócáid a bhí lúaite iontu. D'fhreastal mé ar cheithre ócáid Ghaeilge agus thug mé faoi ndeara nach raibh iarrthóir eile ar bith i láthair ach amháin nuair a bhuail mé le beirt iarrthóir, ach labhair siad Béarla ar fad in ainneoin na hócáide.

Altogether, I can remember attending seventeen public meetings of one form or another. Apart from canvassing, this was the most time-consuming activity in the campaign.

Early on in the campaign, the Green office at 5a Fownes Street, off Dame Street, was really not equipped to deal with the media interest that could have been generated by these public events. The office had to issue statements as best it could with volunteer staff coping with a portable typewriter and a temperamental photocopier - using recycled paper, of course.

On a personal note, I got the distinct impression that Greens close to the national office in Fownes Street hoped that most of the required media liaison could be established from the candidate's base in Dublin North. On the other hand, I detected a feeling among Fingal Greens that as I was a Euro-candidate for all Dublin, city Green groups would collectively provide a service for the media. Consequently, much of the typing, phoning and design work was done by myself. By May, Steve Rawson, from Dublin North-Central Greens, had been appointed press officer, and statements began to appear in the newspapers and to be heard on radio and television. From then on, the office began to function effectively.

Whatever time was left for canvassing was quite well used, thanks to a number of selfless volunteers (and their vehicles) who offered to come around with me. As I was teaching up to two weeks before the election, my time was limited anyway. However, door-to-door canvassing was the part of the campaign I enjoyed most. As it is, I like to spend time with people, which cuts back still further on the number of houses covered. The best canvassing for me was in groups of four, but two worked well sometimes.

As you might gather, vast stretches of Dublin were not touched except by "free" election post. One of our yellow leaflets was delivered to almost every household in the constituency. The writing, design and printing of this leaflet was another aspect of this campaign which consumed an enormous amount of my time. However, when it was sent out, workers in An Post passed a remark on how useful the leaflet's shape was as it had been used by post(wo)men to divide up the bundles of election literature destined for each house.

Unlike the February 1987 general election, it was not difficult this time around to find people to copy addresses from the register onto leaflets for the "free" post. If only more addressers had been willing to become canvassers, we would, I believe, have had an even better result. Ultimately, I believe canvassing at doors gives the voters the best opportunity of assessing the candidate and the policies of his or her party.

Second to canvassing in terms of effectiveness is television. I was fortunate enough to be asked onto the panel of "Questions and Answers" on 15 May 1989. I also presented a political broadcast, some pieces on "Nuacht" and on "agallamh ar Chúrsaí". Some radio pieces on RTE 1, FM2, Raidió na Gaeltachta and Millenium Radio gave good feedback also.

My most memorable time during the whole campaign was an afternoon spent talking to people around St Stephen's Green and down Grafton Street in the company of Eileen Battersby from *The Irish Times* on Monday 12 June 1989. Try as she did, Ms Battersby found it quite difficult to find people who did not support the Greens. True, some of these good people were French and Italian, but nonetheless the point was well taken, the Greens are growing.

My biggest personal dilemma during the last six weeks of the campaign was trying to canvass as a Euro and a general election candidate at the same time. The confusion in many people's minds was made worse by An Post insisting that no reference to the general election was to be made on a Euro leaflet and vice versa. As I mentioned earlier, in Fingal we had no money to print a second set of leaflets, so I had intended having a rubber stamp made up with "Trevor is also standing in the General Election" on it, but to use it on my Euro leaflet would have been disallowed so confusion reigned amongst many voters.

In the end, I was not elected in the Euro-election which means success has to be measured in some other way. What was won on 15 June 1989 was hope, hope for the planet Earth and hope for the Greens. H.O.P.E. (Help Organise Peaceful Energy) for the next time.

4. The election results and the new Dáil

Michael Gallagher

In 1987, the election results had been dramatic but the composition of the government predictable. In 1989 the sting was in the tail: the election results showed a settling back towards a pre-1987 normality, and it was the government formation process which produced the shocks.

The 1987 election had produced a whole string of superlatives. Each of the traditional three main parties had plunged to its lowest level of support for several decades; the PDs had made the strongest general election debut of any party for nearly 40 years. The overall volatility displayed by voters was greater than at any election since 1943. In comparison, the 1989 outcome seems rather tame. Fine Gael and Labour both regained some of the ground they had lost, though Fianna Fáil gained no votes and lost seats. The PDs were unable to maintain their 1987 position, and it was left to the Workers' Party and the Greens to provide some of the main talking points of the election.

GAINS AND LOSSES

The concept of "volatility" is conventionally defined in terms of the percentage of voters who switch their vote from one election to the next, and so it is measured by simply adding up the percentage gains of the parties which gained votes from the previous general election[1]. By this measure, volatility at the 1987 election had been 16.1 per cent, compared with less than 4 per cent at both 1982 elections. In 1989, volatility was lower, registering at 7.5 per cent. While this is higher than at the 1982 elections, it is not exceptional, as higher figures were recorded for volatility between the elections of 1973 and 1977 (7.7 per cent) and between those of 1977 and 1981 (8.4 per cent). This suggests a certain settling down after the upheaval of 1987. Similarly, only 19 seats changed hands in 18 constituencies (there were two changes in Dun Laoghaire), compared with 30 in 26 constituencies in 1987 (see Table 4.1).

As always, the aggregate figure conceals greater movements in constituencies around the country. The average volatility per constituency was 12.4 per cent, a more realistic assessment than the figure in the previous paragraph of the minimum number of voters who must have changed their vote from 1987. As in 1987, volatility was highest in Dublin (an average of 14.5 per cent in each constituency) and lowest in Connacht-Ulster (11.0 per cent). The most volatile constituency was Dublin South-West (19.5 per cent), followed by Cork South-Central and Mayo West, with volatility lowest in Laois-Offaly (4.8 per cent), followed by Cavan-Monaghan and Mayo East.

Table 4.1: Seats changing hands at 1989 election

FF	Gains (2)	Dublin NC (FG), Dun Laoghaire (PD)
	Losses (6)	Dublin N (Lab), Dublin SW (WP), Longford-Westmeath (FG), Roscommon (Ind), Sligo-Leitrim (FG), Tipperary S (Lab)
FG	Gains (7)	Carlow-Kilkenny (PD), Dublin Cen (PD), Dublin SE (PD), Dublin W (PD), Limerick W (PD), Longford-Westmeath (FF), Sligo-Leitrim (FF)
	Losses (3)	Cork NC (Lab), Dublin NC (FF), Kerry S (Lab)
Lab	Gains (5)	Cork NC (FG), Dublin N (FF), Kerry S (FG), Tipperary S (FF), Waterford (PD)
	Losses (2)	Dublin SC (WP), Dun Laoghaire (WP)
PDs	Gains (0)	
	Losses (8)	Carlow-Kilkenny (FG), Dublin Cen (FG), Dublin S (Greens), Dublin SE (FG), Dublin W (FG), Dun Laoghaire (FF), Limerick W (FG), Waterford (Lab)
WP	Gains (3)	Dublin SC (Lab), Dublin SW (FF), Dun Laoghaire (Lab)
	Losses (0)	
Oths	Gains (2)	Dublin S (PD), Roscommon (FF)
	Losses (0)	

Note: the party in brackets indicates from whom the seat was gained or to whom it was lost.

One striking aspect of the election was the sizeable drop in turnout (see Table 4.2), defined here as valid votes as a proportion of the electorate. At a mere 67.7 per cent, this was the lowest turnout since the same figure was recorded in September 1927. From 76.0 per cent in 1969, turnout dropped at each of the next five elections, rose fractionally in 1987, but has now resumed its decline. It fell from the 1987 level in every

constituency bar one, Dublin South-East (which still recorded the lowest
turnout in the country, 56.7 per cent). This constituency was the exception
to such pattern as can be detected, for the heaviest falls in turnout occurred
in the more middle-class parts of Dublin and in the growing commuter
constituencies of Leinster. Turnout fell by over 7 per cent in nine
constituencies. These included four Dublin constituencies (North-East,
South, South-Central and Dun Laoghaire), the three adjacent Leinster
constituencies of Kildare, Meath and Wicklow, plus Donegal South-West
and Galway East. This ties in with some of the evidence in chapter 2,
showing low (and declining) middle-class viewership of election
broadcasts during the campaign. It also ties in with the opinion poll
findings (see the next chapter) that the middle classes in particular felt
the election was unnecessary in the first place. The overall fall could be
explained in terms of the register becoming increasingly inaccurate due to
accelerating emigration, or in terms of "voter fatigue" brought on by five
general elections, two European Parliament elections, a set of local
elections and four referendums, all in the space of eight years, or a
combination of both.

We now turn to an examination of the fortunes of the parties sepa-
rately. The basic figures of the election outcome are summarised in Tables
4.2 and 4.3; for the full results for each constituency, see the appendix at
the back of the book.

Table 4.2:Party votes 1989 by province, with changes since 1987,
in percentages

	Dublin		Rest of Leinster		Munster		Connacht-Ulster		Ireland	
Fianna Fáil	40.7	+0.2	46.1	+0.3	43.6	+1.0	47.5	-2.2	44.1	0
Fine Gael	23.0	-0.7	30.9	+3.6	30.4	+3.4	34.6	+2.7	29.3	+2.2
Labour	9.5	+2.4	13.5	+3.9	10.9	+4.1	2.4	+1.2	9.5	+3.0
PDs	5.4	-8.2	4.2	-6.8	8.0	-7.0	3.2	-2.4	5.5	-6.4
Workers' Pty	11.4	+3.9	1.7	-0.5	4.0	+0.8	1.4	0	5.0	+1.2
Green Party	5.2	+4.1	0.4	+0.2	0	-0.2	0	0	1.5	+1.1
Sinn Féin	1.9	-0.3	0.8	-0.7	0.2	-0.7	2.3	-0.9	1.2	-0.6
Other	2.9	-1.5	2.5	-0.1	3.0	-1.4	8.6	+1.7	3.9	-0.5
Total	100.0		100.0		100.0		100.0		100.0	
Turnout	63.3	-5.4	68.0	-6.0	71.2	-4.1	68.6	-4.6	67.7	-5.0

Table 4.3: Party seats 1989, with changes since 1987

	Dublin		Rest of Leinster		Munster		Connacht-Ulster		Ireland	
Fianna Fáil	21	0	18	-1	21	-1	17	-2	77	-4
Fine Gael	15	+2	14	+2	15	-1	11	+1	55	+4
Labour	3	-1	5	0	6	+4	1	0	15	+3
PDs	1	-5	0	-1	4	-2	1	0	6	-8
Workers' Pty	6	+3	0	0	1	0	0	0	7	+3
Green Party	1	+1	0	0	0	0	0	0	1	+1
Sinn Féin	0	0	0	0	0	0	0	0	0	0
Others	1	0	0	0	2	0	2	+1	5	+1
Total	48		37		49		32		166	

Fianna Fáil

For the second consecutive election, Fianna Fáil began the campaign expecting to win an overall majority but failed to do so. This time, to make matters worse, it actually lost seats. Only four times since the party first came to power in 1932 has it won fewer than 44.1 per cent of the votes. Although some believe that the party has suffered lean times under Charles Haughey, Table 4.4 shows that this is a little unfair. It is true that its average electoral strength under him is below what the other three leaders achieved, but the differences are not great. Perhaps more importantly, Fianna Fáil has picked up smaller bonuses from the electoral system during the 1980s, so in terms of winning Dáil seats Haughey has indeed been the party's least successful leader.

Table 4.4: Fianna Fáil's electoral record under four leaders 1932-1989

	Elections	Average % of first preference votes	Average % of seats
Eamon de Valera	10	46.2	49.2
Seán Lemass	2	45.8	49.6
Jack Lynch	3	47.5	52.1
Charles Haughey	5	45.2	47.4

Note: the Ceann Comhairle's seat is excluded from the calculations.

The outcome

As Table 4.2 shows, the party made very modest gains in three regions and fell back by just over two per cent in Connacht-Ulster. This led to a net loss of one seat in Leinster and Munster and two in Connacht-Ulster (Table 4.3). Yet, as was the case in 1987, this picture of little overall change conceals considerable shifts in individual constituencies. Altogether, the party gained votes in 19 constituencies and lost in 22. Table 4.5 shows its best and worst performances.

Table 4.5: Parties' best and worst performances in 1989 relative to 1987

	Best constituencies	Change (%)	Worst constituencies	Change (%)
FF	Limerick W	+9.1	Dublin NW	-12.9
	Cork SC	+7.9	Roscommon	-12.2
	Galway E	+7.7	Waterford	-7.8
	Dublin S	+7.6	Kildare	-6.3
	Limerick E	+7.0	Sligo-Leitrim	-5.5
FG	Cork NW	+11.2	Mayo W	-12.7
	Longford-Westmeath	+8.6	Dublin SE	-4.3
	Clare	+8.4	Dublin SW	-4.1
	Tipperary S	+7.9	Dublin NW	-3.9
	Galway E	+7.5	Kerry N	-3.5
Lab	Waterford	+11.4	Dun Laoghaire	-5.9
	Kerry N	+10.3	Longford-Westmeath	-2.3
	Dublin SW	+10.2	Limerick E	-2.3
	Tipperary N	+9.1	Limerick W	-1.5
	Tipperary S	+8.9	Dublin SC	-1.4
PDs	Laois-Offaly	-1.1	Galway E	-16.6
	Sligo-Leitrim	-2.6	Dublin S	-12.4
	Clare	-3.4	Cork SC	-11.5
	Galway W	-3.5	Cork NW	-11.4
	Waterford	-3.6	Dun Laoghaire	-10.8
WP	Dublin NE	+8.3	Wicklow	-2.8
	Dublin NW	+7.9	Kerry S	-2.2
	Dublin SC	+7.6	Louth	-1.2
	Dublin SW	+6.1	Cavan-Monaghan	-1.0
	Dun Laoghaire	+5.5	Tipperary S	-1.0

Note: The PDs lost no votes in eight constituencies because they had had no candidate there in 1987.

72

As in 1987, major gains and losses are spread around the country in what seems at first to be a patternless fashion. Uniform national swing is certainly not a feature of Irish elections. The two seats the party gained (Dublin North-Central and Dun Laoghaire) were statistically its sixth and thirteenth best prospects respectively at the outset of the campaign, while of the six it lost, only two (Sligo-Leitrim and Longford-Westmeath) featured among its ten most marginal seats. Despite the effort expended by the parties to devise and implement national strategies, which was detailed in chapter 2, we saw in the previous chapter that candidates on the ground often find that they have little direct contact with head office during the campaign, and they believe that their own efforts, be it their activity since the previous election or the door-to-door canvass, can contribute significantly to the outcome in their constituency. The very different outcomes in different parts of the country testify to the importance of local and personal factors.

Even so, Fianna Fáil's performance does have a pattern, which has two aspects. First, the party generally picked up votes where the PDs lost them. Of Fianna Fáil's best five performances in Table 4.5, three also feature in the PDs' worst five. Nationwide, there is quite a strong correlation (0.52) between Fianna Fáil gains and PD losses[2]. Second, Fianna Fáil lost votes to the left (Labour and the Workers' Party combined), the correlation between Fianna Fáil's losses and gains for the left being 0.36. Waterford and Dublin North-West, both among Fianna Fáil's worst three performances, marked the second and third biggest gains respectively for the combined left.

Fianna Fáil picked up votes in wealthier constituencies and lost them in poorer ones, as can be illustrated by comparing constituencies within the two major cities. In Dublin, Fianna Fáil recorded an average *gain* of 5.4 per cent in the three most prosperous constituencies (South, South-East and Dun Laoghaire) but an average *loss* of 5.1 per cent in the three least prosperous (Dublin Central, North-West and South-West), with an average loss of 1.3 per cent in the other five Dublin constituencies. Geraldine Kennedy's account of her campaign in Dun Laoghaire in Chapter 3 also bears out the view that there was a swing among middle-class PD voters there to Fianna Fáil. Similarly, in Cork, Fianna Fáil fell back by 4.3 per cent in the more working-class North-Central but advanced by 7.9 per cent in the refined environs of South-Central.

Although this pattern is pronounced, it doesn't entirely explain everything that happened to Fianna Fáil around the country. Many other factors, in some cases purely local ones, were also at work. In Roscommon, unexpectedly strong feeling on the local hospitals issue produced the major shock of the defeat of former Justice Minister Seán Doherty. In Kildare and Sligo-Leitrim the retirement of long-standing deputies Paddy Power and Ray MacSharry, plus internal disharmony in the latter constituency, contributed to the drop in support.

But overall the shifts in votes, and the opinion poll analysis reported in Chapter 5, both point in the same direction. Fianna Fáil made impressive middle-class gains from 1987 - but for every middle-class voter who entered the party fold by one gate, a working-class voter left by another one, leaving its aggregate share of the votes unchanged. The very policies which over the previous two years had won the confidence of former PD voters had alienated others who now switched to the left. The task of building and holding a cross-class coalition of support large enough to give it 84 Dáil seats proved beyond Fianna Fáil.

Fine Gael

Fine Gael gained both votes and seats at the election, but given the nadir to which it had plunged in 1987, what was achieved was the bare minimum the party expected. The gains the party made were very limited, and the overall 29.3 percent of the votes it won leaves it still below its humiliating 1977 level, and at its third weakest point in the last twelve general elections. It won back fewer than a fifth of the votes it had lost in 1987. Its further slip in votes in Dublin sees it at its lowest ever ebb in the capital, though it did make gains in the other three regions of the country. But although the statistics of Fine Gael's performance were unimpressive, the party was reasonably content with the outcome. The election brought to an end a very difficult period for Fine Gael, during which many activists thought that the Tallaght strategy of constructive or muted opposition was giving it responsibility without power, and some had feared a mauling when the election came.

Fine Gael gained seven seats, five from the PDs and two from Fianna Fáil, and lost three (Table 4.1). Although it picked up more PD seats than Fianna Fáil did, Fianna Fáil may have gained more PD votes. Certainly the PDs' losses correlate more strongly with Fianna Fáil gains (0.52) than with Fine Gael gains (0.26). In some of the constituencies where the PDs' losses were greatest, such as Cork South-Central, Dublin North-East, Dublin South, Dublin South-West, Dun Laoghaire and Limerick East, Fine Gael either lost votes itself or made only very small gains. Undoubtedly it won some PD votes, but it seems that many former PD voters concluded that the Fianna Fáil government was doing most of what they had wanted when they had given their backing to the PDs in 1987.

In addition, the growth of the Greens may have damaged Fine Gael, either by direct defections or by former PD voters switching to the Greens rather than to Fine Gael. Green gains correlate more strongly, and negatively (-0.41) with Fine Gael gains than with any other party's fortunes, and the correlation rises to -0.54 for the eleven Dublin constituencies. Fine Gael's biggest loss in Dublin came in the constituency (South-East) where the Greens recorded their largest gain. Generally, Fine Gael actually fell back in votes in some of the southside Dublin constituencies where the PDs sustained major losses, and the Greens were partly responsible for this.

Bright spots for the party came in Cork North-West and Longford-Westmeath, where it recorded major gains despite the retirement of Fine Gael incumbents, and in Clare, where many had tipped it to lose a seat. The party won a majority of the votes in Cork North-West and Cork South-West, feats it had never achieved before in those constituencies and has rarely achieved anywhere else. It also became the strongest party in two other constituencies, Dun Laoghaire and Roscommon. Black spots were its performances in Dublin South-West (where it received a pitiful 8.6 per cent of the votes) and Kerry South, the only constituencies where it did not win a seat. Overall, Fine Gael picked itself up off the floor, but it is still far below the dizzy heights of the early 1980s, when it could seriously believe it was about to displace Fianna Fáil as the largest party in the state.

The Progressive Democrats

In 1987 the PDs' opponents had refused to take seriously the consistent opinion poll evidence pointing to a substantial PD presence in the 25th Dáil. This time it was the PDs' scepticism which was shown to be unjustified. The polls suggested a disaster for the PDs, and once again the polls were right. At a stroke the party lost more than half of its votes and seats. It lost votes in every constituency where it had stood in 1987 (Table 4.5). Most of its seats went to Fine Gael (Table 4.1), but, as we have seen, a sizeable proportion of its voters must also have defected to Fianna Fáil.

The PDs faced the problem of all breakthrough parties. The people from whom they had got support in 1987 were, by definition, voters who were open to changing their allegiance (in many cases because they were young first-time voters), so what was to stop them flooding out of the PD camp as precipitously as they had flooded in? The task of converting volatile voters into long-term loyalists is one which has proved beyond a whole succession of minor parties in Ireland since 1922. The PDs' problem was compounded by their very success in having their central issues of public spending restraint and tax cuts accepted by the two main parties. To many erstwhile supporters, the party seemed to have made itself redundant.

The outcome

The PDs were reduced to just six seats, won in five constituencies. Five of its TDs had previously sat in the Dáil for Fianna Fáil; the sixth, Máirín Quill, had stood as a Fianna Fáil Dáil candidate and had been elected to Cork Corporation in 1985 as a Fianna Fáil councillor. The genuinely new deputies elected in 1987, who had done much to make the PDs an impressive parliamentary force, were blown away in the adverse wind, while those with roots deep in local politics survived. Many, perhaps all, of the party's remaining seats are due more to the personal support base of the TD than to any PD vote per se. The PDs have already, in their second election, fallen to a lower level of votes than Labour has ever reached even in its darkest hour. The party seems to have embarked on the familiar Irish minor party slide from a bright beginning towards oblivion. It will escape this fate only if it can construct a foundation which will outlast the political careers of its current deputies.

The left

The gains made by Labour and the Workers' Party led to talk about a major realignment in Irish politics, the emergence of a left-right divide, and so on. But the picture needs to be kept in perspective. The two parties between them won 14.4 per cent of the votes, the left's strongest performance since 1973 but a figure Labour on its own has exceeded at four previous elections. They may have won 22 seats in the 166-member Dáil in 1989, but Labour alone won 22 seats out of 144 in 1965. The Irish left remains the weakest in Europe, as Peter Mair points out in the final chapter of this book.

Each party made a net gain of three seats. Labour made gains in every region of the country, and in Munster regained most of the seats it had lost in 1987. Its recovery to a respectable level after its 1987 debacle confirms its remarkable resilience. There is a "Labour tradition" in many rural constituencies which, if mobilised by the right candidate in the right circumstances, can produce a seat in the face of unpromising statistics. A case in point is Waterford, where Tom Kyne held a seat for the party for nearly thirty years up to 1977. Although Brian O'Shea lost his deposit there in both elections in 1982, he topped the poll in 1989. Rural Labour seats can be and are handed on from one candidate to another, even if the interregnum is sometimes protracted. It is this enduring, if sometimes latent, vote that the PDs conspicuously lack.

Labour made gains in rural Leinster and Munster, but in Dublin the left's advance was spearheaded by the Workers' Party, which now has six TDs in the capital to Labour's three. Two of its gains were made at Labour's expense, its candidates taking the seats left vacant by Frank Cluskey's death and Barry Desmond's transfer to Strasbourg. Its third gain was in Dublin South-West, where Pat Rabbitte joined Labour's Mervyn Taylor in the Dáil, the first time any constituency has returned two left-wing TDs since Seán Dunne and John O'Connell were both elected for Labour in the old Dublin South-West constituency (covering a different area from the present one) in 1969.

Although the Workers' Party now overshadows Labour in Dublin, its problem is that it has only one seat, Joe Sherlock's personal creation, outside Dublin. In contrast, Labour has a better claim to be a national party, with representation in all four regions, and even in Dublin it was within striking distance of additional seats in four constituencies (Central, North-Central, North-West and South). Labour's share of the combined Labour and Workers' Party vote, which dropped steadily from 85.2 per cent in 1981 to 63.0 per cent in 1987, rose slightly to 65.6 per cent in 1989. The battle between the two parties will continue, and if it expresses itself in intensive constituency activity and policy development rather than mutual public attacks, this may work to the overall benefit of the left.

Others

One of the most surprising, and perhaps surprised, of the new TDs was Roger Garland of the Green Party / Comhaontas Glas, who took the fourth seat in Dublin South. The Greens had never previously managed even to save a Dáil election deposit, but Garland's success was merely a manifestation of an upsurge in support in Dublin, which saw their support there increase nearly fivefold. The party hopes that this, like Joe Sherlock's breakthrough for the Workers' Party in 1981, will boost its credibility and its national profile, helping it to grow further at elections to come. Its critics suggest that if its presence in the Dáil means that its policies on issues other than protecting the environment come under the spotlight, much of its support could rapidly evaporate.

Sinn Féin did even worse than in 1987, losing a third of the few votes it had won on that occasion. Before the 1987 election, the first to arise after it dropped its abstentionist policy, its leader Gerry Adams said several times that the real test of the party's prospects in the south would come not at that election but at the following one[3]. If that is so, its 1989 performance suggests it has little future in the south. Of its fourteen candidates, twelve, along with all of its Euro-candidates, lost their deposits. Its 1.2 per cent of support means that it is scarcely more popular among the southern electorate than it is among northern Protestants, and the "long road" to success on which its activists say it is embarked in the south looks more like a cul-de-sac.

The four outgoing TDs outside the five main parties were all re-elected. Seán Treacy, as outgoing Ceann Comhairle, was returned auto-

77

The outcome

matically, independents Neil Blaney and Tony Gregory each secured election on the first count, and in Limerick East Jim Kemmy increased his vote by over a half and outpolled Des O'Malley. Kemmy's personal standing is in inverse proportion to that of his Democratic Socialist Party, which seems unlikely to remain in existence much longer. These four were joined by a fifth independent, Tom Foxe, who took Seán Doherty's seat in Roscommon, fighting on a platform of preserving the future of the hospital in Roscommon town. Soon after being elected, he was interviewed on the radio by RTE's Shane Kenny, who wondered what role he could play in national politics and suggested that the Roscommon town hospital issue was a purely local one. "Not at all", replied Foxe, "the whole county's concerned about it".

THE TRANSFER PATTERN

At the five elections of 1973-82, with just three main parties present, the flow of transfers between parties was fairly stable and predictable. Fine Gael and Labour voters generally transferred their votes to each other, and this co-operation was crucial in depriving Fianna Fáil of an overall majority at each election except 1977. The picture was altered in 1987 by the appearance of the PDs, the ending of the Fine Gael-Labour entente, and the growth of the Workers' Party. A new pattern emerged, of a close relationship between Fine Gael and the PDs, a rather lukewarm one between the two left-wing parties, and some lingering traces of warmth between Fine Gael and Labour. Fianna Fáil invariably gave few transfers and received few, and in 1987 was deprived of 13 seats by transfers among the other parties.

The following discussion is based on analysis of the transfer of votes of eliminated candidates, and the transfer of surplus votes of elected candidates. The analysis is confined to cases where just one candidate's votes are transferred at a time. This should mean that virtually all transfers are analysed, as multiple eliminations are permitted only in very exceptional circumstances, but unfortunately it doesn't. The rules say that multiple eliminations are allowed only when the total votes of both the candidates to be eliminated comes to less than the number of votes in the possession of the next highest candidate, *and* the number of votes in the possession of each eliminated candidate exceeds a third of the quota (Third Schedule of Electoral Act, Rule 7(2)). This means that multiple elimination of candidates is possible only when each has saved his or her deposit. Despite this, many returning officers, seemingly in clear conflict with the letter of the electoral law, tend to eliminate several candidates together

78

even if the votes of some or all do not exceed a third of the quota. In 1989 there were 11 such cases (in Clare, Cork North-Central, Cork South-Central, Galway West, Longford-Westmeath, Louth, Roscommon, Tipperary North, Tipperary South, Waterford and Wexford), and there were 13 in 1987.

The broad outlines of the transfer pattern were much the same in 1989 as in 1987. Once again, the familiar "Fianna Fáil versus the rest" dimension of the party system (at least, the party system as we used to know it before Fianna Fáil joined a coalition on 12 July 1989) manifested itself in Fianna Fáil's isolation. Few of its transfers passed outside the party fold, and most of its terminal transfers (the votes distributed when there are no other Fianna Fáil candidates available to receive transfers) became non-transferable rather than go to candidates of other parties. Similarly, Fianna Fáil received few transfers from other parties.

The pact between Fine Gael and the PDs tightened up the flow of transfers between them. Terminal transfers from each party went predominantly to the other when it had a candidate available to receive them (Table 4.6). When both Fianna Fáil and Fine Gael were available to receive terminal PD transfers, the proportion going to Fine Gael in 1989 (66 per cent) was up on 1987 (54 per cent).

Table 4.6: Destination of terminal transfers

Trans-fers from	Parties available in each constituency to receive transfers	Percentage of transfers received						
		FF	FG	PD	Lab	WP	Oth	N-T
FG	FF, PD (3)	9.7	–	79.8	2.3	1.0	–	7.4
FG	PD, Lab (1)	6.4	–	74.6	13.4	5.6	–	0
PD	FF, FG (15)	12.7	65.7	–	7.3	2.4	4.1	7.8
Lab	FF, FG (15)	20.8	32.6	3.9	–	11.9	1.3	29.5
Lab	FG, WP (8)	16.0	22.2	2.5	–	44.5	4.9	9.9
WP	FF, FG, Lab (8)	12.9	10.4	4.0	51.8	–	6.9	14.0
Greens	-- (9)	17.8	23.5	5.8	25.5	10.1	0.5	16.8

Note: Figures in brackets show the number of constituencies where the relevant terminal transfer arose. For the Greens, all nine of their terminal transfers are included, without controlling for the availability of other parties.

On the left, too, solidarity was a bit stronger than in 1987. On that occasion, only 38 per cent of Labour terminal transfers went to the Workers'

The outcome

Party when both Fine Gael and the Workers' Party were available to receive them, and in 1989 this rose to 44 per cent. When candidates of Fianna Fáil, Fine Gael and Labour were all available to receive Workers' Party terminal transfers, over half (52 per cent) went to Labour compared with only 36 per cent in 1987. The persistence of some mild affection among Labour voters for Fine Gael is shown by that party receiving markedly more Labour terminal transfers than Fianna Fáil when both parties were available to receive them. Finally, examination of the Greens' terminal transfers does not support the suggestion that the party should be categorised as inherently left-wing. Although Labour and the Workers' Party together generally received slightly more Green transfers than Fianna Fáil and Fine Gael together, in situations where all four parties were available to receive transfers, Green votes tended to go in all directions (see Table 4.6).

The next table, Table 4.7, enables comparisons to be drawn with previous elections. It shows in particular the slow but steady rise in the rate of transfers between the two left-wing parties during the 1980s, though this still falls well short of the degree of solidarity between Fine Gael and the PDs, and indeed between Labour and Fine Gael before 1987.

Table 4.7: Interparty relationships 1981-1989

	1981	Feb 1982	Nov 1982	1987	1989
Fine Gael to Labour	86.8	69.1	80.4	39.8	17.6
Labour to Fine Gael	56.6	59.5	58.6	32.6	31.3
Fine Gael to PDs	--	--	--	72.1	79.8
PDs to Fine Gael	--	--	--	53.5	64.3
Labour to WP	16.2	26.4	37.5	37.8	44.5
WP to Labour	36.8	39.5	50.2	36.5	51.0

Note: The table shows the percentage of terminal transfers going from the first party to the second in situations where the second party had a candidate available to receive them.

As in 1987, transfers played a vital part in depriving Fianna Fáil of an overall majority. On that occasion thirteen seats were snatched from its grasp by transfers among the other parties. This time round it missed out on seven, where one of its candidates would have taken a seat had transfers not altered the balance between the Fianna Fáil candidate and a candidate of another party (see Table 4.8). This is the tangible price Fianna

Fáil has paid in the past for its hostility up to now to any kind of alliance with another party, the other side of the coin being its strong sense of self-identity and high rate of internal transfer solidarity. Fine Gael lost two seats due to transfers, one of them, rather improbably, because Workers' Party transfers took Máirín Quill of the PDs ahead of its outgoing TD Liam Burke.

Table 4.8: Constituencies where transfers affected the outcome

Constituency	Seat won by	At the expense of	Due to transfers from
Cork SC	Toddy O'Sullivan (Lab)	Batt O'Keeffe (FF)	WP
Dublin N	Seán Ryan (Lab)	G V Wright (FF)	Greens, FG
Dublin SE	Garret FitzGerald (FG)	Eoin Ryan (FF)	PD, Greens
Dublin SW	Mary Harney (PD)	Seán Walsh (FF)	FG, Greens
Dublin W	Austin Currie (FG)	Olga Bennett (FF)	PD, Lab
Limerick E	Peadar Clohessy (PD)	Eddie Wade (FF)	FG
Tipperary S	Michael Ferris (Lab)	Seán MacCarthy (FF)	Ind, FG
Cork NC	Máirín Quill (PD)	Liam Burke (FG)	WP, Ind
Kerry S	Michael Moynihan (Lab)	Michael Begley (FG)	FF

There were four other constituencies where transfers could, on realistic assumptions, have affected the outcome but did not. Labour missed out on seats in Dublin Central and Dublin North-West (where its candidate was only 55 votes short of a seat) due to an inadequate transfer from the Workers' Party. The same is probably true of Dublin North-Central, where the Workers' Party to Labour transfer was only 25.5 per cent. Had it been 32.3 per cent, still well below the national average, Labour's Michael O'Halloran would have overhauled Fine Gael's George Birmingham, and would probably have taken the last seat from Fianna Fáil on the transfers resulting from Birmingham's elimination. The final case was in Kerry South, where a better PD transfer could have saved the seat of Fine Gael's Michael Begley.

STV AND VOTE MANAGEMENT

Under STV, parties often have an incentive to "manage" the votes they receive in a particular constituency so as to maximise the number of seats they win. If a party is seeking two seats in a constituency, it wants its votes shared equally between its two leading candidates, in the hope that they will both float up towards the quota on a tide of transfers from other parties. If one reaches the quota on the first count and the other lags way behind, the trailing candidate is liable to be eliminated. The votes are "managed" by dividing the constituency territorially into, it is hoped, two equal sections, and awarding one section to each candidate by asking voters there to give him or her their first preference. The major parties tend to use this technique in most constituencies; examples were given in the accounts by Charlie McCreevy and Ivan Yates in the previous chapter.

A good example of the occasional need for vote management comes from the Waterford constituency. Fine Gael's two candidates won nearly 11,000 votes between them, but the distribution was very unbalanced. Austin Deasy received 7571 first preferences, not far short of the quota of 8265, while Katherine Bulbulia received only 3340. Fine Gael won only one seat while Fianna Fáil won two. But if about 2000 of Deasy's first preferences could have been diverted to Bulbulia, so that the two were roughly level, they would almost certainly have both been elected with the help of the three and a half thousand PD votes. Vote management is not always easy to carry out, partly because the ideal division of the constituency may be apparent only with hindsight, and partly because the party's leading candidate has to put his or her own seat in jeopardy to a running mate to try to win two for the party.

There were at least six constituencies, and possibly nine, where parties forfeited seats through inadequate vote management. Fine Gael missed out on a seat in Waterford, as indicated above, and in Cork North-Central and Cork South-Central it failed to take seats which went instead to the PDs. For example, in Cork North-Central Liam Burke of Fine Gael finished only 91 votes behind the PDs' Máirín Quill, while the other outgoing Fine Gael TD, Bernard Allen, had eleven hundred votes more than Quill. Interestingly, Waterford and Cork South-Central were constituencies where Fine Gael displayed an inability to learn from the past, having lost seats in 1987 through poor vote management[4]. Fianna Fáil forfeited two seats, in Limerick East (to the PDs) and, probably, in Longford-Westmeath (to Fine Gael), while the Workers' Party might well have taken two seats in party leader Proinsias De Rossa's constituency of Dublin North-West, at the expense of Fine Gael, had its 8829 first preferences been divided equally between its two candidates. In addition to these six cases, there are three others, Dublin North, Dublin South and Dublin South-East, where better vote management would have given Fianna Fáil at least a chance of an extra seat, at the expense of Labour, the Greens and Fine Gael respectively.

Mention should also be made of two cases where successful vote management was crucial to the outcome. In Dublin North-Central, on the last count, when three seats remained to be filled, the two Fianna Fáil candidates had only very slightly more votes between them than the two Fine Gael candidates (13855 compared with 13844), but the fact that the former were running almost neck and neck while the two Fine Gael candidates were sixteen hundred votes apart was decisive in giving Fianna Fáil one of its only two seat gains across the country. In Dublin South-East, poor vote management had cost Fine Gael one of their two seats in 1987. Heeding the lesson, this time around Garret FitzGerald embarked on a vote management scheme of his own devising, under which he urged a number of his supporters to switch their first preference to his running mate Joe Doyle. His personal vote dropped by over four thousand, and the overall Fine Gael vote fell, but because of FitzGerald's strategy the party regained its second seat.

THE CONSTITUENCY BOUNDARIES

It has been suggested that the set of constituencies devised by the independent boundaries commission in the early 1980s (and modified very slightly in the mid 1980s) has made it hard for Fianna Fáil to win a majority of seats. However, the boundaries were not an important factor in preventing the party attaining an overall majority in 1989. In its entire history, Fianna Fáil has never won a majority of seats on a vote share as low as the 44.1 per cent it won in 1989, and with 46.7 per cent of the contested seats it can hardly have any complaints about its treatment by the electoral system. The lowest vote share with which it has achieved an overall majority is 45.7 per cent in 1969, when it was helped by the decidedly partisan boundaries drawn up by Kevin Boland and by the low level of transfers passing between Fine Gael and Labour.

By the time the election was held, the constituency boundaries had become clearly unfair, and Mr Justice Hamilton declared in the High Court on 23 May that the Oireachtas was in breach of its constitutional duties by its failure to revise them in line with the findings of the 1986 Census. A table of figures released in the Dáil had given details of the population in each constituency[5]. It revealed that no fewer than 25 of the 41 constituencies had ratios of population to TDs that differed by more than a thousand from the national average of 21,329. Thirteen of these were overrepresented, the most overrepresented being Dublin North-West, where the ratio was 18,632 to one, and which was entitled to only 3.5 members in a 166-member Dáil instead of the four it actually had. The other twelve were underrepresented, the most underrepresented being Dublin South-West, where the ratio was 26,712 to one, and which was entitled to five members rather than the four it had. The obvious question is: did these unfair boundaries damage or benefit any parties specifically, and who would have benefited if a constituency revision had been carried out before the election?

In November 1988, the independent commission had published its recommendations for revised constituencies. The new constituencies, 45 of them, would have brought Dáil representation across the country into line with population, but the proposed scheme was rejected by the opposition parties because it drastically reduced the number of 5-seat constituencies (from fifteen to five), in accordance with the terms of reference laid down by the Fianna Fáil government. It is impossible to be certain how the parties would have fared in an election fought on these constituencies, given that some of the proposed constituencies cut across existing ones, but on the basis of best guesses it seems that although Fianna Fáil might have got a slightly better return from its votes, it would have been unlikely to win more than 80 seats.

On the whole it does not seem that the inequitable constituencies made any great difference to the results. Fianna Fáil and Fine Gael may have benefited slightly and Labour suffered, but the impact was only a seat or two either way. The largest two parties may have benefited in that they drew a disproportionate amount of their strength from the thirteen most over-represented constituencies. Fianna Fáil won 26.6 per cent of its votes but 29.9 per cent of its seats in these constituencies, and Fine Gael won 28.7 per cent of its votes but 30.9 per cent of its seats. Thus, if the most over-represented constituencies collectively had been cut back to their proper proportions, the two major parties would, other things being equal, have been most affected. In contrast, Labour won a disproportionate amount of its seats in the most under-represented constituencies, and stood to benefit if these constituencies had been given the extra seats they were due.

However, the effects of inequitable apportionment are not always easy to separate from the effects of over- and under-representation in individual constituencies. In addition, the imbalances in representation were not great: the thirteen most over-represented constituencies should have had 44.2 seats between them rather than the 49 they had, and the twelve most under-represented should have had 59.2 instead of the 54 they had. If an equitable apportionment had been carried out, without altering the relative numbers of three-, four- and five-seat constituencies, it is quite possible that the parties would have lost on the swings and gained on the roundabouts. The conclusion must be that the inequitable constituencies did not bring any significant benefit to any particular party.

THE 26th DAIL

Having looked at the composition of the new Dáil in terms of party, we now examine it in terms of the type of people who were elected to Leinster House. What are their backgrounds?

Occupation
Table 4.9 shows the occupational backgrounds of deputies. The overall pattern is very similar to those of the Dála elected in November 1982 and 1987[6].

Table 4.9: Occupations of deputies elected in June 1989

		FF	FG	Lab	PDs	WP	Oths	Total
Manual	Number	2	0	2	0	1	2	7
employee	%	2.6	0	13.3	0	14.3	33.3	4.2
Non-manual	Number	8	6	6	1	3	0	24
employee	%	10.4	10.9	40.0	16.7	42.9	0	14.5
Commercial	Number	21	13	1	2	1	2	40
	%	27.3	23.6	6.7	33.3	14.3	33.3	24.1
Farmer	Number	11	7	0	0	0	0	18
	%	14.3	12.7	0	0	0	0	10.8
Lower	Number	14	17	2	2	0	1	36
professional	%	18.2	30.9	13.3	33.3	0	16.7	21.7
Higher	Number	21	12	4	1	2	1	41
professional	%	27.3	21.8	26.7	16.7	28.6	16.7	24.7
Total	Number	77	55	15	6	7	6	166
	%	100.0	100.0	100.0	100.0	100.0	100.0	100.0

Note: For explanation of the classification scheme, see footnote 6.

Again, professionals form the largest component (46 per cent), and manual workers are conspicuous by their absence. Professionals have been growing in strength in the Dáil over the years, while "commercial" TDs and farmers have been shrinking. Commercial deputies have dropped from 34 per cent in 1965 to their present 24 per cent, while farmers have declined more dramatically, from 24 per cent in 1965 to less than half that proportion in 1989. As before, the profiles of the two main parties are very similar, the only notable difference being Fine Gael's slightly greater proportion of professionals.

Education

The slow but steady upward drift in the proportion of deputies with a university degree continued in 1989 (Table 4.10). In 1973 the figure stood at 28 per cent, and this had risen to 41 per cent by 1987. A further small increase in 1989 brought the figure to 43 per cent, still low by the standards of many parliaments. Fine Gael retains its traditional position as the party with the highest proportion of university-educated TDs, but the gap between the two main parties is narrower than has often been the case in the past. University-educated deputies tend on average to be newer (by two years) and younger (by four years) than the others, so the growth in their numbers is likely to continue.

Table 4.10: Educational backgrounds of deputies

		FF	FG	Lab	PDs	WP	Oths	Total
Deputies with university degree	N	31	25	4	4	4	3	71
	%	40.3	45.5	26.7	66.7	57.1	50.0	42.8

Gender

The number of women in the Dáil reached a record fourteen in November 1982, a figure repeated in 1987, but it has now fallen by one (Table 4.11). Although in most countries there are more women among left-wing deputies, the table shows that all Ireland's left-wing TDs are men, a lacuna highlighted by Labour leader Dick Spring's post-election appointment of himself as party spokesperson on women's affairs.

Table 4.11: Women deputies

		FF	FG	Lab	PDs	WP	Oths	Total
Women deputies	N	5	6	0	2	0	0	13
	%	6.5	10.9	0	33.3	0	0	7.8

Of the thirteen women in the Dáil, two are new deputies, bringing to 44 the total number of different women TDs since 1922. As in the previous Dáil, the female TDs are younger and newer than their male counterparts. They are also more likely to be related to a previous TD, to have a university degree and never to have been a local authority member.

Routes to the Dáil
In most countries, it is common for deputies to reach the national parliament via local government, and Ireland is no exception. Table 4.12 shows that only a seventh of TDs have never belonged to a local authority (that is, one of the 27 county councils or the five main city corporations), and over two-thirds joined a local authority before entering the Dáil. Altogether, 117 (70 per cent) of deputies were local authority members at the time of the election. The overall figures differ little from those of 1987, but there is an interesting change among the PD deputies. In 1987, five of the PD deputies had never belonged to a local authority. All of these lost their seats in 1989, but only one of the seven contesting PD deputies with local authority membership in their background suffered the same fate. It seems that for the brand new PD deputies, their two years of constituency activity did not accumulate sufficient personal credit to withstand the rainy day when it came.

Table 4.12: Local government background of deputies

| | When did deputy become member of local authority? | | | | | | | |
| | Before entering Dáil | | After entering Dáil | | Never a member | | Total | |
	N	%	N	%	N	%	N	%
Fianna Fáil	51	66.2	16	20.8	10	13.0	77	100.0
Fine Gael	40	72.7	3	5.5	12	21.8	55	100.0
Labour	13	86.7	2	13.3	0	0	15	100.0
PD	4	66.7	2	33.3	0	0	6	100.0
Workers' Party	6	85.7	1	14.3	0	0	7	100.0
Others	4	66.7	0	0	2	33.3	6	100.0
Total	118	71.1	24	14.5	24	14.5	166	100.0

The other best-known route to the Dáil lies in being related to another TD. In the 26th Dáil, 42 deputies (25 per cent) were related to a present or

The outcome

former TD who preceded them into the Dáil, much the same as in 1987. Of these, the relationship was, on a subjective judgement (based primarily on whether the TDs in question represented the same constituency and on the amount of time, if any, elapsing between their sitting in the Dáil), important in the initial election of 28 of them.

Turnover and experience

When the 25th Dáil was dissolved, two seats were vacant, and a further twelve TDs did not contest the election. In addition, twenty-seven outgoing TDs were defeated at the election. This brought forty-one deputies into the 26th Dáil who had not sat in the 25th, of whom thirty-two were new TDs and nine were former TDs regaining a seat after an absence.

Of the outgoing TDs to be defeated, nearly half (13 out of 27) lost their seat to a running mate of the same party. All the TDs in this category belonged to Fianna Fáil or Fine Gael, and the proportion of defeated TDs of these two parties whose seat went to a running mate was 13 out of 21, or 62 per cent. This is the same rate as in the elections of 1982, though it is higher than in 1987, when the figure was only 28 per cent. Losing one's seat to a running mate rather than to another party's candidate is, of course, an occupational hazard under STV. Some see voters' ability to reject incumbents in favour of other candidates of the same party, and to renew the parliamentary groups by electing deputies they see as more able and active, as enhancing participatory democracy. Others believe that the high rate of TDs' defeats at the hands of running mates reinforces the case for introducing a new electoral system to protect incumbents from the need to respond to the high level of constituents' casework demands [7].

The average deputy first stood for the Dáil in January 1978, and was first elected in May 1980 (Table 4.13). The average is perhaps distorted by the longevity of a handful of deputies, such as Neil Blaney and Charles Haughey, as most TDs (109, or 66 per cent) entered the Dáil in the 1980s. Political generations change rapidly: only two TDs sat in the Dáil with Eamon de Valera, only 16 with Seán Lemass, and only 57 with Liam Cosgrave and Jack Lynch. The occurrence of five general elections within the space of eight years has produced a dramatic degree of turnover in the political elite. There is considerable inter-party variation: the PDs, who had the newest parliamentary group in the previous Dáil, now have the most experienced, because of the survival of their long-established TDs and the disappearance of the newcomers. The short gap between first candidacy and first election for the Fianna Fáil deputies contrasts with the arduous years between the two for Labour and, especially, the Workers' Party.

Table 4.13: Electoral experience of deputies in 26th Dáil

	First stood for Dáil	First elected to Dáil	Elections contested	Elections won	Age in June 1989	Age when first elected
FF	Feb 1978	Mar 1979	5.2	4.6	46.4	36.2
FG	Nov 1979	Nov 1981	4.9	4.0	45.2	37.6
Lab	Sep 1975	Jan 1982	5.9	3.8	50.3	42.9
PD	Feb 1971	Oct 1974	7.2	6.2	50.4	35.8
WP	Sep 1976	Dec 1985	5.9	2.3	45.8	42.3
Oth	Nov 1972	Jul 1975	6.7	5.7	55.8	41.9
All	Jan 1978	May 1980	5.3	4.3	46.8	37.7

Note: all figures are averages. Ages are in years.

Collectively, deputies have stood for the Dáil 882 times and have been elected on 718 occasions, a success rate of 81 per cent. Comparative figures for pre-1982 Dála are not available, but it is likely that the current Dáil is exceptionally battle-hardened because of the spate of elections in the 1980s. Outgoing deputies such as George Birmingham, Hugh Byrne, Denis Foley and Seán MacCarthy, who fought and won the first four of these elections only to lose in 1989, left the Dáil after only eight years, whereas in earlier decades deputies who were elected four times consecutively could expect 12-16 years' Dáil membership. Most deputies (93) were elected the first time they stood; at the other extreme, five (two from Labour and three from the Workers' Party) lost four or more times before succeeding. Nearly half the deputies (79) have never lost an election, and 139, including the 32 first elected in 1989, have been unbeaten since first being elected.

The mean age of deputies has crept up slightly at each of the last two elections, and now stands at nearly 47. The average date of birth of the TDs of the 26th Dáil was August 1942, with only one (Michael Moynihan of Kerry South) being born before the foundation of the state. Labour and the PDs have the oldest Dáil groups, with Fine Gael having the youngest. Taking TDs' ages on the date of the election (15 June 1989), there were 9 deputies in their twenties, 36 in their thirties, 52 in their forties, 54 in their fifties, 14 in their sixties and one in his seventies. The average age of TDs when they were first elected, just under 38, is relatively young by the standards of other parliaments.

THE FUTURE

The next election is likely to be fought on a revised set of constituencies, but it is still worth looking at the post-1989 marginals. The figures in Table 4.14 show how many votes would have needed to switch between Fianna Fáil and one of its opponents to have brought about a different outcome. The figure given under "swing" refers to the percentage of votes which would have needed to change sides between Fianna Fáil and its specified opponent, using best estimates of the way in which any undistributed votes or surpluses would have transferred[8]. The table lists all 19 constituencies where a swing of three per cent or less would have made a difference. In 1989, Fianna Fáil achieved a swing of at least three per cent in nine constituencies, and suffered such a swing against it in fourteen constituencies, so all the constituencies listed are genuine marginals.

Table 4.14: Fianna Fáil marginals at the next election

Constituency	Swing required %	Gain from
Possible FF gains		
Longford-Westmeath	0.4	FG
Limerick E	1.0	PD
Dublin N	1.1	Lab
Dublin SW	1.2 / 2.8	PD / WP
Dublin SE	1.3	FG
Tipperary S	1.8 / 3.0	Lab / FG
Carlow-Kilkenny	2.4	FG
Wexford	2.8	FG
Clare	3.0	FG
Dublin SC	3.0	FG
Possible FF losses		*Loss to*
Cork E	0.5	FG
Dublin NC	0.6 / 1.0	Lab / FG
Waterford	0.6 / 2.0	PD / WP
Dublin Central	0.6	Lab
Tipperary N	0.6	Lab
Dun Laoghaire	0.8	PD
Mayo E	1.2	FG
Cork NC	1.7	FG
Mayo W	2.2	Ind

There are ten constituencies where such a swing would have earned Fianna Fáil an extra seat, compared with nine where it would stand to lose a seat on such a swing away from it. The "super-marginals", where a swing of one per cent or less would switch a seat, are stacked against Fianna Fáil; there are six constituencies where it would lose a seat on such a swing and only two where it would gain one. Other things being equal, the party would have been more likely to lose seats in a July 1989 rerun than to gain them, implying that to have called a fresh election rather than form a coalition would not have resolved Fianna Fáil's dilemma. The most marginal seats tend to be congregated in Dublin and Munster.

Table 4.15 lists the constituencies where seats are marginal as between other parties. Here too it is clear that Dublin and Munster are the key areas, as each of the nine most marginal constituencies is in one of these two regions. The table shows that three of the PDs' remaining seats (as well as Mary Harney's in Dublin South-West, listed in Table 4.14) are vulnerable to a small swing, although the party could also gain some. The tables hold most encouragement for Labour, which is the challenger in rather more marginals than it is the challenged.

Table 4.15: Non-Fianna Fáil marginals at the next election

Constituency	Loss by	Gain by	Swing required (%)
Dublin NW	FG	Lab	0.1
Cork NC	PD	FG	0.1
Tipperary N	FG	Lab	0.6
Cork SC	PD	FG	0.7
Kerry S	Lab	FG	0.8
Cork E	WP	FG	0.9
Dublin S	Green	Lab / PD	0.9 / 2.0
Dublin S	FG	PD	1.5
Dublin SE	FG / Lab	Green	1.5 / 1.5
Dublin SC	FG	Lab	1.7
Cork SC	Lab	WP	1.8
Meath	FG	Lab	2.0
Laois-Offaly	FG	PD	2.1
Sligo-Leitrim	FG	Ind	2.1
Dun Laoghaire	FG	PD	2.4
Limerick E	PD	FG	2.6

The outcome

Of course, the next election is particularly difficult to assess in advance. Even the battle lines are not clear. If the current Fianna Fáil-PD coalition government holds together for a full four- or five-year term, the two parties may fight the election in tandem and agree a transfer pact. It is even conceivable, though highly unlikely, that the PDs might by then have been reabsorbed into a post-Haughey Fianna Fáil. Alternatively, the PDs may revert to an official (as in 1989) or unofficial (as in 1987) liaison with Fine Gael, either as a result of the ideological compatibility between the two parties or as part of a conscious strategy to try to become Ireland's permanent party of government, like the West German Free Democrats, by periodically switching their coalition partners. A third possibility is that the coalition breaks down acrimoniously at some stage, and a bruised Fianna Fáil reverts to its traditional "ourselves against the rest" approach. If a contest for the leadership takes place in the party before the next election, as some expect, or even if one is believed to be in the offing when the election comes, the depth of anti-coalition feeling within the Fianna Fáil organisation will no doubt be carefully assessed, both by aspirants to the position and by TDs when deciding whom to vote for. Fianna Fáil may find itself racked by the same kind of internal divisions on the issue as other parties, especially Labour, have experienced in the past, and there is no certainty that anti-coalitionists will not gain the upper hand before the next election.

The two parties of the left, having prospered between 1987 and 1989 by adopting a position of outright opposition to cuts in public expenditure, can expect to make further gains during the lifetime of the present government by sticking to the same line, while keeping a wary eye on each other. Critics, like Alan Dukes in the Dáil on the day the coalition government was installed, will naturally accuse the left of taking the soft option of carping from the sidelines, but the left undoubtedly sees itself as having a historic opportunity to advance to new peaks of support and to foster the emergence of left versus right politics in Ireland.

The decline of the PDs at the 1989 election could be seen as a sign of the familiar party system fighting back, moving towards re-establishing itself in its traditional mould. But the outcome of the post-election negotiations on the formation of a government immediately plunged it back into the melting pot.

FOOTNOTES

---

1   Mogens S. Pedersen, "The dynamics of European party systems: changing patterns of electoral volatility", *European Journal of Political Research* 7:1 (1979) pp. 1-26.

2   The figure referred to is Pearson's coefficient (r). A value of zero would denote that the two factors were not related at all; a value of 1 would denote that the two match perfectly.

3   *Irish Times* 13 February 1987, p. 8.

4   Michael Gallagher, "The outcome" in Michael Laver, Peter Mair and Richard Sinnott (eds), *How Ireland Voted: the Irish general election 1987* (Swords: Poolbeg, 1987), pp. 85-6.

5   *Dáil Debates* 379:501-4, 22 March 1988.

6   The sources for the new TDs are contemporary newspapers; Jim Farrelly, *Who's Who in Irish Politics: the top 500* (Dublin: Blackwater, 1989); and Ted Nealon, *Nealon's Guide to the 26th Dáil and Seanad* (Dublin: Platform Press, 1989). Full-time politicians are classified according to their previous occupation, and deputies with more than one job are classified according to their main one. The classification scheme used is as follows. Under "commercial" are included business people, mainly small businessmen such as shopkeepers, publicans, auctioneers, contractors and so on. "Lower professionals" are mainly schoolteachers, while "higher professionals" include doctors, lawyers, lecturers, architects, accountants and economists.

7   For an argument closer to the former view, see Michael Gallagher, "Does Ireland need a new electoral system?", *Irish Political Studies* 2 (1987) pp. 27-48. For the latter view see articles by Gemma Hussey in *Irish Times*, 15-17 August 1989. For intra-party turnover between 1948 and 1977 see R. K. Carty, *Party and Parish Pump: electoral politics in Ireland* (Waterloo, Ontario: Wilfrid Laurier University Press, 1981) pp. 112-17.

8   The swing here and in Table 4.15 concerns the number of votes which would need to switch as between the two candidates in contention; it assumes neither party "manages" its votes better or worse than in 1989.

5. How the voters decided

Michael Marsh and Richard Sinnott

The previous chapter looked at what the voters decided. When we move on to try to explain how and why people decided to vote as they did, a whole set of questions about the attitudes and behaviour of the voters presents itself. When, precisely, did the Fianna Fáil push for a majority falter? Was the calling of the election a gamble or a reasonable calculation that went wrong? What effect did the decision to call the election have on the reputation of the man who made it, and what role did his reputation play in the subsequent campaign? Was the health issue as dominant as it seemed? If so, what was the effect on party support? Given the increased vote for the left, was there any ideological coherence beneath the campaign issues? In chapter 3 we read graphic personal accounts of the trials and tribulations of campaigning - how did the efforts of these six candidates and of hundreds of others influence voters' decisions? How many people switched their vote in 1989? Were the gains and losses of the parties class-based? If so, have they brought us any nearer the much-discussed realignment of Irish politics along class lines? This chapter marshals the opinion poll evidence on these matters, beginning with developments in patterns of support for the various parties between 1987 and 1989.

PATTERNS OF PARTY SUPPORT 1987-89

At first sight, the trends in party support revealed in the polls[1] taken between 1987 and the calling of the election in May 1989 seem simple: by July 1988, Fianna Fáil had moved into a reasonably comfortable electoral position with 43 per cent of the declared vote (see Figure 5.1). The improvement in Fianna Fáil support appears to have coincided with the collapse of the PDs between April and July of 1988; (as one would expect, Figure 5.1 suggests that Fine Gael also benefited substantially from that collapse). Fianna Fáil's strong position was then more or less maintained over the course of the following eleven months and even improved slightly in the early days of the election campaign as, with the calling of the election, some of the "don't knows" came off the fence. On this evidence, it might seem that Fianna Fáil went to the country in May 1989 with a reasonable chance of achieving its objective, even if not as a certain winner. However, if we look below the surface at the movements in support for the parties among different social classes over the two year period, a more complicated picture emerges, one which suggests that Fianna Fáil's basis for going to the country was much less secure than appeared at first sight.

Figure 5.1 Trends in party support 1987-1989

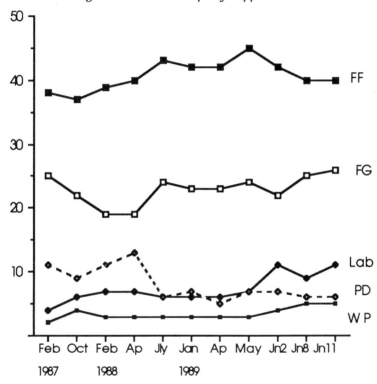

Part of the problem was that, based on past experience in the 1980s, Fianna Fáil knew it was very unlikely to gain an overall majority with less than 46 per cent of the vote. Any significant slippage below this would put paid to its hopes. This was ominous, because the trends in the class composition of Fianna Fáil support in the period 1987-89 were marked by considerable instability and therefore indicated very real potential for just such slippage.

Fluctuations in class voting preferences

In looking at these class trends, it is worth bearing in mind that analysis of the February 1987 election led to the conclusion that "the class basis of Irish politics is more evident now than at any time in the previous twenty years"[2]. Part of the evidence for this conclusion was the marked contrast between Fianna Fáil support among the working class (skilled working class, 45 per cent; unskilled working class, 41 per cent) and its support among the middle class (upper and middle middle class, 26 per cent; lower middle class, 32 per cent). In speculating on the likely course of development of this new class pattern, we suggested then that one crucial factor would be "the effect on the party's working class base of Fianna Fáil's current policy of financial cuts in state services, balanced against the possibly opposite effect of these same cuts on at least some of Fianna Fáil's bourgeois and middle class critics".[3] Figure 5.2 allows us to examine how this actually worked out.

Figure 5.2 Fianna Fáil support in different social classes

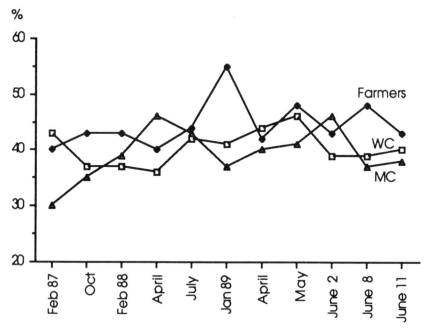

After six months of Fianna Fáil government, a divergence in support had indeed begun to manifest itself. Working class support for Fianna Fáil had dropped significantly (down eight and four percentage points in the skilled and unskilled working class respectively). There was a simultaneous rise in middle class support, though at that stage this was only really noticeable in the AB (upper middle and middle) class, a group which is too small to offset the working class losses. It was not until a full year had elapsed (and a second budget had occurred) that both sections of the middle class really rallied to Fianna Fáil (upper middle and middle, 49 per cent; lower middle, 45 per cent). Two features of this surge in middle class support should be noted. First, it happened prior to the collapse of the PD vote, which, as we have seen, occurred after April 1988. Rather, it seemed to come mainly at the expense of Fine Gael, which hit an all-time low among the middle class in April 1988. Secondly, the surge in middle class support for Fianna Fáil was of remarkably short duration. By January 1989, it had slipped back to 37 per cent and, although there were some subsequent fluctuations, it failed to reestablish the levels reached in the spring and summer of 1988. In fact, despite a reasonable overall level of support of 42 per cent, the January 1989 poll brought very mixed news to Fianna Fáil - an exceptionally high degree of support among the farming community (55 per cent) masked an indifferent showing among all other sectors of the electorate. However, a poll in April 1989, the last published poll before the election, seemed to put the party back on track. Health and other public expenditure cuts notwithstanding, its support among the working class was similar to what it had been in the last election and, although middle class support had slipped substantially from the high points of April and July 1988, it was still way ahead of what it had been in February 1987.

Perhaps, then, Fianna Fáil had rediscovered the old successful cross-class formula, or at least rediscovered enough of it to make it right for Charles Haughey to seize his opportunity and call an election for June 15th? One weakness in the argument for an early election was that, as Figure 5.2 shows, the pattern of cross-class support that was evident in the April poll was too short-lived and too subject to fluctuations to provide a reliable basis for victory. A second weakness in the case for a June election, detectable perhaps only with the benefit of hindsight, was that, given the nature of the policies the government had been pursuing, middle class support would have have needed to have been much stronger to offset the potential leakage to the left.

As late as the first weekend of the campaign that leakage was still only potential (see the lines for Labour and the Workers' Party in Figure 5.1). The growth in support for the left and in particular for the Labour

Party was a product of the election campaign and had not occurred in response to government policy over the two-year period. Obviously one can
argue that such a swing to the left was always likely but, if it was, this
reaction did not manifest itself even with the calling of the election. In
the first poll of the campaign, taken over the first weekend, both left
wing parties were showing only quite modest advances on their poor performance in the previous election. Less than a week later the Labour
Party especially had made significant gains, which, with some slight
faltering a week before voting, it maintained into the election itself.

Individual voter change February 1987 - June 1989
In order to understand why some voters switched, we need to know when
they switched. We are fortunate in having a good stock of information on
this question for this election. From a Eurobarometer poll taken in March
1989, we know how those who had voted for the various parties in
February 1987 were intending to vote at that stage, that is before an election had even been mooted. From the final MRBI poll of the campaign we
have information on how 1987 party voters intended to vote in the election
five days later. Both of these sets of data are subject to the problems of
vote recall over an extended period of time but are nonetheless valuable
indicators of the general trend, in particular for the larger parties. We
also have, for the first time in an Irish election, campaign panel data,
that is responses from the same set of individuals interviewed twice - at
the beginning of the campaign and on the day after voting.[4] This enables
us to compare their voting intention at the outset of the campaign with
the vote they report having cast three weeks later. Table 5.1 shows how
far each of the parties managed to hold on to its support over the three
periods in question. Each figure indicates the percentage of a party's voters whose voting intention (or reported vote) at the later date in each period is unchanged from that reported for the earlier date.

Table 5.1: Stability of voting intention, 1987-1989

Period	All Parties	FF	FG	Lab	WP	PD
	%	%	%	%	%	%
Feb 87 - Mar 89	83	87	80	80	74	65
Feb 87 - June 89	72	74	76	63	71	47
May 89 - June 89	79	85	78	66	81	40

Source: Eurobarometer No 30, MRBI2, Lansdowne 1 and 2

The discussion of trends over the period 1987-89 indicated considerable movement of voters between the parties. However, when we examine a snapshot of the results of these movements in March 1989, it is evident that the result for the parties was, with the exception of the Progressive Democrats, relatively little change. Overall, 83 per cent of the voters were, at that stage, intending to vote for the same party they had voted for in 1987 and for three of the parties (Fianna Fáil, Fine Gael and Labour), there was very little variation from this overall figure.[5]

The second line of data in Table 5.1 compares reported vote in 1987 with intended vote quite close to the end of the 1989 campaign and, as one would expect, it portrays the greatest degree of change. Comparing the first two lines confirms the impression that it was the election period itself rather than the period in government as a whole that was decisive for Fianna Fáil's failure to win its overall majority. As of March 1989, it had lost 13 per cent of its 1987 voters. But by the end of the election campaign, less than three months later, that figure was 26 per cent.

There is an overlap between the second and third periods portrayed in Table 5.1. The panel data, which relates to the third period (i.e., 27th/28th May - 15th June 1989) and which is probably more reliable than the data based on fairly distant recall, further confirms the importance of the campaign itself. Twenty-one per cent of those who declared a preference for one of the five main parties at the outset of the campaign changed their mind between then and polling day. Fianna Fáil suffered the smallest losses (15 per cent). The Workers' Party was next best, losing 19 per cent. Somewhat surprisingly, Fine Gael and especially Labour shed a significant quantity of votes (22 per cent and 34 per cent respectively). As for the Progressive Democrats, they suffered what can only be described as further heavy vote haemorrhage (60 per cent), even after their pre-campaign losses.

Of course, a party's fate is decided not only by how many supporters it loses but also by how many voters it can attract from the other parties, and from amongst those who were undecided. Accordingly, we need to look both at the proportion of votes a party manages to hold on to (Table 5.1) and at the extent and origin of its gains (Table 5.2). Ideally, a party should retain as much as possible of the support it had at the beginning of the campaign (the figure in Table 5.1) and this block of loyal voters should constitute as low a proportion as possible of the party's final vote, in the sense that it should be augmented by as many votes as possible from other parties (Table 5.2). Looking at the matter in this way, one can see where things went wrong for Fianna Fáil. It did better than the other parties in retaining the votes it had at the outset but failed to win over many voters during the campaign. A mere thirteen per cent of its final vote was due to its campaign efforts - not enough to outweigh the losses it suffered.

Table 5.2: Votes retained and won in the course of the campaign

	Actual vote				
Intended vote at the start	FF %	FG %	LAB %	WP %	PD %
FF	87	9	17	12	15
FG	3	77	8	10	18
Labour	1	3	57	7	0
WP	0	0	3	59	5
PD	3	5	3	2	51
DK	5	6	3	5	8
Other/Not Vote	1	1	8	2	10
Total	100	100	100	100	100
N=	412	235	63	41	39

Source: Lansdowne 1 and 2

By contrast, Fine Gael lost a substantial proportion (22 per cent, see Table 5.1) of those who at the outset said they would vote for it, but compensated by winning replacements for these losses - these campaign gains constituted 23 per cent of Fine Gael's final vote. The most frequent source of such gains was Fianna Fáil; voters who had intended voting for Fianna Fáil but switched to Fine Gael made up nine per cent of the total Fine Gael vote, or two in five of all Fine Gael campaign gains. Relatively speaking, Labour did even better at the expense of Fianna Fáil. We have seen (Table 5.1) that Labour lost almost one-third of its intending voters from the outset of the campaign. However, it more than made up the loss, in that two-fifths of its final vote represented gains made during the campaign. Once again the largest block (one-sixth of its total vote) came from Fianna Fáil. The Workers' Party, which did quite well in terms of keeping its early campaign vote (see Table 5.1), showed a pattern of gains that was quite similar to that of the Labour party.

Despite their apparently inexorable decline since April 1988, the Progressive Democrats actually won over (or won back) some voters during the campaign - one-half of their final total consisted of campaign gains.

100

However, the party lost more than it gained - three out of five of those who said they would vote for the PDs at the beginning of the campaign had deserted the ship by voting day.

This, then, was an election in which the events, the agenda-setting, the publicity efforts and the issues of the campaign would appear to have played a crucial role. The first issue was the very calling of the election, a decision that, as we shall see, had considerable implications for the reputation and popularity of Charles Haughey.

THE ELECTION AS AN ISSUE

A popular government
The opinions polls regularly ask voters if they are satisfied or dissatisfied with the performance of the government. By subtracting the per cent dissatisfied from the per cent satisfied we can form a simple index rating a government's performance. Ratings from February 1987 to June 1989 are shown in Figure 5.3.

Figure 5.3   Government's popularity rating 1987-89

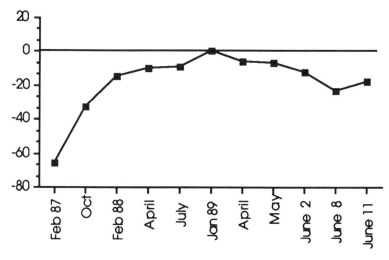

On the eve of the 1987 election the Fine Gael/Labour government stood at -66, with dissatisfied outnumbering satisfied voters by 80 per cent to 14 per cent. The situation improved steadily under the new administration to the extent that in January 1989 the index reached zero, meaning that

101

there were equal numbers of satisfied and dissatisfied voters. This was a high point; from early 1988 until the run-up to the election the approval index was fairly constant at around -8 per cent. However, a small decline was evident in April 1989, and this accelerated once the campaign was well under way, with the index standing at -23 by June 8th.

This pattern, of a regular increase towards a plateau followed by a sharp decline through the campaign, reverses almost exactly the conventional wisdom, which is that a government is most unpopular at mid-term but regains support as the election draws near. These figures provide evidence that some of Fianna Fáil's problems stemmed from the Taoiseach's decision to seek a dissolution of the Dáil. Whilst government's popularity fell through the campaign, the fact is that their rating was at no time a positive one. Certainly this administration was more popular than its predecessor, but it never had more supporters than detractors.

A necessary election?
One reason for the fall in the government's popularity during the campaign may have been that a clear majority of voters (two-thirds according to early polls, as we see in Table 5.3) saw the 1989 election as unnecessary.

Table 5.3: Is it necessary to have an election at this time, or not?

	May 26-27	June 2
	%	%
Necessary	28	29
Unnecessary	67	66
DK	5	5
Total	100	100
N=	1053	1045

Source: Lansdowne1, IMS1

Even Fianna Fáil supporters did not want an election; only 34 per cent of them in the first poll thought an election necessary. As the campaign proceeded, responses became increasingly defined in partisan terms, with Fianna Fáil supporters increasingly believing the election to be necessary and other parties' supporters increasingly thinking it unnecessary. Fianna Fáil voters were nine per cent more likely than those intending to vote for other parties to see the election as "necessary" in the first poll and were 15 per cent more likely to do so in the second poll. Voters either shifted allegiance according to their views on the necessity of an election, or else, more likely, party arguments on the necessity or otherwise of an election were getting through to their followers.[6] Even so, a majority of voters who were intending to vote Fianna Fáil still felt the election was unnecessary a week into the campaign.

Amongst Fianna Fáil supporters the election was most likely to be considered necessary by those who were satisfied with the government's performance, but in other political groupings it was those who were satisfied who were most inclined to see the election as unnecessary. Thus, within Fianna Fáil, the calling of the election served to give already unhappy supporters something more to complain about, and outside Fianna Fáil, those most inclined to support the government were most upset by the election (see Table 5.4). We have seen that the government's popularity declined through the campaign. We shall now look at evidence that suggests that the decision to hold an election may have adversely affected the Taoiseach's popularity even more dramatically.

Table 5.4: Views on necessity of election, by satisfaction with government and voting intention

		Nec	Not nec	DK	Total	N=
FF	%Satisfied	41	54	5	100	316
	%Not satisfied	33	62	5	100	98
Pact	%Satisfied	16	83	1	100	57
	%Not satisfied	24	74	2	100	234
Left	%Satisfied	19	81	0	100	21
	%Not satisfied	26	70	4	100	127

Source: IMS1

THE LEADERSHIP FACTOR

Mr. Haughey's popularity: rehabilitation and reversal
The 1989 election was Mr. Haughey's fifth attempt to win a majority of seats as leader of his party. This was inevitably highlighted in campaign coverage and tended to focus attention on his leadership, which had been a prominent issue both in previous campaigns and, within his own party, through much of 1982-83. Did the widespread support for the 1987-1989 Fianna Fáil government restore public confidence in his leadership? Did the decision to go for an early election undermine what may have been gained? A decade after its first appearance in 1979, did "the

Haughey factor" still exist, and what role, if any, did it play in the 1989 election?

Although the Haughey factor became a matter of parliamentary controversy with the debate on the nomination of the Taoiseach in December 1979, it did not become a marked feature of the attitudes of the electorate until early 1982. Figure 5.4 traces the balance of satisfaction or dissatisfaction with Haughey at various intervals over the period of his leadership of Fianna Fáil. It shows that he enjoyed a surplus of satisfaction over dissatisfaction immediately after his election as party leader and Taoiseach, and that this held good up to and including the the June 1981 election. It was not until January 1982 that this changed substantially, when it slipped into deficit for the first time and then, with the calling of the Budget election of February 1982, plummeted to minus 17 points. After a short but very difficult period in government in 1982, a period replete with political and economic crises, the deficit widened to a huge 34 percentage points in the November 1982 election.

Figure 5.4 Mr Haughey's popularity rating 1981-1989

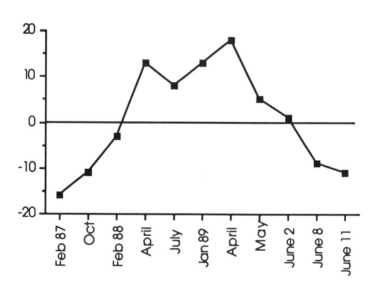

Mr. Haughey emerged from the 1987 election as leader of a minority government but without having managed to secure decisive public approval of his leadership. Six months after the election his satisfaction /

dissatisfaction rating was still at an 11 percentage point deficit and it is notable that dissatisfaction was greatest among the unskilled working class, who had been his staunchest supporters when his leadership was a matter of overt controversy. However, as general approval of the Fianna Fáil minority government grew, so too did satisfaction with Mr. Haughey's leadership. In April 1988, his rating as Taoiseach turned positive for the first time since June 1981. Again the approval was greater among the middle class, but it extended across the social spectrum. With the exception of a dip among middle class voters in January 1989, the positive picture was maintained over the course of the following year, rising to a surplus of 18 points in April 1989.

However, immediately on the calling of the election (i.e., in the Lansdowne / Star poll taken over the first weekend of the campaign), Mr. Haughey's popularity suffered a sharp drop of 12 points, leaving only a marginal surplus of satisfaction over dissatisfaction of five percentage points. It is particularly significant that, whereas the level of *Fianna Fáil* support revealed in the April 1989 poll did not drop much in the first poll of the campaign, approval of the person who had called the election certainly did.

In terms of voters' satisfaction with the way in which he was doing his job, the situation went from bad to worse for Mr. Haughey from there on. The index slipped to a mere one-point surplus within a week of the calling of the election and the slide continued thereafter - to minus nine on June 8th and to minus eleven in the last poll of the campaign. As his popularity declined, some of the old contrast between greater middle class dissatisfaction and less pronounced working class dissatisfaction that had been so clear around 1982 reappeared.

Preference for Taoiseach

Satisfaction with the performance of a particular leader may or may not affect the way people vote. For one thing, choice of Taoiseach may not be an important factor for the individual voter (we present some evidence on this below). If it is important, then the effect on the voting decision will depend also on how the voters see the main contender for the job. For much of the period when electoral contests were between Charles Haughey and Garret FitzGerald, Haughey trailed significantly, that is from the middle of June 1980 until well after the November 1982 election. For most of that time there was a significant class bias in the patterns of support for these leaders, with the middle class strongly favouring FitzGerald and the working class supporting or being less opposed to Haughey.[7] Even on the eve of the 1987 election, when only 14 per cent were satisfied with

How the voters decided

FitzGerald's government, he was still preferred to Haughey as Taoiseach by one point.[8]

Garret FitzGerald's successor, Alan Dukes, inherited a defeated party, but also a record of leadership popularity over an extended period that would be hard to match. Figure 5.5 charts the ensuing contest between Alan Dukes and Charles Haughey up to June 1989.

Figure 5.5 Mr Haughey's lead over Fine Gael leader 1987-1989

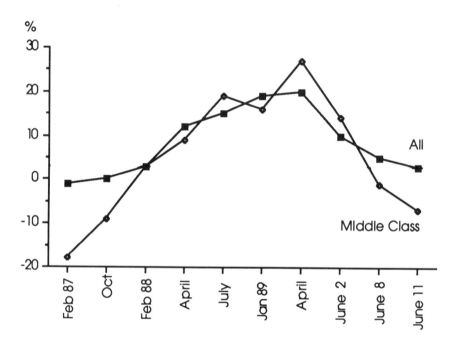

In the first "round" of the series (October 1987), the two were level. The figure makes clear that, while he was level with Dukes among voters as a whole, Haughey was still regarded with suspicion among the middle class. This implies that, despite his party's falling popularity among the working class, he was still ahead of Dukes in that sector. A little more than a year after the 1987 election, however, he moved into a commanding lead. The pattern of this lead differed from the pattern of his party's support in that it developed equally in all classes and, once under way, it held up quite consistently over the following twelve months. A week into the election, however, what on the eve of the election had been a commanding lead was halved.[9] In the second week of the campaign the slide

106

continued and Haughey's lead was reduced to five percentage points. The final poll of the campaign showed a further slight drop and significantly showed Dukes again leading Haughey in preference for Taoiseach among the middle class by seven percentage points. The decline from April was much greater among middle class voters than among working class ones, particularly the unskilled working class. Haughey's loss in the former group was 34 points, but in the latter it was only six points.

This sharp reversal of Mr. Haughey's fortunes early in the campaign, both in his declining index of satisfaction and his rating relative to Dukes as charted in Figures 5.4 and 5.5, suggests strongly that the timing of the election had an adverse effect on Mr. Haughey's image, possibly raising in voters' minds the charges of opportunism that had adversely affected his popularity in earlier periods.

Some evidence that reservations of this sort about Mr. Haughey's leadership may have featured in the 1989 election comes from data on the perception of the characteristics of party leaders collected in the second IMS poll of the 1989 election. Respondents were asked whether they saw a particular set of characteristics (competent, trustworthy, realistic and arrogant) as applicable to the political leaders. Respondents could name as many or as few of the political leaders as they wished in respect of any given characteristic. Haughey is the most likely to be perceived as competent and as realistic, being just ahead of Dukes on both these characteristics (Table 5.5). However he falls significantly behind in the "trustworthy" stakes and he is a full 35 percentage points more likely than Dukes to be seen as arrogant. These are perhaps just the kind of reservations that would have been kindled by the precipitous rush to the hustings in a situation in which, whatever the potential instabilities in the parliamentary situation, most voters saw no grounds for an election.

Table 5.5: Perceptions of party leaders, June 1989

	Haughey %	Dukes %	O'Malley %	Spring %	De Rossa %
Competent	45	39	21	19	15
Trustworthy	23	33	13	17	12
Realistic	33	28	15	14	12
Arrogant	47	12	24	9	5

Source: IMS2

THE ISSUES

The agenda
The election itself was the first issue of the campaign, but it was not long before other matters dominated the political debate. Information from the many polls taken during the campaign about the issues of the election is in some ways disappointing. There is no parallel to the questions asked by MRBI in 1987 which ascertained the respondent's positions on several issues and his or her ranking of the parties on those issues. Nor is there any systematic equivalent to the question asked in most recent elections by at least one polling agency: which party has the best policy on employment, on prices, etc? However, several questions were asked about the importance of some issues, and IMS included some specific items on the health service, which turned out to be the unexpected element of the campaign.

The first wave of the Lansdowne poll, carried out at the start of the campaign, asked people to say, from their own point of view, what were the three most important issues in the general election. A list of fifteen issues and groups of issues were provided and up to three answers recorded. Results are displayed in Table 5.6 which shows those eight issues most commonly chosen as first, second and third in importance and indicates how often mention was made of each issue.

Table 5.6 Important issues in the election

	May 26-27 %	May 27-29 %
Unemployment	73	73
Health	42	45
Emigration	37	27
Tax cuts	31	21
Prices	25}	
Economy	19}	13
Welfare/Pensions	12	16
Education cuts	8	8
N=	1053	1001

Source : Lansdowne1, MRBI1

The second column of Table 5.6 shows the results of an open ended question asked by MRBI at the same time as the Lansdowne poll was conducted. This question invited people to say what were the issues which the parties should be concerned about. There are several interesting features of the responses to these questions.

The first is the overwhelming importance of unemployment, which in both surveys far outweighs the other items in importance. This echoes the situation in earlier elections: unemployment has been top of the electorate's agenda for all the elections of the 1980s. The second feature is the emergence of some issues in unprecedentedly high places on the agenda. Health cuts and the health service emerged as the second most important issue. To a great extent it became *the* issue of the election by virtue of its novelty. Emigration, though hardly a new topic, also emerged as one which the electorate treated more seriously. Seventy-six per cent said it was "very important" in the MRBI survey, compared with only 46 per cent who thought so in 1987.[10] Taxation and general concerns about fiscal problems moved down the agenda, although tax reform was still the fourth item in both surveys. The third feature is the lack of attention given to a number of items that might be considered important, given their coverage in the media: Northern Ireland, the rod licence dispute and army pay. Issues related to Northern Ireland, variously expressed as Northern Ireland/Extradition/Anglo-Irish agreement, were important to under three per cent of respondents in each poll.

These responses, of course, give no direct indication of what should be done to correct the problems, nor of who is to blame for them. In the absence of data about who is judged to have the best policy on individual problems we can only speculate. It might be expected that the government of the day would be blamed for problems that have moved up the agenda, whereas they might take some credit for problems that have moved down. Issues also drop because they cease to be the cause of any partisan difference: the relative absence of Northern Ireland as an issue is a case in point. Unemployment has become a chronic problem, and it is unlikely that many parties gained much from this issue.

The political agenda is also defined in subtly different ways by supporters of the different parties or combinations of parties. Table 5.7 gives combined figures for supporters of "Pact" parties (Fine Gael and Progressive Democrats) and "left" parties (Labour and Workers' Party). Several features deserve mention. While the overall rankings in each party grouping are similar, there are also some systematic differences between the parties.

Table 5.7 : Important issues, by party supported

	Pact	FF	Left
	%	%	%
Unemployment	68	74	80
Health	48	37	47
Emigration	39	36	30
Personal Tax	33	29	28
Prices	23	26	27
Economy	17	21	19
Welfare/Pensions	10	13	21
Education cuts	12	9	12
N=	322	470	105

Source: Lansdowne1

If an issue is more important for the left parties, it is less important for the "Pact" parties. (The Progressive Democrats and the Workers' Party are normally at opposite poles.) Generally, more left voters think unemployment, prices, the economy and pensions are important than do Pact and Fianna Fáil supporters, whereas more Pact voters than left voters think reducing emigration and reducing direct taxation important. Fianna Fáil supporters normally fall between those of the other groupings, but on two issues they clearly break this pattern: health cuts and education cuts. Both are essentially criticisms of the government and as such the relative absence of Fianna Fáil supporters thinking them important is understandable. Even so, 37 per cent of Fianna Fáil supporters thought health cuts were an important issue, and whilst this was 10 per cent below the level found amongst the supporters of other parties, it would not have helped Fianna Fáil's cause in the campaign.

Some of the party-issue links can be understood in class terms. Tax reform was thought important by almost twice as many from the middle class group as from the unskilled working class group. Given the Progressive Democrats' social profile, the concern of their supporters with this issue would be expected, even apart from the PDs' special emphasis on it. Unemployment was most often thought to be important by unskilled workers, which may underlie its salience to left party voters. Concern with the health issue, on the other hand, showed very little variation across the social spectrum. The fact that two out of every five voters, irrespective of social class, agreed that this was an important issue points to the need for a more detailed investigation of the role it played.

110

The health issue

The sudden appearance of health high on the political agenda following the publication of the first Lansdowne and MRBI polls attracted considerable media attention, and there were reports that Fianna Fáil was revising its manifesto to take account of it. Whilst only 13 per cent reported it as being the "most important" issue in the Lansdowne poll, over 40 per cent mentioned the issue as important, and it was perhaps this figure which had most impact. Two weeks into the campaign, an IMS/Sunday Independent poll (IMS2) provided people with a list of "some issues which people have identified as being important in the campaign" - emigration, health, taxation and unemployment - and asked respondents: "From your personal point of view, which ONE of these issues will most influence you in deciding your vote?". Results are displayed in Table 5.8, along with the figures for "most important issue" from the earlier Lansdowne poll.

Table 5.8 : The most important issue

	May 26-27	June 8	
	%	%	
Unemployment	47	30	Unemployment
Health	13	39	Health
Emigration	9	9	Emigration
Personal Tax	7	18	Taxation
Others	23	3	None of these
DK	1	1	DK
Total	100	100	
N=	1053	1050	

Source: Lansdowne1, IMS2

The increase in the salience of health over a period of ten or eleven days is remarkable. Health actually *replaced* unemployment as the major issue by a margin of nine per cent. Further confirmation of the perceived importance of the health issue comes from the panel data, when respondents were asked after the election what had been the most important issues of the campaign for them personally.[11] Table 5.9 shows the relative importance of the issues as seen by the same individuals at the outset of the campaign and on the day after they had voted.

Table 5.9   *Most important election issues, start and end of campaign*

	May 26-27	June 16
Unemployment/jobs	69	53
Health	41	45
Reducing Emigration	34	27
Taxation	33	24
Economy	16	19
Cost of living	26	17
Stable government	7	17
Social Welfare	15	12
Education cuts	12	12
N=	1053	798

Source: Lansdowne1 and 2

Health was the only major issue which more people considered important at the close of the campaign than they did at the beginning. Whilst
overall rankings are a little different to those in Table 5.8, the major features are much the same. (It should be remembered that these are responses to a question asking which issues were important, whereas those
in Table 5.8 are responses to a question asking which issue is the *most* important.) One difference that is highlighted in this table is the growth in
the number of those who saw stable government as important. Fianna Fáil
voters were much less likely than other voters to see health as important
and were much more likely to mention stable government. The pattern on
the health issue repeats that shown earlier, and that on stable government underlines the interpretation that the rising salience of this issue
was helpful to Fianna Fáil.[12] We return to this in more detail below.

Clearly the health issue was seen to be important, but what impact
did it have on how the voters decided? Both IMS surveys (IMS2, IMS3)
late in the campaign asked: "which party has the best policy to deal
with the problems of the health services?". Answers from these two surveys are displayed in Table 5.10, which also gives the voting intention
figures from each survey.

Whilst other parties' health policies attract levels of approval close
to the party's strength in the electorate, Fianna Fáil's lag far behind.
The gap is 12 per cent in the first poll and 15 per cent in the second. With
33 per cent of the respondents to the second of these two polls saying no
party had the best policy, or not knowing which was best, there was

obviously much confusion. In all parties a significant number thought no party had the answer but most voters thought their own party was "best" on health. Although the actual figures varied over the two polls, Pact voters were most confident and left-inclined voters least so.

Table 5.10   Best policy on health and voting intention

	IMS 2		IMS 3	
	Best policy	vote	Best policy	vote
	%	%	%	%
FF	28	40	25	40
FG	25	25	23	26
PD	6	6	4	6
Labour	9	9	11	11
WP	4	5	3	5
Other	1	4	1	4
None/DK	27	11	33	8
Total	100	100	100	100
N=		1050		1055

What is most telling in this regard are the judgements of those who thought that health was the most important issue of the campaign. These are found in Table 5.11 which shows the opinions of each of the main political groupings as to which party had the best policy on health, confining analysis to those who thought health the most important issue. There is a considerable contrast here between the Pact parties and the rest, with 76 per cent of Pact voters thinking their parties are best, compared with 55 per cent of Fianna Fáil voters and 42 per cent of left voters. Undecided voters, too, favoured the Pact promises on the issue, with the numbers favouring Fianna Fáil trailing third behind the numbers favouring the policies of the left. The weakness of Fianna Fáil on the issue is clear, and it is more striking when it is realised that, Fianna Fáil voters generally strongly favour their own party on issues they consider important.

Although Table 5.11 does not show Fianna Fáil losing votes on the issue, it does emphasise the cross-pressures on many Fianna Fáil supporters. Surprisingly, the left does not show up well on the issue, with only 42 per cent of left voters thinking one of the left parties had the best policy on the issue. All of this suggests that knowing the voters' views on who had the best policy on health is not of great use in explaining the net shift in votes from Fianna Fáil to Labour and The Workers' Party. From Table 5.11 we might have expected the voters to have gone to Fine Gael or the Progressive Democrats. In fact, it seems that although almost two out of every five voters said health was the most important issue for them in determining their vote, less than 60 per cent of those who thought health so important had a voting intention that was consistent with their views on that issue. This possibly reflects the impact the media had on setting the campaign agenda, but it also indicates some limitations of the survey method in exploring motivations. One way or another, health became the issue of the election, and hence voters knew what to tell interviewers when asked for their views on what was the most important issue.

Table 5.11: Party with the best policy on health, by vote.

	Best	Policy						
	FF	Pact	Left	Other	None	DK	Total	N=
Voting intention:	%	%	%	%	%	%	%	
FF	55	14	5	1	11	14	100	166
Pact	2	76	5	1	2	14	100	134
Left	5	22	42	2	10	19	100	59
Other	7	43	29	14	7	0	100	14
DK/Ref/Not vote	12	20	15	2	12	39	100	41
Total	25	37	12	1	8	17	100	414

Source: IMS2
Note: analysis confined to those saying health most important issue.

However, this does not mean health did not influence some voters, and even small groups can be decisive in elections. The campaign panel data give us a handle on this question, as least as far as shifts within the campaign are concerned. These shifts are discussed in more detail in a later section but two figures are of interest here. Overall, only seven per cent of switchers actually gave health as the reason for their change of mind. Fifteen per cent of those who switched *from* Fianna Fáil cited the health issue as a reason. In summary, the health issue had considerable prominence in voters' minds; it was not, however, as overwhelmingly decisive as this suggests, but it did play a role in moving some, possibly decisive, votes away from Fianna Fáil.

Perceptions of economic well-being
Our analysis of the health issue focussed on voters' reactions to the prospects offered by the different parties for improving the service. However, it has been argued that "rather than a prospective decision, the voting decision can be more of a retrospective decision . . . elections may constitute a collective evaluation of actual trends from past to present as much as one of proposed trends from present to future"[13] As David Farrell noted in chapter 2, Fianna Fáil's election campaign seems to have been based on this view; it stood on its record of achievement rather than on detailed promises of future action, at least in the early days of the campaign. We can test one aspect of the assumption on which this strategy was based by examining people's opinion of their economic situation over the past two years: had it improved, got worse or remained much the same? Only 33 per cent thought it had got worse, compared with 43 per cent who saw improvement, 22 per cent who thought things were much the same and one per cent who did not know.

Table 5.12 Voting intention by perception of economic improvement

	Perception of economic improvement		
	Better	Worse	Same/DK
Vote:	%	%	%
FF	60	21	39
Pact	23	33	34
Left	8	25	15
Other	3	4	2
DK/Ref/Not vote	6	17	10
Total	100	100	100
N=	452	349	244

Source: IMS1

Table 5.12 shows the link with voting intention. The figure of only 60 per cent who thought things had improved and intended voting Fianna Fáil indicates that many were against the government despite some satisfaction with its economic record. (In fact, 38 per cent of Pact voters and 23 per cent of left-inclined voters acknowledged that there had been some improvement in the economy.) Arguably, those who felt better off and were voting against the government were refusing to give the credit for improvement to the government, or perhaps were not satisfied with the extent of it. The improvement was felt most by the middle class, among whom 58 per cent saw improvement. The figure drops to 40 per cent amongst skilled workers and 29 per cent amongst the unskilled ones, with farmers at 45 per cent. This is a striking class difference and must have contributed to the variations in class voting observed elsewhere in this chapter. However, the analysis in Table 5.13 also shows that class differences in the perception of economic improvement apply within each political grouping, even the left.

Table 5.13 Perception of economic improvement
by class and voting intention

| Vote and class: | | Perception of economic improvement | | | | |
		Better %	Worse %	Same/DK %	Total %	N=
FF	MC	77	13	10	100	145
	WC	51	22	27	100	206
	Farmers	61	11	28	100	85
Pact	MC	42	30	28	100	99
	WC	24	50	26	100	125
	Farmers	42	30	28	100	79
Left	MC	46	27	27	100	30
	WC	19	58	23	100	111
	Farmers	7	79	14	100	14

Middle class Fianna Fáil voters were 26 per cent more likely to say the economy had improved than working class Fianna Fáil voters. The difference within the Pact vote was 18 per cent, and within the left it was 27 per cent. Although it is clear that class-related voting shifts did take place, this result illustrates how class divisions on an issue can be submerged within the Irish party system.

The left: an ideological vote?
We have already argued that a shift to the left occurred in the campaign. This gave rise to much talk of a new left-right divide in Irish politics. To what extent was the vote for the left a reward for traditional grass-roots

work, a protest vote against harsh economic policies, or an indication of an ideological shift in some parts of the Irish electorate?

In the evidence we have examined already, there were some signs that the political agenda of left voters differed from that of those who voted for other parties, particularly for the Pact parties. However, these differences were of degree rather than kind, with all political groups in substantial agreement about the relative importance of the major issues. If we move on from that to more fundamental political attitudes, does this agreement disappear?

In the first IMS/Independent survey respondents were given two statements with which they could agree or disagree:

"taxation must be reduced, even if it means cuts in areas like
health, education and social welfare";
"the only way to bring down unemployment is to continue cutting
back on government expenditure".

Both of these might be expected to divide right from left, and both were highly topical in the context of the 1989 election. The results for the major political parties are displayed in Table 5.14.

Table 5.14 Attitudes to taxation and public expenditure by voting intention

Attitudes:	Voting Intention				
	PD	FG	FF	Lab	WP
	%	%	%	%	%
Reduce taxation even if this means more cuts: % who disagree:	73	77	67	85	83
Can only reduce unemployment by expenditure cuts: % who agree:	59	54	63	57	60
N=	74	229	436	115	40

Source: IMS1

The most striking thing about the results is not any left-right divide but the substantial degree of consensus which exists, with sizeable majorities agreeing with the second proposition and disagreeing with the first. It appears as if left wing opinions are in a majority on the first, and right wing opinions in a majority in all parties on the second statement. Possibly the reference to specific and sensitive policy areas in the first statement and the more bland reference to public expenditure in the second explains something of the differing general response, but this does not explain the relative absence of a left-right division of opinion on both statements. On the taxation/social welfare balance, there is a difference between the left parties and the others, with left voters 12 per cent more likely to disagree with the statement than Pact voters and almost 20 per cent more likely to do so than Fianna Fáil voters. However, on the solution to unemployment, the left voters fall between those of the Pact and those of Fianna Fáil, with a range of only nine per cent covering all of them.

The class bases of these responses are also not sharply defined. In fact, the working class is *more* likely than the middle class to see cuts in public expenditure as the only solution to the unemployment problem: 64 per cent of the unskilled group agree with the second statement, compared with 50 per cent of the middle class group. We have already seen that the working class was not enamoured of the government's economic achievements and that relatively few working class voters thought the economy was improving. However, these objections do not translate clearly into more ideological statements. The earlier analysis of the health issue also suggested that if the left attracted voters from Fianna Fáil it was more because of a dissatisfaction with the government than a belief that the left parties had the answers. The left vote, then, seems not to have been the result of any upsurge of socialist sentiment. To the extent that it was a political statement of support for parties rather than candidates it was a vote of protest against the general economic situation rather than a demand for fundamentally different policies.

Choice of government as an issue

Fianna Fáil made much of its traditional claim to be the only party which could provide stable government. It has always asserted that only single party governments are stable, and that majority single party governments are the most stable. The shape of the government as an issue never emerged as strongly as health or emigration. Initially, as we saw in Table 5.9, "Stable/strong government" was mentioned as important by only seven per cent of respondents, most of them Fianna Fáil supporters, but by the close of the campaign this figure had risen to 17 per cent.

The initial MRBI poll asked whether the situation in which a Fianna Fáil minority government had been supported by the opposition on the ba-

118

sis of a financial policy consensus was satisfactory: 43 per cent said yes. A smaller proportion, 37 per cent, felt a continuation of the same situation would be satisfactory.[14] The difference was a result largely of the opinions of Fianna Fáil supporters who approved the past but wanted something different in the future. Much of the satisfaction with the current state of affairs came from outside Fianna Fáil with a remarkable 40 per cent of non-Fianna Fáil voters satisfied with the existing arrangements and 36 per cent of them prepared to see it continue.

Table 5.15 Preference for government during course of campaign

	June 2 %	June 8 %	June 9 %
FF majority	44	41	37
FF minority	14	15	10
Pact coalition	31	34	23
National Government	na	na	23
Don't Know	10	10	7
Total	100	100	100
N=	1045	1050	1055

Source: IMS1, IMS2, MRBI2

Several later surveys asked people what sort of government they would like to see emerge from the election and provided a number of options.[15] The results are shown in Table 5.15. A comparison of the two IMS polls, conducted a week apart in the middle of the campaign, shows support for Fianna Fáil dropping, whilst support for a Fianna Fáil *minority* government was maintained. With the additional option of "national government" (undefined) in the MRBI poll, the popularity of the "Fianna Fail majority" option drops still further.[16] These figures emphasise the reservations of the Fianna Fáil voter about electing a majority Fianna Fáil administration. In all three of these polls, the relative preference for a minority as opposed to a majority Fianna Fáil administration is greater amongst middle class voters than working class ones.

We showed in the first section of this chapter that Fianna Fáil's position at the start of the campaign was less secure than it appeared. This review of the issues suggests a number of other reasons why Fianna Fáil's lead evaporated. We have also identified the lack of any issue through which Fianna Fáil could mobilise its supporters. The most prominent feature of the campaign, health, was running against it; this put the Fianna Fáil campaign on the defensive and distracted attention from those areas, such as the economy generally, where it could stand on its record. Fianna Fáil's achievements were on "old" issues, and furthermore were those where the government's success could be attributed to the support of other parties. Finally, a sizeable proportion of those who wanted a Fianna Fáil government preferred a minority administration.

HOW THE VOTERS EXPLAINED THEIR DECISION

Leaders, policies and candidates

Leaders, policy-issues and perceptions of well-being all appear to have influenced voters on election day, even if we cannot be certain exactly how much weight these different factors exercised on the final decision. Evidence from polls taken during previous elections suggests that voters see candidates as a more important influence than any of these factors. The question: "which of these will be most important to you in making up your mind how to vote in the General Election?" was asked again in 1989 with a small but significant variation in the range of alternatives offered:

-choosing a Taoiseach;
-choosing ministers who will form a government;
-choosing between the policies of the parties;
-choosing a TD who will look after the local needs of the constituency;
-choosing a TD who will perform well on national issues in the Dáil.[17]

Except for the last option, this is a question that has been asked regularly in this form over several elections, and the responses are shown in Table 5.16. The candidate consistently appears as the most important factor. Although the addition of the "TD for national issues" option does confuse the picture, policies seem to have been less important to voters in 1989 than in earlier years - certainly, they were not more important. There were some party differences on this question, with left voters more likely to cite policies and a good local TD than other political groupings, although these two factors are also most important for Pact voters. Fianna Fáil voters think a local TD and a Taoiseach are most important. These results do not indicate that the left vote was a policy vote, but they do suggest the left wing voters are not indifferent to policies, even if a near majority of them say they vote firstly for an active local representative.[17]

It would be easy to overstate the importance of candidates on the evidence of this question. It is not clear whether people interpret it as referring to only their first preference vote, their early preferences or to their overall ranking of parties and candidates. It seems possible that many would rank the candidates of their chosen party according to their local effectiveness, yet make their party choice according to one of the factors considered earlier. Even so, the fact that candidates are a very important element in the decision is undeniable. Furthermore, it is reinforced by the evidence of the campaign panel study.

Table 5.16 Major factor in vote 1977-89

	Year of election					
	1977	1981	1982	1982	1987	1989
	%	%	%	%	%	%
Taoiseach	8	16	20	19	15	14
Ministers	18	16	17	15	18	9
Policies	21	24	27	25	29	15
TD: local	46	42	35	41	38	40
TD: national	na	na	na	na	na	16

Sources: 1977-82 from R. Sinnott "Voters, Issues and the Party System" in H. Penniman and B.Farrell, Ireland at the Polls 1981,1982, and 1987 (Washington: AEI/Duke, 1987), Table 3.8. 1987 from M. Laver, M. Marsh and R. Sinnott, "Patterns of Party Support" in M. Laver, P. Mair and R. Sinnott (eds), How Ireland Voted: The Irish General Election 1987 (Swords: Poolbeg, 1987), Table 26. 1989 from Lansdowne1. na= not asked

What changed voters' minds during the campaign?
Some 21 per cent of voters reported that they changed their minds during the campaign. How did such voters account for the change? In particular, given that the most dramatic feature of the campaign was the decline in Fianna Fáil support, how did voters who left the Fianna Fáil ranks explain their decision? We have already seen that the health issue was cited by one out of every six of those who deserted Fianna Fáil. There was obviously more to the movements between parties than that.

As already indicated, voters commonly attribute their decision to the candidate factor. Table 5.17 shows that this factor was also important for those who changed their mind during the campaign. However, an almost equal number say that political issues determined their change of mind. Those referring to issues are most likely to mention health, if they are specific at all. Turning now to those who switched from Fianna Fáil, we must note that any conclusion to be drawn from that part of the table must be qualified on account of the small number of cases involved.[18] The evidence suggests that those deserting Fianna Fáil were influenced by candidate factors to a greater extent than switchers in general.

Table 5.17: Reasons for switching (more than one reason given)

	All %	From FF %
Candidate factors:	33	46
Local candidate	20	12
Like candidate	11	25
Candidate known to me	8	14
Received favour from TD/cand	6	5
Issues:	31	43
Policies	13	7
Health	7	19
Local issues	5	17
Stable government	4	0
Rod licences	2	2
Tax	2	7
Schools	1	0
Army	1	0
Other reasons:	28	30
Influenced by RTE programme	7	15
Voted for party before	5	5
Family influence	5	2
Dissatsfd with party's performance	4	5
Reacted against FG/PD pact	4	0
Other reasons	5	3
None/DK:	20	12
N=	166	41

Source: Lansdowne 1 and 2. Subtotals are sometimes smaller than the sum of their components because of multiple responses.

The most frequent category of candidate reference in this context was "a liking for a candidate of one of the other parties". Issues seem to have

122

played a role more or less on a par with that of candidates. We have already seen that health was one of the more frequently cited issues but was not by any means dominant, and was in fact equalled by references to local issues. One other reason given for defection is perhaps worth noting - 15 per cent of those switching from Fianna Fail referred to the influence of RTE programmes, compared with eight per cent making such a reference among switchers in general.

We have no way of knowing how those who were swayed at the last minute by the candidate factor had voted in 1987, but it is possible that many of the voters who gave this reason were in fact returning to the candidates they had voted for in 1987. To the extent that this happens, the candidate factor may serve to inhibit electoral change. Some voters consider changing their party preference in the inter-election period, and say so in the polls, but once the campaign starts, and the particular candidates who attracted their votes last time start campaigning again, this resolve weakens, and a lead in the polls turns out to be no more reliable than a new year's resolution. We cannot tell if this was the explanation for some of Fianna Fáil's decline, but the evidence here, though far from complete, is at least consistent with this.

The analysis so far leads to the conclusion that no one item or issue decided the election. Many factors played a part. The crucial drift away from the government seems to have been a result of both personality and policy factors, with local candidates, local issues and the health issue most evident. No single factor can account for the successes and failures of 1989.

CLASS AND PARTY: TOWARDS A CLASS-BASED REALIGNMENT?

Class profiles of the parties in 1989
The role of social class has been a recurring theme in much of this chapter so far, whether the discussion has been about trends, leadership or issues. It is now time to tackle more directly the obvious underlying question - what does the 1989 election tell us about the relationship between class and politics? In particular, does it suggest a realignment of Irish politics along class lines?

Table 5.18 sets out the data from the final opinion polls of the 1987 and 1989 campaigns on the relationship between voting and social class, using the standard market research measure of class.[19] Categories AB and C1 include the middle and lower middle class, and non-manual workers, whilst categories C2 and DE are skilled manual workers, unskilled manual workers and those not working. F1 and F2 are larger and smaller farmers respectively; separate figures for these two groups are not available for 1989. Quite clearly, there have been considerable changes in the voting behaviour of the social classes between the two elections. Yet the data for 1987 in Table 5.18 were part of the evidence for the conclusion noted above that in some respects the class basis of Irish politics was clearer in 1987 than at any previous time since polls have been taken. What then have the changes that occurred between 1987 and 1989 done to the class pattern that had emerged in 1987?

One of the main developments in 1987 was that Fianna Fáil lost its cross-class character and won considerably more support in the working class than in either section of the middle class. That process was substantially reversed in 1989, with Fianna Fáil winning back most of the support it had lost in the lower middle class and making a modest recovery in the rest of the middle class. The price of these gains was a loss of six percentage points among the skilled working class. Taken together, the effect of these changes was to return Fianna Fáil more or less to its cross-class pattern of support.

Fine Gael showed some slight recovery in the lower middle class, but otherwise its profile did not change significantly. There is in fact some indication here of a reversion by Fine Gael to its pre-1980s somewhat more middle class base. In the case of the Progressive Democrats, not only did their overall vote drop dramatically, it dropped disproportionately among the middle class - down eight points and 12 points in each sub-sector of that social grouping. The somewhat surprising outcome is to make the Progressive Democrats into a substantially cross class party, albeit one with a much lower level of support than before. Thus, of the three parties so frequently categorised as "the right-wing parties", only one - Fine Gael - has a discernible middle class bias in its support base.

What then of the recovery of the left? Surely the very fact of that recovery points to new class alignment? Table 5.18 shows quite clearly that there is now a stronger class base to the left-wing parties. This is especially true of the Workers' Party, whose support among the unskilled working class substantially exceeds its support elsewhere. The Labour Party made significant gains among both sections of the middle class, which would make one hesitate to categorise it as a purely class-based party. However, its most striking gains were in the working class, and from being an party which drew almost equally from both classes in 1987, Labour in 1989 again has a profile clearly weighted in a working class direction.

Table 5.18: Voting intention by social class, 1987 and 1989

DATE	PARTY	ALL	AB	C1	C2	DE	F1	F2	F1&2
		%	%	%	%	%	%	%	
Feb 87	FF	38	26	32	45	41	30	48	
June 89	FF	40	32	42	39	41			43
Feb 87	FG	25	34	24	23	15	45	35	
June 89	FG	26	35	30	21	14			39
Feb 87	Labour	4	1	6	4	7	1	2	
June 89	Labour	11	6	9	14	15			5
Feb 87	PD	11	18	18	9	9	10	2	
June 89	PD	6	10	6	6	7			4
Feb 87	WP	2	1	2	3	4	0	1	
June 89	WP	5	3	2	5	10			2
Feb 87	Other/DK	19	19	18	14	24	13	14	
June 89	Other/DK	12	15	11	16	13			7

Source: IMS/Sunday Independent poll of 14 Feb 1987, and IMS3

In summary, one must conclude that, although 1989 involved significant class-related shifts in voting behaviour, as the middle class went back to Fianna Fáil and significant numbers of working class voters moved left, it did not produce a strong class-based alignment. This was because such movements as occurred mainly served to redress the class pattern that emerged from the 1987 election. Between 1982 and 1987 both middle class groups moved away from Fianna Fáil and both working class groups moved towards it, leaving it with a profile much more biased towards the working class than in previous years. In 1989 these trends substantially reversed themselves, leaving Fianna Fáil again an almost completely cross-class party

Fine Gael's pattern of support, on the other hand, is more class-based now than in the early 1980s. However, the Fine Gael vote is not big enough, and the bias is not sufficiently pronounced, for the party to constitute one end of a class-based political alignment. Similarly, at the other end of the class spectrum, while there has been an increased tendency for the working class to vote left, the tendency is not strong enough to create the other pole of a class-based alignment, especially since it is qualified by the appeal of Labour to a significant minority of middle class voters. In addition, as shown in an earlier section, the left vote shows very little evidence of being an ideologically consistent one. While there may well be potential in the system for class-based alignment, it did not happen in 1989.

CONCLUSION

Contrary to the usual pattern of government unpopularity at mid-term, Fianna Fáil appeared to be doing well in the opinion polls after two years in office. If the basis of the decision to call an election was a reading of these particular omens, however, the decision was ill founded because, as we have seen, Fianna Fáil's overall level of mid-term support masked a good deal of instability and was not to be relied upon. Moreover, the evidence suggests that the decision to go for what was widely perceived to be an unnecessary election damaged the rehabilitated reputation of Mr Haughey.

Having failed to convince the voters of the necessity of an election, Fianna Fáil found itself with very little with which to mobilize support. In two ways it was the victim of its own success. The issue on which it was generally agreed it had made substantial progress - correcting the public finances - was, by virtue of that progress, no longer an issue. Also, it was not easy to win over supporters of other parties on the basis of this performance, because they could always credit it to the hold that Mr Dukes had over the minority Fianna Fáil administration. We have seen evidence that substantial numbers of voters liked the 1987-89 Fianna Fáil administration precisely as a minority administration.

The second way in which Fianna Fáil was a victim of its own success was that the cutbacks in government spending that were the necessary condition of that success came into sharp focus as a highly emotive election issue - health. A substantial part of the salience of this issue was generated by the campaign itself, and, while its overall effect may have been exaggerated at the time, it was responsible for significant vote losses from Fianna Fáil.

The conclusion that the campaign was particularly important on this occasion is reinforced by noting that most of the increased support for the left occurred within the period of the campaign and that the three weeks from May 25 to June 15 were marked by considerable voter volatility. The fact that 21 per cent of those with a declared party preference at the outset of the campaign had changed their minds by polling day brings out the complexity of what goes on in an election, or at least of what went on in this election. The point is further emphasised when we look at voters' own accounts of what influenced their vote: candidates first of all, but also leaders, policy issues (national and local) and ministerial teams all figured in the decision, and the evidence indicates that there was no single factor in the winning and losing of the 1989 election.

This brings us, finally, to the question of the implications the election may have for electoral and party alignments, and especially for the possibility of the emergence of a class based alignment. What is striking about political behaviour in recent years is not any trend towards a class alignment but the variability and volatility of that behaviour. Class-related swings in voting behaviour have certainly occurred in the 1980s. However, the destination of these class-related swings has also varied and has been influenced by government policy and performance rather than by a consistent link between particular parties and stable class interests or by any coherent ideological considerations. There is thus little or no evidence of a trend towards a substantial class polarization of electoral alignments, despite the fact that there is clear evidence that shifts in voting behaviour have been related to social class.

It would be very difficult to predict where this somewhat wayward influence of class will lead in the medium term. One could focus, on the one hand, on the increased support of the left and, projecting a continued trend in that direction, foresee a definition of political issues in left-right terms. This would lead to a political realignment in which, with Fianna Fáil and Fine Gael in government, the left would form the opposition and would grow in virtue of that fact, almost by way of filling a vacuum. In assessing the probability of this line of development, it must be borne in mind that the support for the left is at present about 15 per cent. The alternative scenario is for a continuation of party competition along the lines of the period 1981-89, that is, a competition in which the issues, the class trends and the factors that influence voting decisions are highly diverse and often specific to the circumstances of the particular election. In such a situation, Fianna Fáil's success in resurrecting its cross-class strategy in 1989, and its powerful position in any coalition formation process (as discussed in chapter 11 of this book), would make it likely to be the dominant party in the medium term .

However, one must also remember that, in a series of elections spanning twenty years, there has been a swing against the incumbent government at almost every election. Now, for the first time in that twenty-year period, a party is in government for a second successive term and is therefore doubly vulnerable to such a swing. Therein lies perhaps an opportunity for Fine Gael and as well as for the parties of the left. In regard to these various possibilities, the evidence of this chapter can do no more than confirm that a significant number of voters are "winnable" by the party or parties that can hit on the right combination of candidate, issue and leadership appeal and, particularly underlined in 1989, on the right timing.

FOOTNOTES

1   The following is a list of campaign polls used in the tables, giving the dates of the fieldwork, place of publication and the short name used in this chapter. Details are given in the chapter of other polls used. Thanks are due to Lansdowne Market Research, Irish Marketing Surveys and the Market Research Bureau of Ireland for permitting and facilitating the use of their surveys, and to the *Independent* Newspaper group and the *Irish Times* for commissioning them in the first place!

Lansdowne1	May 27-28	*Star, Irish Independent,* May 29-30
Lansdowne2	June 16	*Sunday Independent,* Sept 10
IMS1	June 2	*Irish Independent,* June 6
IMS2	June 8	*Sunday Independent,* June 11
IMS3	June 11	*Irish Independent,* June 14
MRBI1	May 27-29	*Irish Times,* June 1
MRBI2	June 9	*Irish Times,* June 12

2   Michael Laver, Michael Marsh, Richard Sinnott, "Patterns of Party Support" in Michael Laver, Peter Mair and Richard Sinnott (eds), *How Ireland Voted: The Irish General Election 1987* (Swords: Poolbeg, 1987) p. 112.

3   Laver et al., "Patterns of Party Support", p. 112.

4   Lansdowne Market Research conducted the first survey of the campaign for the *Star* at the end of May. On the day after polling, before the votes had been counted, the company successfully reinterviewed 89 per cent of the same people who had been interviewed in May. Such "panel" studies are common in other countries, but this is the first conducted here.

5   PD losses are in fact underestimated in Table 5.1, because the recalled vote for that party is significantly less than their actual vote in 1987. This may be because former PD supporters have so distanced themselves from the party that they are unwilling to acknowledge ever having voted for it. Alternatively, it may reflect the novelty value of the party and the fact that some 1987 PD supporters may not have had any attachment to the party as such.

6   These data do not enable us to say whether people changed their opinions because of their prior voting preferences, or their voting preference because

of their opinions. The path of causality can run either way, which limits the extent to which we can say that particular issues hurt or helped the government.

7   See Richard Sinnott, "Voters, Issues and the Party System" in Howard Penniman and Brian Farrell (eds), *Ireland at the Polls 1981,1982, and 1987* (Washington: AEI/Duke, 1987) for details.

8   *IMS/Sunday Independent* poll, 14 February 1987.

9   The initial poll of the campaign, Lansdowne 1, did not ask this question in a comparable way.

10 Laver et al., "Patterns of Party Support", Table 7.

11 The question was: "Which issues were most important to you personally in helping you to decide which way to vote in the general election?"

12 At the time it was thought that concern for stable government would drive middle class voters to Fianna Fáil at the last moment. It was the upper middle class and large (and small) farmers who were most likely to see the issue as important, although the magnitude of the differences between these groups combined and the rest is only eight percentage points. The figures in Table 5.9 differ slightly from those in Table 5.6 because the former are based only on those who responded to both surveys whereas the latter are based on all respondents in the first Lansdowne poll.

13 Morris Fiorina, *Retrospective Voting in American National Elections* (New Haven: Yale University Press, 1981) p. 6.

14 "Since the last General Election we have had a minority Government which was supported on major financial issues by the main political parties. In your opinion (a) was this a satisfactory or unsatisfactory state of affairs? (b) would it be satisfactory if it were to continue after this General Election?" IMS asked "which option would you prefer, if it had to be one of them?", whereas MRBI asked "which of the following would be best for the country?"

15 In the first MRBI poll, 40 per cent thought a majority Fianna Fáil administration under Charles Haughey would be "good for the country".

16 The first MRBI poll used a different form of this question, asking people to rate each of the options (except "ministers") in importance.

17 Left voters were several percentage points less likely than those in other parties to rate policy "very important", and also much less likely to rate the choice of Taoiseach as "very important".

18 Too few voters switched to Fianna Fáil, and too few switched to or away from any other party, for any reliable analysis to be carried out on their reasons.

[19] It should be emphasised that this discussion of class and voting is based only on the standard market research measure of social class. Recent discussions have suggested that, for the purposes of analysing political behaviour, this may not be the most appropriate way to measure it, and have proposed an alternative. The analysis of class and voting in *How Ireland Voted 1987* (see footnote 2 above) was able to apply such a revised measure at least partially, because the *Irish Times* / MRBI polls specifically included questions designed for this purpose (see Laver et al, "Patterns of party support", pp. 97-112). Unfortunately, these questions were not repeated in 1989, and the analysis here is confined to the traditional market research categorisation.

6. The European Parliament election

Patrick Keatinge and Michael Marsh

Unlike the two preceding European Parliament elections, that of 1989 took place against the background of rising expectations for integration in western Europe. The policy-making reforms of the Single European Act (SEA) which came into force in 1987, combined with the agreements "to complete the internal market and to establish a five year budgetary commitment" which followed in 1988, seemed to herald a more constructive atmosphere in the European Community than at any time since Ireland had become a member.

The broader international environment was also propitious. The stock market crisis of October 1987 had been overcome, and that great constant of the last forty-odd years, the cold war, seemed to be in the throes of dissolution. At any rate the superpowers had become sufficiently relaxed to take the implications of EC integration more seriously; American fear of commercial rivalry with "fortress Europe" was matched by Gorbachev's rhetoric of the "common European home". The attraction of integration was felt even more directly by the EFTA countries, and particularly by Austria, on the verge of a formal application for EC membership.

This new departure for the brave new world of 1992 was not without its counter-reformation, led by Margaret Thatcher. In September 1988, in a much referred to speech in Bruges, the British prime minister had assumed the mantle of a latter-day de Gaulle, championing the nation-state against the presumptions of an overambitious president of the EC Commission, Jacques Delors. "Europe" threatened to become a matter of high politics, after years of interminable squabbling over a minuscule budget.

The government's presentation of Ireland's European policy reflected the euphoric rather than the problematic aspects of these developments.[1] On coming to power in March 1987, Mr Haughey very swiftly cast aside the doubts aired by Fianna Fáil during the previous administration. None of the Dáil parties seemed altogether at ease with the high politics that emerged during the referendum campaign on the SEA two months later, though in the end they obtained what was for most of them the right answer, albeit from less than half of a bewildered electorate. By the middle of 1988 this aberrant event was a dim memory as the public awareness campaign for the 1992 deadline was launched, and in the autumn a new "special relationship" was established between the government and the EC Commission. By this stage it was clear that EC membership, through an increase in the structural funds promised by Brussels, was being presented as a central element in the government's overall economic strategy. The National Development Plan 1989-1993, published just two and a half months before the election, indicated how and where these additional resources were to be spent, some compensation perhaps for the much harsher side of recent economic policy.[2]

Fine Gael and the Progressive Democrats could do little but smile wanly at this bravura performance, since their own enthusiasm for "Europe" matched the government's. At best the National Development Plan could be attacked for its form and particularly its failure to take account of specific regional consultation. Both these parties showed some signs of looking at the long-term implications of a revived European Community, including the eventual compatibility of Irish neutrality with an evolving political union.[3]

On the left the Labour Party's divisions on the EC, so evident during the drawn-out ratification of the SEA, had been eased with the removal of the burdens of government. For the Workers' Party there was a major change in policy. In 1987 it had been the only Dáil party to side with Raymond Crotty's anti-SEA campaign, but its new leader, Proinsias De Rossa, proclaimed the party's European vocation at the Ard Fheis on 8 April 1989. Thus the Dáil's consensus on EC membership, which had looked somewhat shopworn in the previous European election was revitalised and extended. If there was to be a radical critique of EC integration or Ireland's participation in it, it would have to come from parties outside the Dáil, such as the Green Party or Sinn Féin, or from independent voices, such as Raymond Crotty.

THE MANIFESTOES

However, that is not to say that a quantum leap had occurred in the Europeanisation of the Irish political system between 1987 and 1989. A comparison between the manifestoes published by those Irish parties possessing formal links with European Parliament party groups and the latter's composite programmes illustrates the limits of integration in this regard.[4] Even allowing for differences between national interests and electoral strategies, as well for a necessary simplification of an untidy listing of uneasy compromises, it is noticeable that the national manifestoes are effectively purged of potentially awkward questions relating to the pace and direction of political integration itself.

The most topical issue of the "high politics" of the Community's development was undoubtedly that of Economic and Monetary Union (EMU), with the publication of the Delors report of the Community's central bankers on 17 April, but this was perhaps too topical - and almost certainly too technical - to receive more than a passing reference at either level of manifesto. No such excuse could be offered for the rather patchy treatment accorded to the European Parliament's claim for greater powers in Community policy-making, which naturally took a central place in most of the party groups' programmes. Fianna Fáil's French Gaullist partners in the European Democratic Alliance (EDA) are among the least enthusiastic on this score, but the controversial implications of their position were hardly reflected in the Irish party's bland recital of the existing powers of the Strasbourg assembly. Fine Gael ignored what was clearly a priority for their counterparts in the European People's Party (EPP). Thus it was left to the two smaller parties, the Progressive Democrats and Labour, to present the matter as a real issue. The former, though as yet holding no seat in the European Parliament, pressed for more powers, as did their associated group, the European Liberal Democratic and Reform Parties (ELDR), while the Labour Party also endorsed the Socialist Group's emphasis on the need for more democratic control.

One of the most telling indicators of Irish sensitivities about a contradiction between national sovereignty and an evolving political union is the issue of neutrality. Here too the inconvenient questions about a possible extension of the EC into the field of defence were heavily laundered in the national party manifestoes. Fianna Fáil, ignoring its associates' flirtation with Atlanticism and their advocacy of the military alliance within NATO, the Western European Union (WEU), sang the praises of Ireland's neutrality at some length; with its eyes firmly fixed on the (immutable?) present, it asserted that there was no pressure to make a defence commitment. Fine Gael's manifesto referred to the EPP's strong emphasis on "security" as if it were concerned solely with police activities to combat drugs and terrorism. The PDs had persuaded the European Liberals to "recognise" that Ireland was militarily neutral, but their national manifesto confusingly combined a call for debate on the issue - a hint of change - with a reference to Ireland being a precedent for the admission of other neutrals being admitted to the Community. The Labour Party, having extracted a similar "recognition" of Ireland's special position, warned of concessions being made by some of their rivals and listed objectives to be pursued by an independent foreign policy within the process of foreign policy consultation, European Political Cooperation.

There was little sign, therefore, in the national manifestoes that the Irish parties were envisaging an explicit commitment to the development of political integration that went beyond the level already achieved in the Single European Act. Indeed, they seemed reluctant even to consider the question one way or another, preferring to fall back on an agenda composed of the "European dimension" of the usual national issues.

THE CAMPAIGN

The campaign proper started with the deadline for the selection of candidates on 20 May, but given the early notification of polling day most of the candidates had been chosen by the end of March. Fianna Fáil relied mainly on its sitting MEPs, but also introduced the former (and controversial) Minister for Justice, Seán Doherty, in Connacht-Ulster and the former president of the Irish Farmers Association, Paddy Lane, in Munster, where incumbents were standing down. Fianna Fáil hoped that Lane would take votes from another former IFA president, the independent MEP T. J. Maher. Fine Gael replaced the retiring Mark Clinton and Tom O'Donnell (Leinster and Munster respectively) with two other big names, the former Minister for Justice and for Defence Paddy Cooney, and - in the most imaginative selection of the election - the former leader of the Alliance Party of Northern Ireland, John Cushnahan.

The smaller parties also fielded some of their senior national personalities. In Dublin Barry Desmond was chosen for Labour, and with his namesake Eileen again being nominated for Munster and Michael Bell nominated for Leinster the party had high hopes of improving on its disastrous showing in 1984. The Progressive Democrats, in their first European election and against a background of decline in the opinion polls, selected two Dáil deputies, Bobby Molloy (Connacht-Ulster) and Mary Harney (Dublin), and their former general secretary and TV presenter, Pat Cox, in Munster. The Workers' Party made a strong bid in Dublin with no less a person than their new leader, Proinsias De Rossa, though most of their other candidates could expect little more than the joys of participation. The same seemed to be the case with the Green Party, an unknown quantity which put up candidates in Dublin and Leinster with a programme that was sharply critical of the European Community. That was also true of Sinn Féin, which advocated withdrawal from the EC as well as treating the election as a protest against extradition.

The latter issue was also the focal point for several independents, ensuring that the 'national question' was raised in this supposedly European campaign. Kevin Boland in Leinster and Neil Blaney, trying to recapture his seat in Connacht-Ulster, represented a threat to their former Fianna Fáil colleagues, and they were joined in Munster by the election's most controversial candidate. The Reverend Patrick Ryan, whose extradition from Belgium and then from Ireland had been unsuccessfully sought by an indignant Mrs Thatcher the previous December, emerged from hiding in full clerical garb with the comment that he "would not particularly object" to the IRA's activities; Sinn Féin returned the compliment by withdrawing its three Munster candidates in his favour.

Other notable independent candidates included the sitting MEP, T. J. Maher in Munster, who almost pulled out of the election for health reasons, and the hero of the Single European Act referendum, Raymond Crotty, who stood in Dublin on a programme which called for a less rather than more integrated EC. Mr Crotty's associate of the 1987 referendum campaign, Joe Noonan, stood in the Munster constituency as the candidate of "People First - Meitheal".

The first party to launch its official campaign, nearly two months before polling day, was Fine Gael, perhaps mindful of the need to establish the position of its several new candidates. The other parties kept their powder dry and may have felt doubly justified when, ten days later, the defeat of the government on the issue of support for haemophiliac victims of AIDS provoked what proved to be a terminal case of general election fever. By the time the other parties and independents presented their programmes, between 16 and 23 May, the dissolution of the Dáil was widely regarded as a virtual fait accompli. Indeed, on 22 May, Chris O'Malley, one of the two Fine Gael candidates in Dublin, tried to obtain a High Court injunction against a general election, mainly on the grounds of the failure to carry out a review of the Dáil constituencies, but also because it would detract from the European election.[5] He failed to achieve his stated objective, but his warning about the effects of a concurrent general election campaign proved to be only too accurate. Speculation about a dissolution had already kept the European contest on hold; when it actually occurred on 25 May the latter became simply "the other election".

This was reflected above all in the poor media coverage. At best, newspapers found space for a constituency report on each of the four European constituencies alongside those of the forty-one Dáil constituencies, occasional excerpts from candidates' supplied scripts, and intermittent editorials and commentaries bemoaning this unfortunate state of affairs and exhorting the electorate to cast a European vote on the day. Such an approach came more naturally for a paper like the *Irish Times*, with its tradition of being a paper of record, than for the *Irish Independent*, which appeared to have decided to put all its eggs in the general election basket. The only nationwide opinion poll was published by the *Irish Times* (in conjunction with MRBI) on 15 May, well before the general election was announced. Television coverage dutifully attempted the former approach, but even the candidates' usual complaints about unfair allocation of time barely filtered through into the printed media. The issue-based independent candidates seemed to be particularly badly affected; whatever complaints Raymond Crotty may have had about the 1987 referendum campaign, the attention he received then must have seemed like a golden age.

Elsewhere in the EC transnational campaigning was encouraged. To see John Cushnahan's candidacy in this light might raise too many hares of national identity, though it was reported that the Irish National Caucus, in a letter campaign directed from the non-European side of the Atlantic, attacked him as a stooge of the British government. The intervention by European Greens, such as Petra Kelly, on behalf of Joe Noonan in Munster and the Green candidates elsewhere, was perhaps closer to the ethos of Strasbourg, but visiting Gaullists, Liberals and Christian Democrats were not observed.

According to one commentator the campaign would have remained doggedly parochial even with better transmission through the media; "to judge by the bulk of daily reports of the candidates' scripts, you would be forgiven for thinking that the only issues at stake in this election are handouts for motorways or grants to clear large areas of bog".[6] Nevertheless, some broader issues persisted fitfully up to polling day. Predictably, these included the commitment to neutrality and, given the coincidence of the national and European votes, the question of the dual mandate. This proved particularly embarrassing for the Progressive Democrats, who had condemned the practice in principle but then felt compelled to deploy Mary Harney and Bobby Molloy on both fronts. It also seemed to put Proinsias De Rossa at a disadvantage compared to his left wing rival, Barry Desmond, but did not disturb Neil Blaney, in a constituency where the practice seemed to be regarded with equanimity.[7]

The fact remains that without serious coverage by the media the issues raised in the European campaign, whether parochial or European, were not exposed to sustained discussion, eventually involving confrontations between the party leaders. The latter had other things on their minds; on the eve of the election it seemed that the European "campaign has vanished and only the posters remain".[8]

THE RESULTS

The results are summarised in Table 6.1. The vote was more fragmented than at any recent election for either the Dáil or the EP. Fianna Fáil and Fine Gael attracted the support of only 53.1 per cent, just over one half of the voters. Labour, the WP and the PDs all showed significantly in at least one constituency and each attracted around 10 per cent of voters, whilst the Green Party beat the PDs into sixth place in Dublin and the WP into sixth place in Leinster, the only two constituencies in which it ran official candidates. Independent candidates also attracted a lot of support, particularly in Munster and Connacht-Ulster where T.J. Maher and Neil Blaney respectively won a substantial vote and succeeded in getting elected. The high Munster figure also owes something to the decision by the Green Party not to oppose Noonan, and to Sinn Féin's decision not to oppose Ryan.

Table 6.1 Party shares of seats and votes at 1989 EP election

	Dublin		Leinster		Munster		Conn-Ulster		Ireland	
	%V	S	%V	S	%V	S	%V	S	%V	S
Fianna Fáil	29.1	1	36.9	2	28.8	2	32.7	1	31.5	6
Fine Gael	17.2	1	26.9	1	17.6	1	28.0	1	21.6	4
Labour	12.8	1	13.2		8.9		1.6		9.5	1
PDs	8.1		8.4		17.3	1	13.0		11.9	1
Workers' Party	15.8	1	4.4		5.4		2.8		7.5	1
Green Party	8.3		6.3						3.7	
Sinn Féin	2.6		2.6				5.0		2.3	
Others	6.1		1.3		22.0	1	16.9	1	11.9	2
TURNOUT (Valid vote)	63.0		66.0		70.2		67.2		66.6	

Source: European Parliament Information Office, Dublin
Note: Percentages do not all sum to 100 due to rounding.

The seats, too, were spread more widely than in the previous two European Parliament elections, particularly that of 1984. Only T.J. Maher broke the two main parties' duopoly last time; now there are five MEPs from outside these two parties and all of them represent different political outlooks. Fianna Fáil lost one seat in Dublin and another in Connacht-Ulster, while Fine Gael lost one in Dublin and another in Munster.

Three MEPs lost their seats: Chris O'Malley (Fine Gael) and Eileen Lemass (Fianna Fáil) in Dublin, and Tom Raftery (Fine Gael) in Munster.

The two Dublin candidates were replaced by new MEPs from other parties, with Labour and the Workers' Party gaining a seat each in Dublin. The PDs succeeded in taking one of the two Fine Gael seats in Munster and Raftery's new running mate, John Cushnahan, won the other seat. Neil Blaney's success in Connacht-Ulster was at the expense of Fianna Fáil. He may have benefited from the absence of Ray MacSharry, who had ousted him in 1984, but he effectively took the seat vacated by Seán Flanagan who had retired. Blaney had been an MEP from 1979-84, and so became the first MEP to regain his seat!

Blaney and De Rossa were the only candidates who emerged from the election holding a dual mandate. Almost all of the sitting TDs who looked for a dual mandate were re-elected, despite the burden of running two campaigns simultaneously. The exception was Seán Doherty, who was eclipsed on the big stage in Connacht-Ulster by Neil Blaney and was unexpectedly pushed off the smaller one by the voters of Roscommon, who chose instead an independent candidate standing on a platform of defending the local hospital.

For some enthusiasts, the best thing about the election was the turnout, which at 67 per cent was well above the 1984 figure of 46 per cent. It had appeared in April that the latter figure might not be exceeded in 1989. Eurobarometer survey data from November 1988 and April 1989 found the proportion of those who said they were "certain" to vote in the forthcoming EP election was below that at the corresponding stage in 1984. The final figure was far in excess of the proportion of those "certain" to vote and nearer to what would have been expected had both "certain" and "probable" voters gone to the polls. [9]

Obviously, the conjunction of the general and European Parliament elections greatly boosted turnout at the latter, even if it did not help publicise the election itself. Did that conjunction affect the result itself? Did a high turnout help any particular party or parties? It might have been expected that big parties would gain from the attention given to the general election and that smaller ones would have an even harder time trying to become visible to the electorate, given the glare of publicity surrounding the other election. However, the results suggest that this was not the case, since the "big" parties did not do at all well. In addition, a comparison between the party choices of those who said in the Eurobarometer surveys they would "certainly" vote and those who would "probably" vote shows no significant differences.

138

CHANGES FROM 1984

The changes in the pattern of support since 1984 are shown in Table 6.2, which also shows where seats were won and lost and provides an index of the overall degree of change.[10] The figure of 21 on the index of change for Ireland as a whole indicates that if we assumed no-one left or entered the electorate, at least 1 in 5 people must have changed their vote since 1984. Overall, the biggest changes were the 10.6 per cent drop in the Fine Gael vote and the 11.9 per cent won by the PDs, who had been no more than a gleam in their leader's eye in 1984. This shift is similar to that which characterised the PDs' debut in the Dáil election of 1987.

Table 6.2: Gains and losses from 1984 EP election

	Dublin %v	seats	Leinster %v	seats	Munster %v	seats	Conn/Ulster %v	seats	Ireland %v	seats
FF	-4.3	-1	-6.9		-10.0		-8.7	-1	-7.7	-2
FG	-15.0	-1	-9.7		-11.0	-1	-5.3		-10.6	-2
Labour	2.8	+1	1.3		1.3		-1.9		1.1	+1
WP	8.9	+1	1.0		0.4		1.7		3.2	+1
PD	8.1		8.4		17.3	+1	13.0		11.9	+1
Greens	6.4		6.3						3.2	
SF	-2.6		-1.7		-3.7		-1.8		-2.6	
Others	-4.8		1.3		5.9		3.1	+1	1.4	+1
Index	26		18		23		18		21	

Source: European Parliament Information Office, Dublin

The PDs perhaps took votes from Fianna Fáil as well as Fine Gael, as Fianna Fáil's vote dropped by almost 7.7 per cent from its 1984 level. The Green Party ran in 1984 (as the Green Alliance) and greatly improved its performance this time, winning over six times as many votes and increasing its share from 0.5 per cent to 3.7 per cent. Dublin saw the greatest change in voting patterns, and two seats changed hands, while Leinster, where the result did not disturb the status quo, saw the least change.

The political *déjà vu* provoked by the sight of the PDs taking votes from Fine Gael prompts the inevitable question about the nature of the European Parliament election: to what extent is it the product of national concerns? The most striking changes from 1984 echo those seen in 1987 in the national arena, which have been delayed in their effect on the European scene only because of the different electoral timetable. Some other features are easily explicable in solely national terms. Fianna Fáil's decline to a level close to that of 1979 could be seen to stem from its position in government, a position it also occupied at the time of the first European Parliament elections. Labour, arguably, gained from its current freedom from the cares of office. The perception of Euro-elections as largely an electoral comment on the performance of the national government is a common one, and one which gains some support from these figures.[11] However, such a position would lead to the expectation that when a European Parliament election and a national election were held on the same day, the results would be very similar. This expectation was far from being realised in the 1989 results.

COMPARISONS WITH GENERAL ELECTION RESULTS

A comparison of the two sets of results in Table 6.3 reveals some marked differences. The "big two" parties both fared relatively poorly in the European Parliament election with Fianna Fáil 12.6 per cent down on its Dáil vote and Fine Gael 7.7 per cent down. Much more attractive in the European arena, by comparison with the national one, were the PDs, the Greens and the independents. The two standard bearers of the left, Labour and the Workers' Party, achieved a similar overall result in each election. Their success in Dublin, where the left vote was up 7.7 per cent on the general election figure, owed a lot to the fact that both parties fielded big name candidates. They did not have this quality of candidate elsewhere, and perhaps in consequence failed to improve notably on their Dáil showing.

In some ways these differences are similar to those which result from comparing the outcomes of earlier European Parliament elections with those of the preceding Dáil election, although the overall extent of change as measured by the index is greater this time, despite the fact the EP election was held concurrently. In 1979 and 1984, too, the "big" parties combined won fewer votes and independents won a lot more than at the preceding general election.

There are several ways in which to account for differences between European Parliament and general elections. We have considered the notion of the elections as simply a referendum on the government already, and whilst it has some plausibility, it is clearly not the whole story. Karlheinz Reif has developed an interpretation of European parliament elections as "second-order" elections. He argues that they have to be un-

140

derstood in national terms but are not directly related to the question of who controls the national government.[12]

Table 6.3: Differences between EP and general election results, 1989

	Dublin %v	Leinster %v	Munster %v	Conn/Ulst %v	Ireland %v
FF	-12.0	-9.2	-15.0	-15.0	-12.6
FG	-5.0	-4.0	-13.0	-6.6	-7.7
Labour	3.3	-0.3	-2.0	-0.8	0
WP	4.4	2.7	1.4	1.4	2.5
PD	2.9	4.2	9.3	9.7	6.4
Greens	2.6	5.9			3.7
SF	0.7	1.8	2.7		1.1
Others	3.7	-1.1	19.0	8.3	6.5
Index	17	15	30	22	20

Note: the figures show European Parliament vote minus general election vote.

Several considerations accompany this perception. The first is that the result will be strongly influenced by the timing of the second-order election, relative to the most recent first-order election: in Ireland, a general election. The second is that such elections are less salient to the electorate as there is less at stake. Reif suggests that lower turnout, a swing to smaller parties and a swing against the government are all likely characteristics of such elections. Turnout will be lower because for parties and electors the result is less important. Small parties will do better because voters will not be concerned with the composition of government, whilst governing parties will normally lose votes since they tend to be unpopular, particularly in mid-term.[13] This last proposition cannot be applied to the current election, and nor is the proposition about turnout really appropriate, but the election confirms the other expectations of the model. The biggest two parties lost and many smaller ones gained. Reif's model may not provide answers to all the features of the results, at least not without a degree of elaboration which would not be appropriate here. What we can do is look at those who did change their vote between the two elections and ask what reasons those voters gave for their decision. How far are their reasons specific to the European election?

REASONS FOR VOTING

Two questions asked in a survey immediately after the election suggest that European as opposed to national concerns were of limited importance.[14] People were asked:

"When considering which party or candidate to vote for, which was more important to you :
- the parties' stands on domestic matters (60.5 per cent)
- or their stands on European matters? (13.8 per cent)
- don't know/no reply (25.7 per cent)"

Those who gave domestic matters as their answer were asked a follow-up question:

"Among the following reasons, which one best explains the way you voted in the recent European elections?
-I wanted to express my support for the government (21.9 per cent)
-I wanted give a warning to the government (6.4 per cent)
-I wanted to express my opposition to the government (9.8 per cent)
-I was not thinking of the government when I voted in the European election (20.1 per cent)
-don't know/no reply/not applicable" (41.7 per cent)

The distribution of responses is given above. Only a small minority, 13.8 per cent, voted on predominantly European issues with three out of every five voters saying that domestic criteria were most important. In the 1979 election the weighting of European and domestic was a little more evenly balanced.[15] This emphasis on domestic factors may be due in part to the accompanying general election, but is still a disappointing finding for those hoping for the development of a less parochial outlook. For a substantial minority, 38.1 per cent, their vote is in some direct way connected with the government and for another sizeable group, 20.1 per cent, the most important reasons are domestic but unconnected with the government. It is in this group that we would expect the strength or weakness of particular candidates to have most effect, and the substantial proportion of voters in this category suggests that the candidates themselves were vital factors in the local success or failure of some parties.

Respondents were also asked how they voted in the European election and how they would vote in the next general election. The results understate the degree of difference between Dáil and European voting in June but are in accord with its pattern.[16] Taking respondents' voting intentions at the next election as an indication of how they voted at the 1989 Dáil election, we find that altogether at least 53.2 per cent were consistent in their party support, and 17.4 per cent changed party. The remainder either abstained, or could not or did not say in the case of one of the two "elections". Only a third of the switchers fell into the major categories of net change: from one of the two main parties to the PDs, Greens or independents. There was actually a greater shift between the five more established parties (Fianna Fáil, Fine Gael, PDs, Labour and Workers' Party) than between these and Greens and independents.

Two questions can be examined here. Firstly, which of the reasons given by respondents above can explain more of the switches in votes between national and European elections? Is it European issues, as some pro-integrationists might hope, reasons connected with the government, or other reasons, unconnected with Europe or the government? Secondly, which parties do the different types of voter support? Is it the case that "European issue" voters tend to be more supportive of those parties who did relatively well in the European Parliament election?

Table 6.4 answers the first set of questions, showing the proportions of switchers and stayers in each of the categories of reasons. The groups most likely to switch were those for whom domestic considerations unconnected with the government were most important, followed by those stressing European issues. Given our interpretation of nongovernmental reasons as candidate factors the volatility of this group is unsurprising, and the relative volatility of the European group is also expected, not least because it has been observed before.[17] Those giving something connected to the government as the reason for their electoral choice are unlikely to switch. Altogether only 11 per cent do so.

Table 6.4 Switchers, stayers and reasons for voting

Voting by:	Switchers	Stayers	DKs	N
Stand on European issues	31.0	56.3	12.7	126
Stand on Domestic issues:				
Supporting government	5.5	86.1	8.5	201
Warning government	27.1	59.3	13.6	59
Opposing government	13.3	63.3	23.3	90
Not thinking of govt	35.9	51.1	13.0	184
Don't Know	5.9	22.3	71.9	256

Table 6.5 shows voting choice according to the reasons given for making that choice. To what extent can we see any particular reasons accounting for the pattern of gains and losses that occurred?

Table 6.5 Party choice at EP election and reason for vote

| | ----------------Domestic---------------- | | | | European | DK | All |
	Support Govt	Warn Govt	Oppose Govt	Non- Govt			
FF	81.1	15.3	2.2	25.0	34.9	41.6	41.2
FG	9.0	28.8	52.2	26.1	22.2	24.3	24.3
PD	2.0	0.5	5.1	10.0	7.6	6.5	7.1
Labour	3.5	16.9	18.9	15.8	4.0	7.8	10.3
WP	3.0	8.5	11.1	8.2	3.2	18.2	7.5
Green	0.5	6.8	0	4.9	8.7	0	3.5
Ind/Other	1.0	13.6	2.2	8.2	7.9	5.2	6.0
Total	100.0	100.0	100.0	100.0	100.0	100.0	100.0
N=	198	56	87	176	123	77	717

Even if it were possible to say that European Parliament elections were characterised by more voters stressing European issues than in a general election, this would certainly not account for the difference between the European Parliament election and the national election. The same is true of nongovernmental concerns. Looking first at those voters motivated primarily by European concerns, we see that the groups who did better in the EP election than in the general election - Greens, independents and PDs - were all relatively popular. (In fact a near majority of Greens, 11 out of 25, voted on European grounds.) Of the "losers" only Fianna Fáil did badly, and the left was unpopular among this group. Greens, independents and the PDs also did well and Fianna Fáil badly amongst the nongovernmental voters; the left was relatively popular here, making up for its weakness amongst voters who emphasised European issues. These patterns are generally reversed amongst "governmental" voters. Fianna Fáil does well overall whilst Greens, independents and the PDs did poorly. However, this was also the group in which Fine Gael did worst.

We observed earlier that it was left to the parties outside the Dáil, such as the Green Party or Sinn Féin, and some independent voices, to provide any radical critique of EC integration or Ireland's participation in it. Since it was the Greens and independents who enjoyed a marked success in the EP election, does this mean that their support was a vote against integration or at least one critical of the style and pace of EC development? Some 30 per cent of those voting demonstrated their reservations in the referendum on the SEA; did that group make its voice heard in this election? Not all independents were in any sense anti-European, and the Green Party's reservations about the EC were probably not its most striking features. Even so, we might expect that the "anti" vote would have chosen these outlets. In fact, the data provide relatively little support for this. As we have shown already, few voters decided on the basis of European issues. Furthermore, those who did were no more or less pro-European than those choosing on the basis of domestic factors.

Table 6.6 shows the differences between three political groups - "right" (Fianna Fáil/Fine Gael/PDs), "left" (Labour/Workers' Party) and "other" voters - on a number of indicators of such enthusiasm. There is a tendency for "others" (Green Party, Sinn Féin and independent) voters to be a little less enthusiastic about the EC. In general, they are some ten to fifteen percent less supportive than voters for the "right". However, Labour and the Workers' Party also attracted more electors doubtful of the benefits of the EC, and those supportive of the EC outweigh those who are critical in all groupings. The absence of a sharp division of opinions between the different political groups further emphasises the conclusion that the domestic party system has not articulated divisions over the EC with any clarity.

Table 6.6   Supportive attitudes to the EC by EP vote

	FF/FG/PD *per cent*	*WP/Lab* *per cent*	*Others* *per cent*
In favour of efforts to unify W. Europe	72	73	66
EC membership a good thing	77	64	63
Ireland has benefited from EC	84	66	72
Would be very sorry if EC abandoned	59	45	42
Single market will be a good thing	58	54	46
Feels hopeful about 1992	71	61	62

145

THE EUROPEAN IMPACT

The fifteen deputies elected to the European parliament subsequently joined a broad range of party groups. Fianna Fáil and Fine Gael deputies again took their place in the European Democratic Alliance and European People's Party respectively. T.J. Maher again joined the Liberal grouping, as did the PDs who were already a member of the international Liberal federation. Labour's MEP, Barry Desmond, joined the Socialist group, the largest of the party groupings in the new parliament. With Proinsias De Rossa in Left Unity, one of the two communist groups, and Neil Blaney in the Regionalist group, Irish representatives are more widely placed across the political spectrum than ever before.

Another change may flow from the Dáil election. The Fianna Fáil-PD Programme for Government 1989-1993 included a proposal that in future MEPs should "qualify for membership of the Oireachtas committees relevant to EC affairs". Should this idea, which had been an important element in the PD manifesto, be realised, the two elections of 1989 may prove to have marked a further incremental change in the "Europeanisation" of the Irish political process despite their essentially domestic nature.

FOOTNOTES

1   For the course of Ireland's European policy since the 1984 European elections, see the annual reviews of Ireland's foreign relations by Patrick Keatinge, *Irish Studies in International Affairs*, vol. 2, nos 1-5 (1985-1989).

2   The National Economic and Social Council (NESC) was at this time coming to a less optimistic appraisal of the effects of EC 'cohesion' policies. But its detailed report, *Ireland in the European Community: Performance, Prospects and Strategy*, NESC Report No. 88, proved to be a dog that did not bark in time for the European election, as it was not published until September 1989.

3   See especially "1992" (Fine Gael, June 1988), sections 369-373.

4   See the articles by Joe Carroll, *Irish Times* 30 May, 2 and 6 June 1989.

5   Chris O'Malley's energetic, though ultimately unsuccessful campaign, included the novel feature in Irish electoral tactics of writing and publishing a book on European issues a year before the election: See Chris O'Malley, *Over in Europe* (Dublin: Chris O'Malley, 1988).

6   See Mary Holland on "Our European campaign of misconduct", *Irish Times* 7 June 1989.

7   A full list of those standing in both elections is:

Dublin: M. Harney TD (PD), P. De Rossa TD (WP), T. Sargent (GP).
Leinster: M. Bell TD (Lab), M. Enright (WP), C. Murphy (WP), S. English (GP).
Munster: J.Fahey TD (FF), M. Ferris (Lab), J. Sherlock TD (WP), W. Fitzsimon (Ind).
Connacht/Ulster: S. Doherty TD (FF), P. Harte TD (FG), B. Molloy TD (PD), J. Brick (WP), S. Rodgers (WP), P. Doherty (SF), C. O Caoláin (SF), N. Blaney TD (Ind).

8   Breandán O hEithir, *Irish Times* 14 June 1989.

9   The April 1989 proportions were 47 per cent certain and 30 per cent probable. In April 1984 55 per cent had said they were certain to vote. Only 46 per cent actually voted.

10   This is often called the Pedersen Volatility index, obtained by halving the total difference between the two elections.

11   Dick Spring suggested the electorate should perceive the election in this way, and vote against the government's record. *Irish Times* 18 May 1989.

12   Karlheinz Reif, Ten second-order national elections, in K.Reif (ed), *Ten European Elections*. (Aldershot: Gower, 1985) pp. 7-9, and Karlheinz Reif, "National electoral cycles and European Elections 1979 and 1984", *Electoral Studies* 3:3 (1984) pp. 244-255.

13   Michael Gallagher has made some similar observations in a recent analysis of local elections results: "Subnational elections and electoral behaviour in the Republic of Ireland", *Irish Political Studies* 4 (1989), pp. 21-42.

14   The survey was carried out through Eurobarometer as part of the European Elections Study 1989.

15   In the earlier question there were more options. Results were: domestic reasons 45 per cent, European reasons 11 per cent, both 32 per cent, neither 7 per cent and don't know 4 per cent. J. G. Blumler and A .D. Fox, *The European Voter: Popular responses to the first Community election* (London: Policy Studies Institute, 1982) p. 143.

16   Comparing the responses with the actual result of the European Parliament election shows that recall of the Fianna Fáil vote was exaggerated at the expense of that for PDs, 'Others' and independents. Full details are available from the authors.

17   Blumler and Fox (*The European Voter*, p. 140) reported that in 1979 17 per cent of switchers voted on European grounds compared with 9 per cent of stayers.

7. The Senate election

John Coakley

The clearly secondary role of the Senate in the Irish legislative and governmental process ensures that Senate elections are always overshadowed by elections to the Dáil. Unlike Ireland's first Senate (1922-1936), whose life-span was independent of that of the Dáil, the electoral schedule of the present Senate is closely tied to that of the lower house. The Constitution provides for a general election to the Senate within 90 days of a dissolution of the Dáil, and the fact that the Senate election follows the Dáil election after so short a lapse encourages a perception of the Senate election as a mere coda in a single electoral process.

In addition to possessing inferior powers to the Dáil, the Senate is considerably smaller, with only 60 members, as opposed to 166 in the other chamber. In 1989, it was the prolonged delay in the nomination of the Taoiseach's 11 appointees to the Senate that attracted greatest interest, principally out of public curiosity about the manner in which the Fianna Fáil - Progressive Democrat pact would be implemented in this domain. The election of the other 49 senators attracted, as usual, little interest, justifying once again the label "silent election".[1]

In this chapter we will analyse the 1989 Senate election, compare the results with those of the 1987 election, and comment on certain aspects of the Senate electoral process which have attracted criticism. The constitutional and legal framework within which the election took place has already been the subject of extensive analysis and so will be touched on only briefly; similarly, those aspects of the electoral process (such as the mechanics of the count and management of the campaign) which show little variation from election to election and which have also been analysed elsewhere will receive little emphasis.[2]

The makeup of the three components of the Senate - the vocational panels, which account for 43 members, the universities, which contribute another six, and the Taoiseach's 11 nominees - will first be examined in turn. Two more general questions regarding Senate elections will then be addressed. The first relates to the extent to which the Senate has failed to become a genuinely "vocational" chamber. The second has to do with the Senate's alleged role as ante-chamber to the Dáil: the extent to which it serves as a training ground for new, hopeful Dáil candidates or as a consolation prize for old, defeated ones.

THE PANELS

The election of the 43 members from the five so-called vocational panels has the largest impact on the composition of the Senate. Candidates may be nominated either by four members of the Oireachtas (none of whom may propose more than one candidate) or by a nominating body registered with the Clerk of the Senate as being entitled to make such nominations. The electorate consists of the members of all county and county borough councils, all newly-elected Dáil deputies and all outgoing senators, but no elector may vote in respect of more than one qualification.

This rather cumbersome procedure was ostensibly designed to ensure that the Senate would be "vocational" in character: that it would contrast with a Dáil dominated by political parties by representing instead certain sectoral interests. Thus, the nomination of candidates was opened to external, non-political bodies (such as the Royal Irish Academy, the Central Fisheries Board, the Irish Congress of Trade Unions and the Licensed Vintners Association, to name only a few selected at random). Furthermore, the electoral rules stipulate that the "nominating body subpanels", as the lists of candidates proposed by these bodies are known, are entitled to certain minimum representation in the Senate itself. On the five-member Cultural and Educational panel, at least two of those elected must have been proposed by nominating bodies; on the seven-member Administrative panel and the nine-member Industrial and Commercial panel, the minimum is three; and on the two 11-member panels, the Agricultural and Labour ones, at least four of the elected senators must have been proposed by nominating bodies. In the case of each panel, the position of candidates nominated by members of the Oireachtas is protected by the same minimum representation requirements. This means that, of the 43 panel seats, a minimum of 16 must go to nominating body nominees and another 16 to Oireachtas nominees; the remaining 11 may come from either group.

The composition of the electorate has the effect, however, of negating the idea of vocational representation. Since Dáil deputies, outgoing senators and county councillors are almost all active party politicians, the Senate elections have a highly political flavour. Each member of the electoral college receives five ballot papers, one for each of the five panels. Even though the ballot paper for each panel does not explicitly indicate candidates' party affiliations, and voting is by secret postal ballot, a highly partisan outcome is ensured by the "guidance" offered by the parties to their members of the electorate.

The 1989 election exemplified again the dominance of party politics in Irish public life. The Senate nominating bodies put forward a total of 71 validly-nominated candidates, five fewer than in 1987. As usual, these

149

were almost all associated with Fianna Fáil, Fine Gael or the Labour Party, though on the Administrative panel one nominating body, the Irish Kidney Association, nominated as an independent candidate Mr Desmond Kenny, Chief Executive of the National Association of the Blind (in 1987 seven independents had been put forward by nominating bodies). The five panels of candidates were completed when the Oireachtas candidates were named. These came to 39, three fewer than in 1987, and were also almost entirely official party nominees (in 1987 there had been no non-party Oireachtas nominees). As in 1987, they included one member of the Workers' Party; a former Fine Gael senator who had failed to get a party nomination, Larry McMahon, was subsequently nominated by two Progressive Democrat deputies and two independent senators; and for technical reasons the Taoiseach nominated a farmer from Kinsealy to stand on the Agricultural panel.[3]

The electorate had changed little in composition since 1987. It consisted overwhelmingly of councillors elected at the 1985 local elections or coopted since then (many of them combining local office with Dáil or Senate membership), together with those newly-elected or re-elected Dáil deputies and outgoing senators who were not council members. The total size of the electoral college came to 956, four fewer than in 1987. Table 7.1 shows the political composition of the 1989 electorate, comparing it with that of 1981 (which resembled the position also in 1982 and 1983, since the 1979 local elections were the dominant influence) and that of 1977 (determined by the 1974 local elections). The precise electoral strength of each party is difficult to establish definitively, but the figures in Table 7.1 probably represent fairly accurately their minimum strength as measured by formal affiliation.

The 1985 local elections had major implications for the probable outcome of any Senate election. Panel results are relatively predictable if one makes certain realistic assumptions about the behaviour of the electoral college. These may be summarised as follows:

1. party loyalty among voters in the Senate elections is extremely strong;

2. voters in the "others" category (in 1989, the Progressive Democrats, the Workers' Party, Sinn Féin, smaller parties and independents) will not vote as a single block but will distribute their support among candidates of the principal parties; and

3. certain patterns of transfers between mutually sympathetic parties will take place.

Table 7.1: *Approximate political composition of the Senate electorate in 1977, 1981 and 1989*

Year	Fianna Fáil	Fine Gael	Labour	Others	Total
1977	379	307	90	92	868
	(43.7)	(35.4)	(10.4)	(10.6)	(100.0)
1981	404	335	82	82	903
	(44.7)	(37.1)	(9.1)	(9.1)	(100.0)
1989	463	298	54	141	956
	(48.4)	(31.2)	(5.6)	(14.7)	(100.0)

Note: Figures in brackets are percentages.
Source: for 1977, John Coakley, "The Irish Senate election of 1977: voting in a small electorate", Parliamentary Affairs, 33:3 (1980), pp. 322-331; for 1981, John Coakley, "The Senate elections" in Howard R Penniman and Brian Farrell (eds), Ireland at the Polls 1981, 1982, and 1987: a study of four general elections (Durham, NC: Duke University Press, for the American Enterprise Institute, 1987), pp. 192-205; for 1989, calculated from data in Irís Oifigiúil supplement number 59, 25 August 1989, from data supplied by the Department of the Environment and from other sources.

Thus, for the three Senate elections where the composition of the electorate was determined overwhelmingly by the results of the 1979 local elections, it was possible to predict the following outcome by calculating the number of electoral quotas available to each party. On each panel, the Labour Party stood to win one seat, with Fianna Fáil and Fine Gael dividing the remainder evenly between them, giving a 19-19-5 ratio between these parties for the whole 43 panel seats. In the event, this is almost exactly what happened in the three elections of August 1981, April 1982 and January 1983; the only exception was on the Administrative panel in 1982 when Fine Gael lost a seat to Fianna Fáil for an unusual technical reason.[4]

Fianna Fáil's exceptionally good performance in the 1985 local elections, when the party was in opposition, brought about a considerable shift in the balance of power in the Senate electorate, and even the defection of some councillors to the Progressive Democrats did not seriously damage its strong position.[5] This altered the predicted outcome. Because of the Labour Party's electoral setback, it was now too weak to have a realistic chance of winning a seat on the five-member Cultural and Educational panel; on each of the others, it could expect a single seat. Fianna Fáil and Fine Gael would no longer divide the remainder evenly between them; in fact, Fianna Fáil could expect a two-seat advantage over Fine Gael on the seven-, nine- and 11-seat panels, giving it a total of 24 seats, to Fine Gael's 15 and the Labour Party's four.

This predicted outcome materialised almost exactly in both 1987 and 1989. On each occasion, Fianna Fáil won its expected number of seats, but among the other parties there was one deviation from the prediction. In 1987, the seat on the seven-member Administrative panel supposedly destined for Labour went instead to Fine Gael, while in 1989 independent Fine Gael candidate Larry McMahon took one seat away from his party.

The mechanics of this process are illustrated in Table 7.2, in which the actual vote on each panel is broken down by party. The valid poll, ranging between 943 and 945, represented 99 per cent of the electorate. The high degree of party voting is clear; much of the variation from one panel to another may be explained in terms of variation in the behaviour of the non-aligned vote.

Table 7.2: Distribution of electorate and of first preference votes in Senate panel elections 1989, by party

Panel	Fianna Fáil	Fine Gael	Labour Party	Workers' Party	Others	Total
Culture & Education	552	329	63	-	-	944
(Candidates)	(12)	(8)	(1)	(0)	(0)	(21)
Agriculture	531	346	66	-	0	943
(Candidates)	(13)	(8)	(1)	(0)	(1)	(23)
Labour	532	278	90	-	45	945
(Candidates)	(12)	(7)	(2)	(0)	(1)	(22)
Industry & Commerce	500	347	68	30	-	945
(Candidates)	(16)	(12)	(1)	(1)	(0)	(30)
Administration	486	335	73	-	50	944
(Candidates)	(6)	(6)	(1)	(0)	(1)	(14)
Electorate	463	298	54	21	120	956
(Total candidates)	(59)	(41)	(6)	(1)	(3)	(110)

Source: Calculated from data published in Irish Times, 19 August 1989, and from information supplied by the Clerk of Seanad Eireann.

Fianna Fáil won between 23 and 89 votes more than its strict party maximum (of 463, if all Fianna Fáil electors voted); Fine Gael won between 31 and 49 above its party maximum (298) on four panels, but dropped to 20 below this on the panel contested by the independent Fine Gael member; and the Labour vote ranged from 9 to 36 above its number of electoral college votes (54). On the only panel contested by the Workers' Party, its candidate won some nine votes more than its number of electoral college votes (21).

It was observed of earlier Senate elections that "invariably, the candidates on the Oireachtas sub-panels are more acceptable to the electorate than those on the vocational sub-panels" and that "vocational candidates" (those proposed by nominating bodies) rarely fill more than the minimum number of seats required by statute.[6] It is, indeed, true that from 1954 to 1977 nominating body nominees tended to gain only minimum representation in the Senate. In 1981 this began to change, when nominating body candidates won two seats more than the minimum. The trend was confirmed in 1982 and 1983, when the number of nominating body candidates elected reached five more than the minimum. As Table 7.3 shows, this pattern has continued; in 1987 nominating body candidates constituted a majority of those elected, and their lead was further increased in 1989.

Table 7.3: Distribution of seats by sub-panel at Senate panel elections 1954-1989

Year	Nominating bodies sub-panel	Oireachtas sub-panel
1954-1977	16	27
1981	18	25
1982	21	22
1983	21	22
1987	23	20
1989	24	19

It is not clear why this change has been taking place in the 1980s. Analysis of the pattern of voting in the 1981 Senate election, in which candidates on either type of subpanel were placed in four groups (candidates with a high political profile; those with a moderately high political profile; those engaged in local political activity only; and those not actively engaged in politics) showed that Oireachtas nominees tended, on average, to win more votes, regardless of the category into which they fell.[7] The increased success of candidates proposed by nominating bodies more recently can be explained, then, only by an increased tendency for prominent political figures to seek nominations of this type, rather than relying on their colleagues in the Oireachtas, though evidence for this is far from conclusive. It is possible that Oireachtas nominations are increasingly used to repay political debts.

THE UNIVERSITY CONSTITUENCIES

Although the campaigns for the three National University of Ireland and the three Trinity College seats attracted much more public debate, the outcome here was more predictable than usual. It is true that the electorates, and consequently the numbers of voters, were very much larger than in the case of the panel elections. The Trinity College electorate numbered over 18,000, of whom 49.9 per cent voted (in 1987 turnout amounted to 58.1 per cent of an electorate of almost 15,000). In the National University almost 74,000 electors were registered, and the turnout was rather lower, at 34.1 per cent (the corresponding figures for 1987 were an electorate of 64,000 and a turnout rate of 44.1 per cent). In addition, the influence of the political parties was marginal rather than central and, hence, voting patterns were likely to be less structured.

Nevertheless, because the three National University senators were securely entrenched, it was clear that they would be re-elected without difficulty, as indeed happened. In Trinity College, one senator, Mary Robinson, did not stand for re-election, and her seat was won by former Lord Mayor of Dublin Carmencita Hederman, who came in third after the two outgoing senators. All six university senators were independents, though, as usual, individuals with strong party associations had contested the election.

THE TAOISEACH'S NOMINEES

By comparison with the position in 1987, when he had had a relatively free hand, the Taoiseach found himself with less room for manoeuvre in 1989. On the former occasion, he had been generous in the appointment of senators from outside the ranks of his own party. These included no fewer than five independents, one of them from Northern Ireland.

In 1989, however, it was known that in negotiations before the formation of the new government Mr Haughey had agreed with Progressive Democrat leader Desmond O'Malley that three of his 11 Senate nominations would go to the minority coalition partner. The anger caused within Fianna Fáil by this agreement, together with deep-seated unease at the very idea of coalition, left the Taoiseach under considerable pressure from his own party activists. When efforts to have one place from the Progressive Democrat quota allocated to a Northern unionist failed, the appointments were made on a strict party political basis, with eight going to Fianna Fáil and three to the Progressive Democrats.

The final balance between the parties is illustrated in Table 7.4. Because of its success in the panel elections, Fianna Fáil was in a position to control a Senate majority despite the fact that it won none of the University seats. In 1987 the appointment of six Fianna Fáil members as Taoiseach's nominees had been sufficient to give it control of half of the Senate. In 1989, the appointment of eight Fianna Fáil members gave it a secure majority, contrasting with its position in the Dáil. The importance of this numerical dominance was to become clear in the vote on the chairmanship of the house, when the Progressive Democrats abandoned Fianna Fáil because of their reservations about that party's candidate for the post, former Minister for Justice Seán Doherty.

Table 7.4: Party composition of Senate after 1987 and 1989 general elections

Section	Party	1987	1989
Vocational Panels	Fianna Fáil	24	24
(43)	Fine Gael	16	14
	Labour Party	3	4
	Independents	-	1
Universities	Independents	6	6
(6)			
Taoiseach's Nominees	Fianna Fáil	6	8
(11)	Progressive Democrats	-	3
	Independents	5	-
Total	Fianna Fáil	30	32
(60)	Fine Gael	16	14
	Labour Party	3	4
	Progressive Democrats	-	3
	Independents	11	7

155

PARTY, REGION AND VOCATIONAL GROUP

Who, exactly, does the Senate represent? How valid is the perception that it is "merely another selection of party politicians chosen in an unnecessarily complicated manner"?[8] In this section we will examine the extent to which, if at all, deeply ingrained party loyalties are challenged by other forms of group affiliation, including most notably regional and vocational ties.

As we have seen, party allegiance has entirely displaced vocational affiliation in the electoral battlefield; Senate electors vote as members of Fianna Fáil or Fine Gael, not as trade unionists, as farmers or as members of professional groups. Indeed, it has for long been clear that the concept of vocationalism in Irish society is almost meaningless, and that it is not rooted in any of the profound sectoral divisions that are implied by traditional corporatism and the old notion of estate representation.

This is seen repeatedly in the nomination process itself. All candidates on the vocational panels are required to have "knowledge or practical experience" relevant to the panel on which they have been nominated. While it is true that candidates are sometimes disqualified by the Returning Officer on the grounds that they do not satisfy this condition, there are many instances where the same individual has contested successive Senate elections but switched panels at least once. In 1989, for instance, five candidates who had also contested the 1987 election now did so on a different panel. While this might be seen as reflecting an exceptional breadth of experience on the part of Irish Senate candidates, it points more obviously to the fact that the sectors to which the five panels correspond are not, in the classic corporatist sense, mutually exclusive.

Given the strength of regional loyalties and the wide geographical dispersal of the Senate electoral college, it would be interesting to examine the extent to which local factors affect voting patterns within parties. While data on senate electoral behaviour are not broken down by region, it is possible to get an impression of regional behavioural patterns by examining certain aggregate data. For instance, examination of the relationship between the regional distribution of the Fianna Fáil senate electorate on the one hand, and the range of variation in support for Fianna Fáil candidates across panels within each province on the other, shows some evidence of a tendency towards cross-regional voting. Analysis of the position within Fine Gael shows a similar pattern: in no province do Fine Gael voters opt en bloc for their local candidates. It seems, then, that regional considerations are of limited concern to the senate electorate, and that they certainly do not challenge party loyalty. Indeed, it is not improbable that in certain cases party activists may fail to vote for the local candidate with a view to preventing the development of a potential challenge to a political rival within the same party.

The regional distribution of Senate seats is described in Table 7.5. This may be compared with the distribution of the Senate electorate, which tends not to follow the distribution of the population very closely; sparsely-populated counties tend to have a much higher ratio of councillors to population than the Dublin area does. What is most striking is that, by comparison with the distribution of the electorate, the overall spread of seats showed a heavy bias in favour of Dublin and against the rest of Leinster, while Munster was over-represented and Connacht-Ulster under-represented in both 1987 and 1989. (By comparison with the distribution of the total population, though, Dublin tends to win something close to its due share, while Leinster is still under-represented and Munster over-represented.)

Table 7.5: Regional distribution of Senate seats, 1989

Section	Dublin	Rest of Leinster	Munster	Connacht-Ulster	Total
Taoiseach's nominees	4	3	4	-	11
Universities	4	-	2	-	6
Culture & Education	1	-	1	3	5
Agriculture	1	2	4	4	11
Labour	3	1	5	2	11
Industry & Commerce	3	1	3	2	9
Administration	2	-	3	2	7
Total, 1989	18	7	22	13	60
Total, 1987	14	11	23	12	60
Seats in proportion to:					
Electorate, 1989	10	17	18	15	60
Population, 1986	18	14	17	11	60

Whatever the extent to which Dublin is over-represented, it is striking that precisely as the population of the capital has been increasing as a proportion of the total population its Senate representation has been dropping to a figure close to its "due" representation; over the period 1938-1965 Dublin was represented in the Senate, on average, by 25 senators.[9]

THE SENATE AS A CHAMBER OF TRANSIT

Among the less kind descriptions that have been applied to the Senate by its critics, a recurring one is the allegation that it is seen all too often as "a place for grooming new Dáil candidates and as a political resting place for defeated deputies"[10]. It is certainly true that a number of political careers in the Dáil were initiated by Senate membership, and each Senate election is contested by several outgoing deputies who lost their Dáil seats and by others who had been unsuccessful candidates in the Dáil election.[11]

The circulation of Irish parliamentarians in the two most recent elections is illustrated in Figure 7.1.

Figure 7.1: The flow of Irish parliamentarians 1987-89

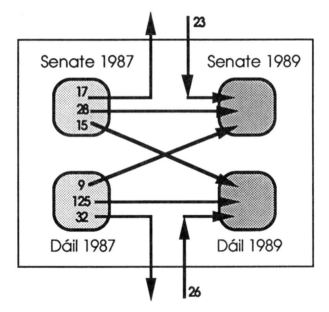

As was noted in chapter 4 above, 41 TDs elected in 1989 had not been members of the previous Dáil, though nine of them had been deputies at an earlier stage. In the case of the Senate, 32 of those elected in 1989 had not been members of the outgoing Senate: of these, nine had been members of the 1987 Dáil, three had been TDs at an earlier stage, two had previously been senators, one was both a former deputy and a former senator, and one had been a member of the European Parliament. Since the number

158

of senators retiring or losing their seats was higher, as a proportion of total house membership, than the corresponding number of deputies, overlap in the membership of the 1987 and 1989 Senates was considerably lower than that for the Dála. Only 47 per cent of senators elected in 1987 became members of the 1989 Senate, a proportion comparable with that in earlier Senates; but 75 per cent of Dáil deputies elected in 1987 were returned again in 1989.

Figure 7.1 also illustrates the extent of circulation between the two chambers. The forces responsible for movements between the two houses are not symmetrical. Outgoing senators who contest Dáil elections are attracted by the superior prestige of that house, though some may have the option of re-election or re-nomination to the Senate closed to them. Outgoing deputies who contest Senate elections, however, have little choice if they wish to remain in public life. Indeed, Figure 7.1 understates the number of refugees from one house knocking at the door of the other; to avoid making the illustration too complicated, the considerable number of unsuccessful candidates has been omitted.

CONCLUSION

The 1989 Senate election, then, was fairly typical of all elections to the second chamber. Its outcome was more or less predictable in terms of party representation (though not, of course, in terms of individuals elected), and it attracted little public interest. The most interesting new feature, the presence in the house of a small group of members of the minority coalition partner whose Senate representation is solely attributable to nomination by a Fianna Fáil Taoiseach, may have further consequences. It is, of course, well known that the Progressive Democrats have as one of their objectives the abolition of the Senate. It remains to be seen whether their involvement in the work of the second chamber will lead to a reassessment on their part of its usefulness in the Irish political process.

The Senate election

FOOTNOTES

I am indebted to Mr Edward O'Reilly, General Secretary, Fine Gael, and to Mr Seán Sherwin, National Organiser, Fianna Fáil, for their assistance in the preparation of this chapter. I am grateful to Mr Kieran Coughlan, Clerk, Seanad Eireann, for advice on technical matters.

1   Dick Walsh, "The silent election", *Irish Times* 4-14 April 1973.

2   The two standard texts on the Senate in general and on its electoral law are Thomas Garvin, *The Irish Senate* (Dublin: Institute of Public Administration, 1969) and John MacG Smyth, *The Theory and Practice of the Irish Senate* (Dublin: Institute of Public Administration, 1972). A more recent review will be found in Jean Grangé, "Irlande: le Sénat (Seanad Éireann)" in Jean Mastias and Jean Grangé (eds), *Les secondes chambres du parlement en Europe occidentale* (Paris: Economica, 1987), pp. 291-316. The 1977 Senate election was the first to be the subject of extensive analysis; see Maurice Manning, "The Senate election" in Howard R Penniman (ed), *Ireland at the Polls: The Dáil elections of 1977* (Washington, DC: American Enterprise Institute for Public Policy Research, 1978) pp. 165-173, and John Coakley, "The Irish Senate election of 1977: voting in a small electorate" *Parliamentary Affairs* 33:3 (1980), pp. 322-331; the elections of 1981, 1982 and 1983 have been examined in John Coakley, "The Senate elections" in Howard R Penniman and Brian Farrell (eds), *Ireland at the Polls 1981, 1982, and 1987: a study of four general elections* (Durham, NC: Duke University Press, for the American Enterprise Institute, 1987) pp. 192-205.

3   The Seanad Electoral (Panel Members) Act, 1947, requires that the number of members nominated to any subpanel shall be at least two greater than the maximum number of senators that may be elected from that subpanel. On the Agricultural panel, this would require the nomination of at least nine candidates on each subpanel (each of which was to return a minimum of four and a maximum of seven senators). In 1987, only eight candidates were nominated by members of the Oireachtas. Mr Haughey was therefore required as Taoiseach to make an additional nomination. Not surprisingly, given the technical nature of this device, Mr Haughey's nominee did not win any first preference votes.

4   The Fine Gael candidate who had headed the poll for his party was excluded to prevent the nominating bodies subpanel being overrepresented; as there was no continuing Fine Gael candidate on the Oireachtas subpanel, Fianna Fáil won an extra seat.

5   On the 1985 local elections see Neil Collins, "The 1985 local government elections in the Republic of Ireland", *Irish Political Studies* 1 (1986), pp. 97-102.

6   Garvin, *Senate*, pp. 32, 35.

7 Coakley, "Senate elections", pp. 199-201.
8 Basil Chubb, *The Government and Politics of Ireland* (London: Oxford University Press, 1974) p. 205.
9 Garvin, *Senate*, pp. 74-75.
10 Manning, "Senate election", p. 167.
11 Biographical data on the new senators and deputies will be found in Ted Nealon, *Nealon's Guide to the 26th Dáil and Seanad Election '89* (Dublin: Platform Press, 1989) and Jim Farrelly, *Who's Who in Irish Politics: the top 500* (Dublin: Blackwater, 1989).

8. The Udarás na Gaeltachta Election

Tony Parker

In some parts of the Republic of Ireland, three elections were held on 15 June 1989. These were the Gaeltacht areas, the officially designated areas of Irish speakers, who voted not only in the general and European Parliament elections but also for seven members of the Udarás na Gaeltachta authority. The election has been referred to in the media as the "Forgotten Election"[1], since it was overshadowed throughout much of the country by the two larger-scale elections. However, to the people in the Gaeltacht areas, the Udarás na Gaeltachta authority plays an important role in economic and social development.

The Gaeltacht areas are officially-designated districts where the Irish language is used in day to day affairs by the vast majority of the population. They are largely concentrated along the western seaboard, in some of the most economically, socially and physically disadvantaged parts of the country. The largest Gaeltacht areas are in Galway, Mayo and Donegal with smaller ones in Kerry, Cork, Waterford (Ring) and Meath (Figure 8.1).

THE UDARAS NA GAELTACHTA AUTHORITY

From 1957 to 1980 infrastructural development in the Gaeltacht was the responsibility not only of national and local government but also of Gaeltarra Éireann, a specific Gaeltacht authority. In 1980 Udarás na Gaeltachta took over from Gaeltarra Éireann, acquiring responsibility for managing various industries and encouraging new ones, and the power to acquire land, premises and plant. The Udarás has a wider role than its predecessor in that it was established to "encourage the preservation and extension of the use of Irish in the Gaeltachta and to promote the economic, social, cultural, linguistic and physical development of the Gaeltacht"[2]. It has been suggested therefore that the Udarás legislation gave the authority "development agency status with a mission to preserve and extend Irish as a spoken language"[3]. While the more extensive powers have differentiated the Udarás from Gaeltarra, a further major distinction is that a majority - seven - of the thirteen members of the board of Udarás na Gaeltachta are elected by residents of the Gaeltacht (the other six are appointed by the Minister for the Gaeltacht). This means that residents of the Gaeltacht areas have had an input into the selection of local representatives to look after their needs and ensure that their area obtains its share of the benefits that the Udarás can provide.

Figure 8.1: Udarás na Gaeltachta constituencies and candidates, 1989

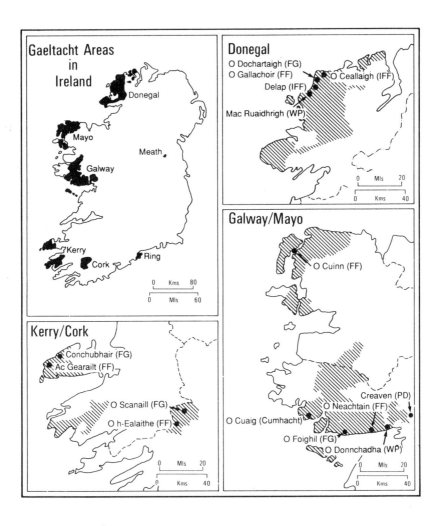

The emphasis in the Udarás na Gaeltachta authority, and therefore in the Udarás elections, has been upon the local area. Localism is a major feature in Irish elections and has been well documented in a variety of contexts,[4] with political parties utilising the effect to advantage in order to maintain party solidarity in the transfer of votes under the PR-STV system of election. Even so, there are situations where party solidarity has broken down in the face of localism.

The Udarás na Gaeltachta elections have followed this localist pattern in all three elections that have been held to date - in 1979, 1984 and 1989. Given the local role of the Udarás authority, no party affiliations appear on the ballot papers in the elections. However, in all three elections the two major political parties, Fianna Fáil and Fine Gael, have nominated candidates in all constituencies, while other national political parties have also nominated candidates in selected constituencies. While party solidarity in general elections has usually been quite high, particularly for Fianna Fáil and Fine Gael, the evidence is that quite frequently local issues represented by local candidates have eroded the degree of party solidarity in the Udarás na Gaeltachta elections. Even where local issues have not been particularly strong, instances occur of voters transferring to other local candidates of a rival party rather than maintaining party solidarity by transferring to a party colleague, primarily because, given the structure of the Udarás constituencies, the latter may come from not just another locality but even another county or part of the country.

The seven elected members to the Udarás board are elected from three constituencies. Three members are elected from the Galway-Mayo constituency, the Meath Gaeltacht voters also being included in this constituency. Two members are elected from the Donegal constituency and from the Cork-Kerry constituency, the latter including voters from the Ring Gaeltacht in Waterford. The dispersed nature of even a single constituency inevitably means that localism will be a particularly strong force not only in the voting patterns of the electorate but also in their transfer patterns. In general elections the localism effect is generally accommodated by the major political parties by selecting a geographical spread of candidates[5] who usually maintain the party vote in subsequent transfer patterns. By contrast, in the Udarás elections, given the direct benefits that can accrue to localities and the inter-county rivalries that exist, no such guarantee of party solidarity exists. Even so, those party organisations who wish to gain representation on the Udarás board must nominate candidates from diverse parts of each constituency.

In the first Udarás election in 1979, a large number of independent and local group candidates were nominated, particularly in the Galway-

164

Mayo-Meath and Cork-Kerry-Ring constituencies, with candidates from the Meath and Ring Gaeltachta also standing[6]. Although in that election only one independent was elected, the overall pattern of voting - particularly in the context of transfers - was localism first and party solidarity second. In the 1984 election the importance of local issues was highlighted by a candidate for Cumhacht, the west Galway political action group who stood specifically on the bad state of the roads in that area, being elected for the Galway-Mayo constituency.

For comparative purposes, the number of votes and proportion of the total valid poll obtained by different political groupings in the 1979 and 1984 Udarás elections are presented in Table 8.1.

Table 8.1: The 1979 and 1984 Udarás na Gaeltachta elections

	1979		1984	
	Votes	Percentage	Votes	Percentage
Cork-Kerry-Ring				
Fianna Fáil	2,289	34.6	2,224	33.6
Fine Gael	1,506	22.8	2,193	33.2
Sinn Féin	-	-	337	5.1
Independents	2,813	42.6	1,853	28.5
Donegal				
Fianna Fáil	3,926	34.4	2,664	22.2
Fine Gael	2,024	17.7	2,818	23.4
SFWP/Workers' Party	2,378	20.8	1,794	14.9
Independent Fianna Fáil	2,756	24.2	4,342	36.1
Sinn Féin	-	-	404	3.4
Independents	328	2.9	-	-
Galway-Mayo-Meath				
Fianna Fáil	5,911	47.1	6,020	48.8
Fine Gael	3,420	27.3	2,575	20.9
Workers' Party	-	-	274	2.2
Cumhacht	-	-	2,577	20.9
Sinn Féin	-	-	290	2.3
Independents	1,322	10.5	818	6.6

As the table shows, Fianna Fáil largely held its share of the votes between the two earlier elections in the Cork-Kerry-Ring and Galway-Mayo-Meath constituencies, but in Donegal its vote declined while those

165

of Independent Fianna Fáil and Fine Gael increased. The Fine Gael vote also increased in the Cork-Kerry-Ring constituency between the two elections, but in Galway-Mayo-Meath the party lost ground, notably with the rise of Cumhacht. Local political groupings made major electoral inroads in the two more northern Udarás constituencies in the first two elections, with Independent Fianna Fáil taking almost a quarter of the vote in Donegal in 1979 and over one-third of the vote in 1984, while Gluaiseacht na Gaeltachta received 15 per cent of the vote in 1979 and Cumhacht achieved a fifth of the first preference vote in 1984. This localist pattern was to be continued in the 1989 Udarás election through the medium of candidate nominations, local issues during the campaign and the results of the election.

THE CANDIDATES

In the 1989 election there were fifteen candidates nominated in the three constituencies. Although the election is ostensibly non-party and, as we have said, party affiliations do not appear on the ballot papers, no candidate in the 1989 election was truly an independent. The Fianna Fáil and Fine Gael parties nominated candidates in all three Udarás constituencies, while the Workers' Party nominated candidates in both the Donegal and Galway-Mayo-Meath constituencies. The Progressive Democrats also nominated a candidate in the latter constituency, while regionally-based political groups nominated candidates in Donegal (Independent Fianna Fáil) and the Connacht constituency (Cumhacht).

Nomination patterns have altered over the three Udarás na Gaeltachta elections. At the first, in 1979, there were thirty-four candidates for the seven seats, with independents standing in all three constituencies. In both the Cork-Kerry-Ring and Galway-Mayo-Meath constituencies more than half the candidates did not belong to established political parties, although a number of the 'independents' belonged to civil rights groups. In the 1984 election, the situation had polarised somewhat with only three independents standing, none of whom came from the Donegal constituency, and the total number of candidates had declined to twenty-three. Of the fifteen candidates standing in 1989, four were running in the Cork-Kerry-Ring constituency, five in Donegal and six in Galway-Mayo-Meath.

In the Cork-Kerry-Ring constituency the four candidates were equally divided between the Fianna Fáil and Fine Gael parties, and between County Kerry and County Cork. In the Donegal constituency, Fianna Fáil, Fine Gael and the Workers' Party each nominated one candidate while Independent Fianna Fáil nominated two, all of whom came from broadly the same part of the constituency. In the Galway-Mayo-Meath constituency, Fianna Fáil nominated two candidates, one from Galway and one from Mayo, while Fine Gael, the Workers' Party, the Progressive Democrats and Cumhacht nominated one candidate each, all of whom came from the Galway part of the constituency. The nominated candidates, their party affiliations and home locations are indicated in table 8.2 and illustrated in figure 8.1.

Table 8.2: Candidates, party allegiance and home location

Cork-Kerry-Ring Constituency		
Brendán Ac Gearailt	(Fianna Fáil)	Ballyferriter
T.P. Conchobhair	(Fine Gael)	Gallarus, Dingle
Donal O h-Éalaithe	(Fianna Fáil)	Coolea
Michéal O Scanaill	(Fine Gael)	Baile Mhúirne
Donegal Constituency		
Antóin Delap	(Ind. Fianna Fáil)	Bun Beag
Séamus Mac Ruaidhrigh	(Workers' Party)	Anngaire
Pádraig O Ceallaigh	(Ind. Fianna Fáil)	Falcarragh
Pádraig O Dochartaigh	(Fine Gael)	Doire Beaga
Seán O Gallachoir	(Fianna Fáil)	Doire Beaga
Galway-Mayo-Meath Constituency		
Seán Creaven	(Prog Dem)	Mionloch
Seosamh O Cuaig	(Cumhacht)	Cill Chiaráin
Tadhg O Cuinn	(Fianna Fáil)	Béal an Mhuirthead
Colm O Donnchadha	(Workers' Party)	An Spidéal
Pól O Foighil	(Fine Gael)	Indreabhán
Seán O Neachtain	(Fianna Fáil)	An Spidéal

A number of the candidates were incumbent members of the Udarás na Gaeltachta authority or, in some instances, had been members from 1979-84. Brendán Ac Gearailt and Michéal O Scanaill were incumbents from the Cork-Kerry-Ring constituency, Ac Gearailt having been elected as an independent in both 1984 and 1979, but being a Fianna Fáil candidate on this occasion. In the same constituency, T.P. Conchobhair had been a member of the authority from 1979-84, before being supplanted by his Fine Gael party colleague, Scanaill. In Donegal, Pádraig O Ceallaigh and Seán O Gallachoir were the incumbents, the former having served on the authority since its inception. A third candidate in the 1989 election,

Pádraig O Dochartaigh, had also served on the Udarás authority between 1979-84, having been appointed Chairman of the authority by the government. In the Galway-Mayo-Meath constituency Tadhg O Cuinn and Seán O Neachtain were two of the sitting members of the authority, the third, Peadar O Tuathail of Cumhacht, not running on this occasion. Pól O Foighil, the Fine Gael candidate, had also served on the Udarás authority from 1979 to 1984.

THE ISSUES

The 1989 Udarás election was fought around a mixture of local issues and party politics. The problem of local job creation was particularly important in all the constituencies; the Fianna Fáil party was blamed for the lack of progress, with an inevitable consequence at the polls. Periodic announcements of new job creation schemes were made during the campaign in an effort to counter this problem. For example, the *Western People* (14 June, 1989) reports an announcement by O Cuinn, the Belmullet-based Fianna Fáil candidate in the Galway-Mayo-Meath constituency, of a new textile industry for the town "which will provide eighty jobs at start-up, rising to three hundred by 1991". In Donegal, emigration and unemployment were very strong, emotive issues in view of the high rate of emigration from the Gaeltacht areas. Local issues dominated the campaign throughout the constituencies, many relating to the fishing industry. On Arranmore Island, in Donegal, problems with monofilament nets and overfishing were important, as was the lack of a post-primary school. In the Cork-Kerry-Ring constituency, local proposals for fish farming formed an election issue, while in the Galway-Mayo-Meath constituency, and in west Galway in particular, the rod licence dispute was a major local issue in all the elections of 1989, with an active anti-Fianna Fáil campaign being mounted. Although all the candidates came from established political groupings, and - in the case of the Fianna Fáil and Fine Gael candidates - were included on party election advertising together with general and European election candidates, many Udarás candidates emphasised their attachment to their locality first and foremost. This was reflected in the votes achieved by some of the leading candidates.

THE RESULTS

Over 61,000 people were eligible to vote in the Udarás na Gaeltachta election and the total poll was 39,631. This represents a turnout of 64 per cent, slightly lower than that of the general election held on the same day (see Chapter 4 above). The turnout varied between the three con-

168

stituencies: Cork-Kerry-Ring recorded the highest (77 per cent), while Donegal and Galway-Mayo-Meath it was lower, at 63 per cent and 62 per cent respectively. Spoilt votes constituted 3.5 per cent of the total poll, with a higher than average concentration in the Galway-Mayo-Meath constituency. This might be partly explained, as might the lower turnout, by the presence of predominantly English-speaking areas around Galway city being included in the officially defined Gaeltacht areas.

Table 8.3: Results of the 1989 Udarás na Gaeltachta Election

	Count			
	1st	2nd	3rd	4th
Cork-Kerry-Ring Constituency				
Brendán Ac Gearailt (FF)	3,194	elected		
Michéal O Scanaill (FG)	1,735	1,845	2,163	
T.P. Conchobhair (FG)	1,527	2,082	2,167	
Donal O h-Éalaithe (FF)	599	776	elim.	
Donegal Constituency				
Pádraig O Dochartaigh (FG)	2,884	3,102	3,611	
Pádraig O Ceallaigh (IFF)	2,738	3,390	3,803	
Seán O Gallachoir (FF)	2,557	2,902	3,327	
Séamus Mac Ruaidhrigh (WP)	2,265	2,587	elim.	
Antóin Delap (IFF)	2,067	elim.		
Galway-Mayo-Meath Constituency				
Tadhg O Cuinn (FF)	5,037	elected		
Pól O Foighil (FG)	3,834	3,989	4,648	4,739
Seosamh O Cuaig (Cumhacht)	3,637	3,790	4,235	4,289
Seán O Neachtain (FF)	3,270	3,405	3,914	4,132
Seán Creaven (PD)	2,212	2,301	elim.	
Colm O Donnchadha (WP)	704	elim.		

The results of the election including the first and subsequent counts are given in Table 8.3. In the Cork-Kerry-Ring constituency Brendán Ac Gearailt received 45 per cent of the first preference vote and was elected on the first count, with the two Fine Gael candidates each receiving between 21 per cent and 25 per cent of the vote, while the Cork-based Fianna Fáil candidate received less than 9 per cent of the poll. In Donegal, the Fine Gael candidate, O Dochartaigh, headed the poll with 23 per cent of the vote, closely followed by O Ceallaigh of Independent Fianna Fáil and O

Gallachoir of Fianna Fáil. Overall, the votes were more evenly spread in this constituency than elsewhere, with only 817 votes separating the first and last candidate on a total valid poll of over 12,500 votes. In the Galway-Mayo-Meath constituency, O Cuinn headed the poll with almost 27 per cent of the vote and was elected on the first count, while O Foighil of Fine Gael and O Cuaig of Cumhacht each received around 20 per cent of the vote.

As the table indicates, on subsequent counts Conchobhair was elected to the second seat in Cork-Kerry-Ring; O Ceallaigh and O Dochartaigh were elected to the two seats in Donegal, and O Foighil and O Cuaig were elected to the two remaining seats in Galway-Mayo-Meath. How the candidates gained election illustrates the critical importance of localism over party politics and each constituency will be considered in turn in the following sections. First, though, the proportion of the first preference vote gained by different political groupings will be discused and compared with the previous Udarás elections.

Collectively, the Fianna Fáil party candidates gleaned little more than 38 per cent of the total valid poll from the three constituencies, while Fine Gael candidates took 22 per cent in this election. Independent Fianna Fáil, who only contested one constituency took over 12.5 per cent of the total vote cast in the election, while Cumhacht - also contesting only the one constituency - gained 9.5 per cent of the vote. The Workers' Party and the Progressive Democrats took 7.8 per cent and 5.8 per cent of the vote respectively.

Table 8.4 indicates the number and proportion of first preference votes gained by each party in the three constituencies. Comparison with Table 8.1 reveals a decline in the Fianna Fáil vote in the Donegal and Galway-Mayo-Meath constituencies from the 1984 election, something which might well have occurred in the Cork-Kerry-Ring constituency as well, had Ac Gearailt not stood on the Fianna Fáil ticket. The Fine Gael vote held firm in the two more northern Udarás constituencies and increased quite substantially in the Cork-Kerry-Ring constituency. The Workers' Party increased its share of the vote in both constituencies in which they stood. The two locally-based political groupings, Independent Fianna Fáil and Cumhacht, continued to make substantial inroads; the former increased its share of the first preference vote by over 2 per cent, while Cumhacht dropped only 1.4 per cent of the vote in a constituency where the Progressive Democrats went from nothing to 11.8 per cent of the vote.

Table 8.4: *Political Parties' Votes and Proportion of the First Preference*
Poll in the 1989 Udarás na Gaeltachta Election

	Votes	Percentage
Cork-Kerry-Ring		
Fianna Fáil	3,793	53.8
Fine Gael	3,262	46.2
Donegal		
Fianna Fáil	2,557	20.4
Fine Gael	2,884	23.1
Workers' Party	2,265	18.1
Independent Fianna Fáil	4,805	38.4
Galway-Mayo-Meath		
Fianna Fáil	8,307	44.4
Fine Gael	3,834	20.5
Progressive Democrats	2,212	11.8
Workers' Party	704	3.8
Cumhacht	3,637	19.5

The Cork-Kerry-Ring constituency
The election of Ac Gearailt on the first count with 3,194 votes could be attributed to a number of factors. He was the only candidate in the constituency to have served on the Udarás authority since its inception ten
years ago, and continuity of service is clearly an advantage in Irish politics, particularly at the local scale. Reportedly, he polled strongly not
only in his own bailiwick but also in the Ring Gaeltacht. Although nominated on this occasion as a Fianna Fáil candidate he had been elected on
the two previous occasions as an independent, and as such was known for
his independent stance on local issues. Furthermore, a name change from
Mac Gearailt to Ac Gearailt resulted in his appearing first on the ballot
paper, above his Kerry rival, Conchobhair, and this may have proven an
advantage if the phenomenon of alphabetical voting noted in general
elections also operates in a local election.
    The local effect is particularly evident in the transfer of Ac Gearailt's
surplus. This is shown in table 8.5 which indicates candidates' share of
the vote on the first count and proportionate share of redistributed votes
on subsequent counts. Almost two-thirds of Ac Gearailt's surplus went to

Conchobhair who was not a party colleague but came from the same local-ity near Dingle. Party solidarity accounted for only 21 per cent of the transfers in the second count in the constituency, and given O h-Éalaithe's low vote on the first count this was insufficient to prevent his elimination and the distribution of his votes. The third and final count resulted in the election of Conchobhair by just four votes.

Table 8.5: Candidates' Percentage Share of the Vote in the Cork-Kerry-Ring Constituency

	Count		
	1st	*2nd*	*3rd*
		FF	*FF*
		surplus	*elimination*
Brendán Ac Gearailt (FF)	45.3%	elected	
Michéal O Scanaill (FG)	24.6%	13.1%	41.0%
T.P. Conchobhair (FG)	21.6%	65.9%	11.0%
Donal O h-Éalaithe (FF)	8.5%	21.0%	48.0%*

* Proportion of non-transferable votes

The distribution of O h-Éalaithe's transfers is interesting in as much as there was no party colleague to transfer votes to, both remaining candi-dates being from Fine Gael. However one came from County Kerry while the other came from the same Gaeltacht area as O h-Éalaithe. Party solidarity was such that 48 per cent of O h-Éalaithe's votes were non-transferable. Forty one per cent went to the closer Fine Gael candidate, compared with only 11 per cent for the one from Kerry. The 41 per cent of local transfers indicates that for many people in the Gaeltacht areas a lo-cal candidate is important, irrespective of party. However it was the 85 votes which went to Conchobhair that resulted in his election. It is quite likely that many of these votes were Ac Gearailt's third preferences which, having first gone to a party colleague in another Gaeltacht area, transferred back to a local candidate, ensuring his election by the slimmest of margins and resulting in two representatives from the Kerry Gaeltacht.

The Donegal constituency
The fact that the Fianna Fáil candidate came third with 2,557 votes com-pared to the Fine Gael candidate's 2,884 votes and one of the Independent

Fianna Fáil candidate's 2,738 votes is evidence of the strong feelings on local issues and the attachment to local personalities. The Udarás constituency is predominantly located in the Dáil constituency of Donegal
South-West, where Fianna Fáil took 55 per cent of the vote in the 1989
general election and where there was no Independent Fianna Fáil candidate. Part of the Udarás constituency, the Milford area, lies in Donegal
North-East though, where there is strong support for the Independent Fianna Fáil party, and this is reflected in O Ceallaigh's first preference
vote. O Ceallaigh also benefited from a strong personal vote due to his
having been an elected member of the Udarás authority since its inception
in 1979.

*Table 8.6: Candidates' Percentage Share of the Vote in the Donegal Con-
stituency*

	Count		
	1st	*2nd* *IFF*	*3rd* *WP*
		elimination	
Pádraig O Dochartaigh (FG)	23.1%	10.5%	19.7%
Pádraig O Ceallaigh (IFF)	21.9%	31.5%	16.0%
Seán O Gallachoir (FF)	20.4%	16.7%	16.4%
Séamus Mac Ruaidhrigh (WP)	18.1%	15.6%	47.8%*
Antóin Delap (IFF)	16.5%	25.6%*	

* Proportion of non-transferable votes

The close spread of the vote in Donegal resulted in a tight contest
throughout for the two seats. The proportionate distribution of transfers
shows some interesting patterns (table 8.6). As a result of the first count,
Delap of Independent Fianna Fáil was eliminated and his votes redistributed on the second count. With a party colleague in contention it might
be expected that party solidarity would result in a substantial transfer to
O Ceallaigh. However he received less than a third of Delap's transfers,
while a quarter of the votes were non-transferable. The other three candidates each received between 10 per cent and 17 per cent of the transfers,
with the Fine Gael candidate receiving fewest. The elimination of Mac
Ruaidhrigh on the third count resulted in almost half of his votes becom-

ing non-transferable, and of the remainder some 20 per cent went to O Dochartaigh, the Fine Gael candidate, while 16 per cent each went to O Ceallaigh (of Independent Fianna Fáil) and O Gallachoir (of Fianna Fáil). O Ceallaigh and O Dochartaigh were both elected on this final count without having reached the quota, the latter being only 284 votes ahead of O Gallachoir. O Dochartaigh's success may in part at least be attributable to attracting an anti-Fianna Fáil protest vote from some of the electorate.

The Galway-Mayo-Meath constituency

The election of O Cuinn on the first count was in some ways inevitable for he was the only Mayo candidate to be nominated and it is estimated that he took around 90 per cent of the valid poll from the county's Gaeltacht areas. As such he is likely to have gained both Fianna Fáil votes and cross-party support from other Mayo Gaeltacht voters who did not have an opportunity to consider any other locally based candidate. The strong showing of O Foighil of Fine Gael is due primarily to his involvement with the local community over the years - developing Irish summer colleges, piped water schemes and managing cooperatives - rather than any inherent support for Fine Gael in the Gaeltacht areas of Galway. That the Cumhacht candidate, O Cuaig, should attract votes is equally unsurprising. Cumhacht were founded in the early 1980s to press for infrastructure development generally in Connemara, particularly the Gaeltacht areas, and especially for improvement in the poor condition of the local roads. They gained electoral success in the 1984 Udarás na Gaeltachta election when Peadar O Tuathail was elected to the authority[7] and subsequently to the County Council in the 1985 local elections. O Cuaig has built upon an already successful base although with a marginally lower proportion of the first preference vote than that achieved by O Tuathail five years ago.

The second count saw the beginnings of the struggle between the five Galway-based candidates with the distribution of O Donnchadha's votes, the Workers' Party candidate from An Spidéal (Table 8.7). This resulted in almost a quarter of his votes being non-transferable and some 20 per cent each being distributed to O Foighil, O Neachtain and O Cuaig, the first two of whom live close to O Donnchadha's home. The PD candidate, Creaven, trailed somewhat, gaining only 12.6 per cent of the transfers, and his votes were redistributed on the third count, with almost 30 per cent of them being non-transferable. This relatively high level of non-transferability may have been due to the fact that the candidate was from Mionloch on the outskirts of Galway city, a locality which had no other candidate and which might well have viewed the Udarás election in a dif-

174

ferent light compared with the more Irish-speaking areas to the west. Of Creaven's transferable votes, O Foighil gained the largest share (28.6 per cent), perhaps reflecting in limited form the transfer agreement between the Fine Gael and Progressive Democrat parties at the general election. Even so, O Neachtain and O Cuaig gained 22 per cent and 19 per cent respectively of Creaven's transfers.

Table 8.7: Candidates' Share of the Vote and Transfer Patterns in the Galway-Mayo-Meath Constituency

	Count			
	1st	*2nd*	*3rd*	*4th*
		WP	*PD*	*FF*
		elimination		*surplus*
Tadhg O Cuinn (FF)	26.9%	elected		
Pól O Foighil (FG)	20.5%	22.0%	28.6%	25.1%
Seosamh O Cuaig (Cumhacht)	19.5%	21.7%	19.3%	14.9%
Seán O Neachtain (FF)	17.4%	19.2%	22.1%	60.1%
Seán Creaven (PD)	11.8%	12.6%	29.9%*	
Colm O Donnchadha (WP)	3.8%	24.4%*		

* Proportion of non-transferable votes

Perhaps the greatest interest attaches to the fourth count, not merely because it was the final count, which elected O Foighil and O Cuaig, but because it was the distribution of O Cuinn's surplus at a stage when a second Fianna Fáil candidate, the incumbent O Neachtain, was still in contention. Only 60 per cent of O Cuinn's surplus passed to his party colleague, with O Foighil of Fine Gael gaining over 25 per cent and O Cuaig of Cumhacht receiving some 15 per cent of the votes. It is likely that this is not a breakdown of party solidarity between two Fianna Fáil candidates but more a reflection of the fact that O Cuinn attracted votes across the political spectrum from Mayo voters. Their second choices to some extent reflected their traditional political persuasions yielding a windfall for O Foighil of 'returned' Fine Gael votes. At the same time the opportunity to vote for a candidate, O Cuaig of Cumhacht, from a locally-based pressure group concerned with primarily local issues was also availed of by a number of Mayo voters.

175

LOCALITY OR PARTY SOLIDARITY?

The evidence from the 1989 Udarás na Gaeltachta election is that, as in the elections of 1979 and 1984, the local effect is particularly important. Party solidarity can stumble in the face of localism and this is indicated in a number of instances in this election. In particular, the relatively low poll for Fianna Fáil in the Udarás constituencies - even when compared to the party's performance in the general election in these western areas - is indicative of a local message being sent by Gaeltacht voters. It may well be that they continued to support Fianna Fáil in the general election, but voted for other candidates in what was for them potentially a more vital, locally-based election. The heavy transfer of surplus votes from Ac Gearailt to the local Fine Gael candidate, Conchobhair, rather than to his County Cork-based party colleague, was critical in enabling Conchobhair to catch up the Cork-based Fine Gael candidate and eventually defeat him by just four votes. In Donegal, party solidarity in the transfer of Independent Fianna Fáil votes broke down in the face of a multiplicity of recipients and a high proportion of non-transferable votes. In the Galway-Mayo-Meath constituency, localism played an important role, both in O Cuinn's large first preference total and election on the first count, and in the distribution of his surplus when some Mayo voters reverted to their traditional Fine Gael party allegiance or voted for the Cumhacht candidate who won by a mere 157 votes from the second Fianna Fáil candidate. The very election of a candidate from a locally-based pressure group, Cumhacht, in 1984 was a triumph of localism over the party machine[8]. That the seat should be retained by another Cumhacht candidate is continuing evidence of the importance of localism in this constituency, and the same is true of the 1989 Udarás na Gaeltachta election overall.

FOOTNOTES

1 *Donegal Democrat* 9 June 1989.
2 Translation of a statement made by the Minister for the Gaeltacht during the debate on the Udarás na Gaeltachta Bill, 1978.
3 F. Flynn, "Gaeltacht development", page 25 in P. Breathnach (ed.), *Rural Development in the West of Ireland* (Department of Geography, Maynooth College: Occasional Paper No 3, 1983) pp. 23-35.
4 See for example, M. Marsh, "Localism, candidate selection and electoral preferences in Ireland: the general election of 1977", *The Economic and Social Review* 12 (1981) pp. 267-86; A. J. Parker, "The 'friends and neighbours' voting effect in the Galway West constituency", *Political Studies Quarterly* 1:3 (1982) pp. 243-62; A. J. Parker, "Localism and bailiwicks: the Galway West constituency in the 1977 general election", *Proceedings of the Royal Irish Academy* 83C:2 (1983) pp. 17-36; and P. M. Sacks, "Bailiwicks, locality and religion: three elements in an Irish Dáil constituency election", *The Economic and Social Review* 1 (1970) pp. 531-54.
5 See A. J. Parker, "Geography and the Irish electoral system", *Irish Geography* 19:1 (1986) pp. 1-14.
6 See A. J. Parker, "A note upon localism and party solidarity: the transfer of votes in the 'Udarás na Gaeltachta election of 1979", *The Economic and Social Review* 15:3 (1984) pp. 209-24.
7 See A. J. Parker, "Localism, the local issue and the 1984 Udarás na Gaeltachta election in Galway", paper presented at the Conference of Irish Geographers, Carysfort College, 1985.
8 See Parker, "Localism, the local issue and the 1984 Udarás election".

9. Forming the government
Brian Farrell

The ostensible occasion of the 1989 general election was a parliamentary defeat on the issue of funding for AIDS patients. It was the sixth occasion that the 25th Dáil had challenged the minority Fianna Fáil government. Scarcely a crisis, it escalated- or drifted - into a decision to seek a fresh mandate. Charles Haughey and his colleagues argued in the course of the campaign that only a single-party majority government could provide the stable and enduring administration required for Ireland as it headed into the 1990s.

For the fifth time in a decade, the voters refused to oblige; Fianna Fáil's total of Dáil seats was reduced by four. Far from resolving an allegedly unmanageable problem of parliamentary uncertainty and government instability, the election results imposed new burdens on a system already showing signs of fragility. Immediately after the election there was no single-party majority; there was no viable alternative in sight. Neither a plausible minority single-party government nor a likely agreed coalition was available. The only consensus - among politicians, public and commentators alike - was that a new election would not resolve the impasse.

Yet this was a situation that was not only predictable, but had been predicted. Following three general elections of 1981-1982, it was noted:

> Present electoral arrangements and the narrow ideological and social
> cleavage between the major parties suggest that variations of the coali-
> tion and minority models are more likely in the future. The intervention
> of independent and smaller-party deputies in close parliamentary divi-
> sions and the continuing local and pressure-group influence point to the
> need for more definite procedures (perhaps drawing on the European
> experience of coalition formation) and possibly for more time (between
> dissolution and the summoning of a new Dáil) to permit government
> formation. In particular, it seems likely that Fianna Fáil will be forced
> to reconsider its traditional opposition to coalition.[1]

Similarly, after the 1987 election, there could be no doubt that "government formation is no longer a neat ceremonial function following on, in some clear cut and predictable liturgical sequence, from the declaration of the results".[2] What was manifest in the late 1980s had been foreseen by percipient politicians from the inception of the new Irish state system. Kevin O'Higgins, Minister for Home Affairs, told the Dáil in 1922 that, because of proportional representation, small groups rather than large political parties would dominate the Dáil. As a result "you will not have the thing that is most needed in Ireland for many a long year - you will not have a strong or stable government. You will have frequent changes in Government, and no continuity of policy in your Departments. You will have a state of affairs pretty much like what you had in Italy or France."[3]

The solution proposed at that time was a marked departure from the Westminister-style single-party government and envisaged a small core Cabinet bound by collective responsibility but supplemented with 'extern' ministers. That proposal was only partially implemented; in practice the few "extern" ministers appointed were all party men and indistinguishable from Cabinet ministers.[4] The Westminster model, including two large "majority-bent" parties, was firmly in place by the late 1920s.

The problem of securing stable government formation remained. During the 1937 debate on the new constitution there was an illuminating exchange between two men destined to lead Irish governments. Proposing an amendment to the draft constitution that would retain proportional representation but not specify the single transferable vote mode, John A. Costello argued "We always understood that the real defect under any system of proportional representation, and particularly the system of the single transferable vote, was that it led, in circumstances where there are no big economic issues before the country, to a large number of small Parties being returned making for instability in government."[5] De Valera opposed the amendment and concluded his observations on the issue with the remark: "I am honestly afraid of the temptation there might be to political Parties to start manoeuvring with various systems of proportional representation for purely Party purposes."[6]

More than twenty years later, in 1959, de Valera came back to the stability problem and, as an attempted parting-gift to the party he had founded, combined his own campaign for the presidency with a constitutional referendum to substitute a simple majority system for STV. It was rejected.

In the following decade the all-party Oireachtas Committee on the Constitution again addressed the problem of reconciling popular representation and governmental stability.[7] Arguments for and against electoral reform were canvassed. Another referendum followed, containing two proposals. One, following on the decision in the O'Donovan case[8], would allow a "tolerance" in the ratio of seats to votes; the other involved substituting the simple plurality vote in single-seat constituencies. Both proposals were decisively rejected.

THE MAJORITY GOVERNMENT MYTH

Despite these efforts to cope with a recognised problem of government formation, there has been a persistent belief that single-party government has been the norm for the Irish system. In part fostered by Fianna Fáil's two periods of sixteen continuous years in government, it has been particularly strong in that party, perhaps because Fianna Fáil has been the only party to achieve single-party majority government.[9]

An examination of the electoral record reveals the need to modify the myth. The continuity in government achieved during 1932-48 required considerable management. Fianna Fáil first took office as a minority government in 1932. It required a snap election early in the following year to secure an overall majority of seats. A similar strategy was required in 1937-38 and 1943-44. In the whole period de Valera only once secured a majority of the popular vote. During the second extended period of Fianna Fáil rule, 1957-73, Lemass failed to get an overall majority in 1961 and secured exactly half the Dáil seats in 1965. The party's popular vote fluctuated between 43.8 per cent and 48.3 per cent. Both the electoral system and the electoral record 1922-89 militate against any confident assumption of an overall majority as a normal outcome.

Table 9.1: Composition and duration of Irish governments 1922 - 1989 [10]

	Single Party Majority	Single Party Minority	Coalition
Total duration, years	34.7	17.0	15.5
Average duration, years	3.8	1.9	3.2
Number of cases	9	9	5

As Table 9.1 indicates, it was possible to form single-party majority governments in only nine cases over the whole period; the two original Cumann na nGaedhael governments are included although their parliamentary majorities arose from republican abstentionist policies. It is also clear that the average duration of single-party majority governments is not that much greater than that of coalition administrations. Moreover, three minority single-party governments survived for more than three years.

By 1989 there had not been an overall majority for a dozen years. It was clear that calling an election was a high-risk strategy. There were calculations on both sides of the argument. Some ministers pointed to the apparently favourable trends in the public opinion polls and the evident disarray on the Opposition benches; they favoured a preemptive dissolution and quick campaign. Others stressed that a continuing series of parliamentary defeats - even on relatively minor issues - must breed uncertainty and instability; they argued that the Tallaght strategy was breaking down and that the health and defence estimates could not be carried; better call an election than have it forced. But more cautious and experienced ministers favoured soldiering on; they argued that the public did not want an early election and that the government should be seen to be forced into a contest - it would be the clinch argument for an overall Fianna Fáil majority. One way or another, both sides were certain that the issue of strong, single-party government versus weak coalition or vulnerable minority government would be central to the campaign. It was an emphasis, from a Fianna Fáil perspective, that could be justified on the basis of present circumstance and past experience. But it did not work.

THE OPTIONS FOR GOVERNMENT

It was one thing to press for a particular electoral outcome. It was another to accommodate to the actual results. As the pattern became distinct, the rhetorical reiteration of Fianna Fáil opposition to any kind of coalition arrangements took on the air of a thoughtless mantra. The Taoiseach's response in his first public comment on radio and television on Saturday 17 June was uncompromising. Asked whether in these new circumstances Fianna Fáil would now contemplate coalition, he replied: "No. I don't think that would be a good solution in this situation. Maybe some time in the future. Coalitions do not work in our circumstances, are not satisfactory and have a kind of political paralysis".[11] He went on to dismiss the point that it was precisely Fianna Fáil's refusal to participate in coalition which had limited Irish government options in the past.

Despite these protestations, in the aftermath of the election there was immediate speculation about how a government might be formed. Most observers quickly recognised that another minority-led Fianna Fáil administration was no longer feasible, although Haughey persistently offered this option. It was generally accepted that if the Tallaght strategy was already showing signs of strain before the contest, it was beyond resurrection afterwards. Nor would any other party accept such a position of responsibility without power. In essence, it was plain, there were only two practical options; each depended on Fianna Fáil relinquishing its principled objection to coalition.

Once that taboo was broken, an historic reconcilation could be envisaged. This would embrace the two partisan wings of an earlier Sinn Féin in a grand alliance of Fianna Fáil and Fine Gael. On the night of the count the former Taoiseach and leader of Fine Gael, Garret FitzGerald, argued vigorously against any such prospect; it would become a monolith impervious to parliamentary criticism or control.[12] The same viewpoint was consciously echoed on the following morning by Haughey.

Yet, in terms of government formation and endurance, such a grand coalition had much to recommend it. Once negotiated, even against considerable opposition within each party, it would have a large, assured majority. Leaders could not be easily threatened by backbench revolts. At an organisational level the traditional rivalry between the two parties could continue. Each could contest local elections and even bye-elections without any undue strain on government stability.

The other alternative was a Fianna Fáil - Progressive Democrat coalition. This, as Richard Sinnott was quick to point out, fitted neatly the "minimum-winning" combination of coalition theory.[13] But, at a practical level there were formidable objections. In the first instance, the parliamentary arithmetic left little room for relaxation; Fianna Fáil's seventy-seven seats plus the Progressive Democrats' six was a lean working majority, requiring an "independent" Ceann Comhairle. There was the additional strain arising from the fact that all six PD deputies were former Fianna Fáil candidates, deputies and ministers; former colleagues regarded them not merely as rivals but as traitors. Any governmental coalition would generate organisational tensions that could lead to further splits. There was the further objection that a long-term history of personal suspicion between Charles Haughey and Desmond O'Malley had led to a notorious breakdown of trust during their last shared period in office.

WHAT HAPPENED?

Whatever the general consideration of options, the immediate practical problem was that Fianna Fáil seemed incapable of considering any kind of coalition arrangement. Mesmerised by its own instinctive dislike for, and traditional opposition to, coalition, the party seemed unable either to initiate or to respond to any resolution of the dilemma created by the election result. Neither Haughey nor his senior colleagues seemed capable of action. One experienced observer commented that that they seemed paralysed by the outcome, Haughey assuming that somehow the other parties would offer a way out: "The first week after the defeat he spent in generalised talks with the other party leaders. They found him, in the main, to be very substantially detached from political reality. Moreover he was getting little useful support from his cabinet; people like Gerry Collins were simply saying very little, others, like Albert Reynolds and Pádraig Flynn, argued consistently for toughing it out: the opposition parties would blink first."[14]

The first open shift in party positions was in fact signalled by PD deputy Mary Harney in a radio interview for the *This Week* programme. She indicated that the party might have to vote for a Taoiseach they did not like.[15] This encouraged the Fianna Fáil backbencher Charlie McCreevy to make contact. It also provoked two other PD deputies, Pearse Wyse and Máirín Quill, both from Cork, to repeat publicly their opposition to any support for Haughey as Taoiseach. The issue of whether the Progressive Democrats were still bound by their preelection pact with Fine Gael became the focus for a much deeper and more passionate internal debate. It occupied a series of meetings and much attention.[16]

Meantime, the Fine Gael leader, Alan Dukes, put forward his own proposals for government formation. These envisaged a grand coalition of the two main parties. Perhaps conscious of the need to satisfy critics of his Tallaght strategy, Dukes pitched his opening demands high. Ignoring the discrepancy in seats between Fianna Fáil and Fine Gael, he proposed an equal share of Cabinet seats, an alternation of the office of Taoiseach between the party leaders, each to hold office as Taoiseach for a two-year period.[17] This bold bargain, not unexpectedly, was rejected by Haughey as "totally unacceptable"; it would be "a betrayal by us of the electorate who voted for Fianna Fáil on our clearly-stated policy of single-party government". Although the two leaders met on a number of occasions subsequently, there was never any serious effort at negotiation between them.

Instead, Haughey asked O'Malley to suggest a basis on which the Progressive Democrats might support a minority Fianna Fáil government.[18] The small PD group continued its deliberations. After a six-hour meeting of the parliamentary party on Tuesday 27 June the party rejected this overture and decided to honour its pre-election pact with Fine Gael.[19] However, a spokesman confirmed that the position would be reviewed subsequently; a door was being left open to resume negotiation.

The scene was set for an abortive first meeting of the 26th Dáil on Thursday 29 June. The morning papers carried a statement by a Fianna

Fáil party spokesman offering "serious and realistic negotiations",[20] but they did not extend to the acceptance of coalition. Dáil proceedings followed a predictable course. Seán Treacy was elected Ceann Comhairle. Haughey, Dukes and Spring were nominated as Taoiseach; each, in turn, failed to achieve a majority. Haughey now proposed an adjournment until the following Monday to allow interim consultations with the other parties. But the Labour leader, subsequently supported by Dukes, insisted that under Article 28.10 of the Constitution, Haughey must resign forthwith as Taoiseach, on failing to secure nomination. This view was rejected by Haughey. He insisted that the Attorney-General had advised that "it is perfectly in order for me to take a reasonable amount of time to reflect, consider and, if necessary, consent. That is what I propose to do."[21] However, he was forced to give way.

Following a two-and-a-quarter hour suspension of the Dáil, Haughey still reiterated that an immediate resignation was not necessary. But he agreed to resign and the Dáil agreed to meet on Monday 3 July. This was an important piece of parliamentary theatre - although it left the constitutional interpretation unresolved. It dramatically confirmed the failure of the 1989 election strategy to deliver an overall majority. Yet on his return from Aras an Uachtarain, having resigned as Taoiseach, Haughey still insisted dismissively, "I don't believe in coalitions."[22] Flanked by six Cabinet ministers, he spoke confidently of achieving a "policy-based agreement or an arrangement specifically with the Progressive Democrats."[23]

These events did not encourage confidence among the ranks of the smaller party. Many were disturbed by Haughey's reluctance to resign as Taoiseach and resented his cavalier assumption that they would accept a Fianna Fáil proposal. Nevertheless, the Progressive Democrats put forward a tightly-drafted 9-point framework for dialogue.[24] Coalition, the sensitive key issue, was not specifically mentioned but was scarcely concealed in the neutral terms of point 7 : "that prior to any negotiations taking place all discussions on all matters be open and that nothing be ruled in or ruled out in advance." It was a formula that did not prevent almost immediate breakdown at an initial meeting on the evening of Friday 30 June.[25]

The negotiators on both sides had been carefully balanced: Albert Reynolds and Bertie Ahern for Fianna Fáil, Bobby Molloy and Pat Cox for the Progressive Democrats. The immediate question was whether any negotiation could take place until the principle of coalition was accepted; the Fianna Fáil negotiators said that was imposing preconditions. When talks resumed at 8.50 on Saturday morning, there was no movement on either side. By mid-morning Fianna Fáil were blaming the Progressive Democrats for a breakdown. At noon, Haughey told political correspondents "coalition is completely ruled out".[26] These views were repeated at further meetings between Haughey, O'Malley and the two negotiating teams.

The positions seemed irreconcilable. A series of week-end meetings with Dukes produced no new proposals. On the radio programme *This Week* on Sunday 2 July, Haughey was suggesting that "the negotiations had resulted in stalemate. He hinted that 'the only final, unsatisfactory and unhelpful solution would be a general election' and suggested that the 'accepted wisdom' would require the President to accede to his request should he seek a dissolution."[27]

Once again it was the controversy regarding this constitutional gloss, rather than what Haughey described as the "doomsday" prospect of a new election, that dominated proceedings in a short sitting of the Dáil on Monday 3 July. Other party leaders took turns to reject and denounce what they described as an attempt to preempt a constitutional power specifically designed to be exercised at the absolute discretion of the president. In an article published in that morning's *Irish Independent*, O'Malley wrote that Haughey seemed "determined to defy the will of the people".[28] But in the Dáil Haughey was unrepentant and unyielding.

He refused to acknowledge that there was a 'crisis' and insisted that Fianna Fáil had a positive response to this 'problem': "We are specifically offering the people - as we believe it is our duty to do - a Government, albeit a minority Government, a Fianna Fáil Government, which will carry on the work, the successful work, of the last two-and-a-quarter years".[29] This appeared a formal endorsement of the hard-line anti-coalition tone of the Fianna Fáil parliamentary party held that morning. But it is worth noting that, after an amount of rhetorical release, the resolution actually put to the meeting had shifted the focus. Put forward by Brian Lenihan, it did not explicitly commit the parliamentary party to reject coalition; "instead it approved the conduct of negotiations to date and gave Haughey freedom to continue these efforts".[30]

Superficially it seemed the stalemate was set to continue. A statement by Pádraig Flynn, after a Cabinet meeting on Tuesday 4 July appeared to remove all prospects of compromise: "the Government is very strong. All the members of the Cabinet are unanimous for no coalition. The national executive, the parliamentary party and the grass roots have indicated that this is a core value which we must preserve."[31] But this assertion of traditional orthodoxy was misleading. No such unanimity existed.

Most noticeably, at Cabinet level those most vociferously prepared to opt for a new election had been those who had pressed for the original dissolution and election that was now compounding the problem. Some colleagues interpreted this eagerness as a generational bid to gain party leadership. Other ministers - most easily identified was Bertie Ahern - were convinced that a compromise, however painful, was preferable to another electoral rejection. At the same time, they were cautious about initiating discussion of coalition, conscious that it was the rock on which Haughey's leadership might founder. Haughey, himself, according to close observers, appeared uncharacteristically passive and listless. In fact, he had prepared the ground and was now at last ready to act. The breakthrough was revealed during Wednesday 5 July. A terse joint statement by Haughey and O'Malley issued at 5.00 p.m. stated: "negotiations towards the formation of a government are being resumed by our two parties in accordance with the terms of the framework for dialogue agreed last week."[32]

In the spirit of point 3 of that framework, no further clarification was offered. It seems likely that by now Haughey was assured of a Cabinet majority for his judgment that O'Malley and the Progressive Democrats would not move and carried that view at the Cabinet meeting on the morning of Wednesday 5 July. In the light of these developments, Flynn's strong "core value" statement may be seen less as a clarion call than as a rearguard action.

Public opinion polls published in the *Irish Times* and *Cork Examiner* on Thursday 6 July confirmed that there was overwhelming support for some kind of power-sharing arrangement between the political parties and widespread opposition to any new election. The pressure for government formation was now unstoppable. At the same time, in the course of that day's brief Dáil sitting O'Malley insisted: "I want to make it clear that the negotiations which the Progressive Democrats have entered into are barely started and their outcome cannot and ought not be presumed."[33]

But, in effect, Haughey in coded language had effectively conceded the principle of coalition: "the Irish people should always have the option of a single party Government. However, if our entry into some form of political alliance is the only possible way forward at this stage, the only way in which a Government can be formed in this Dáil without causing another immediate general election, then clearly in the higher national interest our duty is positively and constructively to explore the possibility of finding some agreed basis for Government."[34]

That exploration still had to navigate the shoals of the Progressive Democrats' insistence on securing two places in Cabinet and the details of policy formulations on a variety of issues, including the question of constituency revision. But, implicitly, from the outset, these had been minor, even if contentious, matters. They were scarcely cliffhanger decisions - despite much exaggerated speculation and rumour up to the last minute - compared with the momentous reversal of policy by Fianna Fáil on the principle of coalition.

Just when that Rubicon was crossed in the mind of Charles Haughey may never be known. There are some indications that the public chronology given above may underestimate his readiness to recognise the new political reality. It is worth noting that at his first preliminary meeting with O'Malley on Tuesday 20 June (when something like a formalised Tallaght strategy was on the table) Haughey "made it clear that this was not the final word."[35] These two leaders had had a long political relationship and ample opportunity to gauge each other's intentions in tough bargaining situations. Haughey could scarcely have failed to recognise that Cabinet membership was an imperative for O'Malley's party; O'Malley, for his part, recognised that converting Fianna Fáil to accepting coalition required time and patience.

Indeed each leader needed time to bring party colleagues round. O'Malley managed this relatively quickly. In measure because of his own predominance and capacity within the Progressive Democrats; in measure, assisted by the support of defeated Dáil candidates who nevertheless accepted the logic of the post-electoral situation. Once the major, emotional stumbling blocks to an agreement with Fianna Fáil had been resolved the remaining issues were all negotiable.

For Haughey, leading a much larger and longer established party, the process inevitably took more time. He was acutely aware that any precipitate action or statement on his part might engender internal splits. There was ample evidence of unease at parliamentary party and grassroots level. The circumstances dictated that Haughey must not be seen to be eager to embrace an historic (and irreversible) strategic U-turn; he had to lead, passively, from the middle. He described the process to the Dáil: "As the days passed into weeks following the reassembly of the Dáil, the reality became clear, the conclusion inescapable, that the only possible alliance that could give this country four years of stable Government, at this crucial period in our history, was one between Fianna Fáil and the Progressive Democrats."[36]

It now seems probable that the two principals had reached an understanding (possibly unspoken) well in advance. Before the final breakthrough sources close to O'Malley were remarking, rather wistfully, that the only prospect worse than a new election was the prospect of being back in government under Haughey. It was a heavy hint that the two leaders had already accepted the broad lines of a necessary compromise.

If this interpretation is correct, it helps to explain why no serious effort was made to explore possible arrangements with Fine Gael; after all, there was no reason to regard Dukes's initial offer as more than a bargaining bid. It also explains the apparent willingness of Haughey to allow matters to drift over a period of weeks. And it provides a context both for O'Malley's acknowledgement of sympathy for Haughey[37] and for his otherwise extremely fulsome praise. "I take this opportunity here to acknowledge in particular the courage and skill exhibited by Deputy Haughey in recent weeks, courage and skill which I know he possesses in abundance and which have been utilised in the national interest during this time."[38] Certainly the two men's shared experience during the protracted period of uncertainty and negotiation appears to have created new bonds between them.

This augurs well for the survival of the present coalition. It will not be all plain sailing. Dissatisfaction within Fianna Fáil continues to simmer, undoubtedly sometimes stirred by local rivalries and ambitions. But the parties in government have managed the tricky issue of Senate nominations; once again, allowing time and familiarity to defuse disagreement and discontent. Ironically, the long history of relations between Haughey and O'Malley, which had been envisaged as the insurmountable barrier to any Fianna Fáil - Progressive Democrat understanding, may yet prove to be the cement that holds it together.

THE CONSEQUENCES

One thing is evident: coalition, like the Oath, has now been swallowed by Fianna Fáil. Once it has proved willing to enter a coalition - and, equally important, to maintain that coalition agreement - a new vista opens up in Irish government formation. Fianna Fáil must be seen as the potential leading force in a series of future Irish governments (see chapter 11). As the single largest party in the state, it can anticipate a constant role as the semi-permanent party of government. The only challenge depends upon Fine Gael's capacity to offer itself as a credible alternative pole around which a coalition might be constructed.

But for both main parties (and more especially for Fianna Fáil) the role of coalition leader will impose new demands. They will need to balance their traditional claims to be "catch-all" parties against the need to identify specific segments of the electoral market on which they can target their appeal. They will need to clarify, if not their ideologies, at least their policy priorities. Otherwise in future coalition negotiations they are likely to find themselves at a loss when confronted by the more precise shopping-lists drawn up by potential partners. In particular for Fianna Fáil, the question of translating and balancing its class support against specific policy objectives presents a delicate new challenge. If Fianna Fáil is to exchange its traditional goal of single-party government for the more realistic role of being the dominant party in a series of coalitions, it must make an effort to keep a door open to the parties of the left and right. That will require new skills in party management and leadership. In turn, it will involve a level of renewal, reform and recruitment which is not yet in evidence.

But the abiding lesson of the 1989 election is a reinforcement of what was revealed after earlier elections in this decade. There is an urgent need for new mechanisms to assist in the negotiation and formation of governments. The time gap between the general election of 15 June and the creation of the Fianna Fáil - Progressive Democrat administration on 12 July was not exceptionally long by comparison with some other European political systems. On the other hand, the lack of any coherent conventions or organised structures within which the coalition agreement could be formulated gave rise to a great deal of unnecessary uncertainty. Attention has already been drawn to this procedural deficiency and some role for either the President or the Ceann Comhairle has been suggested.[39] Any such reforms would have clear implications for the selection of candidates to these high offices. The possibility of exploring the Dutch model and providing for a formal *formateur* has also been suggested. Consideration might also be given to adopting fixed terms of office and fixed dates for elections as a method of ensuring government stability, especially as a means of ensuring coalition survival.

One thing is clear. There is an institutional vacuum between the voters' expression of their choice and the business of government formation. It should be addressed well in advance of the next general election.

FOOTNOTES

1   Brian Farrell, "Government Formation and Ministerial Selection" in H. Penniman and B. Farrell, eds., *Ireland at the Polls, 1981, 1982 and 1987: a study of four general elections* (Durham, N.C.: Duke University Press, 1987), pp.141-2

2   Brian Farrell, "The road from 1987: government formation and institutional inertia" in M. Laver, P. Mair and R. Sinnott, (eds), *How Ireland Voted: the Irish general election of 1987*, (Swords: Poolbeg 1987.)

3   *Dáil Debates*, vol. 1, cols. 1556-7, 12 October 1922.

4   For a fuller discussion of the 'extern' minister proposals see Brian Farrell, "The Drafting of the Irish Free State Constitution: 1", *Irish Jurist*, vol. V, n.s., Part 1 (Summer 1970), especially pp. 130-134.

5   *Dáil Debates*, vol. 67, col. 1345, 1 June 1937.

6   *Ibid*, col. 1346.

7   Report of the Committee on the Constitution, December 1967, Stationary Office, Dublin Pr. 9817. The main arguments relating to electoral reform are usefully summarised in *Irish Times*, 'Committee anticipated difficulties 22 years ago', 30 June 1989, p.7.

8   O'Donovan v. Attorney General (1961), IR 114. The case was well reported in *Irish Times*. See also *Dáil Debates*, vol. 339, *passim*. p. 25

9   The Dáil majorities of the original Cumann na nGaedheal governments, 1922-23 and 1923-27, are directly attributable to the republican policy of abstention.

10 This table is adopted from Table 5.1 in Farrell, 'Government Formation' in Penniman and Farrell, which contains a fuller discussion.

11 *Today Tonight Election Special*, RTE, morning transmission, 17 June 1989.

12 *Today Tonight Election Special*, RTE, evening transmission, 16 June 1989.

13 Richard Sinnott, "Voters are dividing along class lines", *Election '89*, a supplement to *Irish Times*, 19 June 1989, p.10.

14 Gerald Barry, "Good Enough for Me and Bobby Molloy", *Sunday Tribune*, 16 July 1989.

15 *This Week*, RTE, 25 June 1989.

16 There is a useful account by Stephen Collins, "Coalition is still the crunch issue" in *Sunday Press*, 2 July 1989, p.10.

17 Mark Brennock, "Haughey turns to PDs as FG deal rejected", *Irish Times*, 23 June 1989, p.1

18 *Ibid*.

19 Denis Coghlan, "PDs not to back Haughey in Dáil vote", *Irish Times*, 28 June 1989, p.1,

20 Denis Coghlan, "FF makes new offer on eve of likely defeat", *Irish Times*, 29 June 1989, p.1.

21 Dáil Debates, vol. 391, col. 54, 29 June 1989 .

22 Mark Brennock, "FF strategy is based on hope", *Irish Times*, 30 June 1989, p.7.

23 Denis Coghlan, "No preconditions as FF and PD talks open today", *Irish Times*, 30 June 1989, p.1.

24 These are listed as "PD Framework", *Irish Times*, 30 June 1989, p.2.

25 Mark Brennock, "Frenetic series of weekend meetings yields no progress", *Irish Times*, 3 July 1989, p.2.

26 Stephen Collins, *Sunday Press* , 2 July 1989.

27 Denis Coghlan, "Deadlock likely as Haughey says no to coalition", *Irish Times*, 3 July 1989, p.1.

28 Desmond O'Malley, "Sharing power is only real solution", *Irish Independent*, 3 July 1989, p.11.

29 *Dáil Debates*, vol. 391, col. 84, 3 July 1989.

30 Denis Coghlan, "FF expected to resume talks with PDs today", *Irish Times*, 4 July 1989, p.1. See also Gerald Barry article as cited *Sunday Tribune*, 16 July 1989.

31 Denis Coghlan, "Coalition remains stumbling block to FF-PD deal", Irish Times, 5 July 1989, carried over to p.8.

32 Stephen Collins, "Will Charlie, PDs now make it up?", Sunday Press, 25 June 1989, p.9.

33 *Dáil Debates*, vol. 391, col. 108, 6 July 1989.

34 *Ibid.*, col. 120.

35 Stephen Collins, "Will Charlie, PDs now make make it up?", *Sunday Press*, 25 June 1989, p.9.

36 *Dáil Debates*, vol. 391, col. 149, 12 July 1989.

37 Gerald Barry, *Sunday Tribune*, 16 July 1989.

38 *Dáil Debates*, vol. 391, col. 129, 12 July 1989.

39 See Farrell citations supra. Also John Coakley, "The general election in context" in Laver, op. cit. and Jim Duffy, "The choice for the President", *Irish Times*, 29 June 1989, p.7.

10. Coalition and Fianna Fáil

Michael Laver and Audrey Arkins

In most of Western Europe, coalition government is the rule rather than the exception. Government formation in Ireland, on the other hand, has generally involved a straightforward process of deciding whether the cabinet that runs the country will contain only Fianna Fáil ministers or whether it will be a coalition of Fianna Fáil's opponents.[1] Since the beginning of the 1980s, however, the situation seems to have been changing inexorably as single party majority government has moved ever further from Fianna Fáil's grasp. Wheeling and dealing between politicians over who will get into the cabinet has become a routine post-election spectacle. Yet the very idea of coalition remains anathema to many within Fianna Fáil, who associate it historically with electoral defeat, followed by an opportunistic liaison between an ideological odd couple of Fianna Fáil's old enemies, Fine Gael and Labour.

After generations of disparaging the very concept of coalition, Fianna Fáil changed tack in 1989. The party of single party government gave cabinet seats to Dessie O'Malley and Bobby Molloy, former Fianna Fáil dissidents who had jumped ship. O'Malley had founded, and Molloy had been a key early sponsor of, a rival party, the Progressive Democrats (PDs). The intervention of the PDs in the 1987 and 1989 elections was almost certainly the crucial factor that robbed Fianna Fáil of a parliamentary majority. Even so, Charles Haughey, despite controlling only a minority of seats in the previous Dáil, had faced down the opposition for two years. Each time he was challenged, he had gone eyeball to eyeball with his enemies, daring them to call an election and suffer the consequences. The question that intrigued everyone with an interest in Irish politics in the aftermath of the 1989 election, therefore, was: "Could Haughey have done it again? Could he have faced down the opposition one more time?"

Before we can settle the matter of whether Haughey could indeed have hung tough, we must first understand how Fianna Fáil has been able to get away with refusing to do coalition deals for so long. This has to do with the fact that quite often, while Fianna Fáil has lacked a majority, it has been able to govern alone because it has faced an opposition that was deeply divided over policy. In such cases, of course, the party's lack of a majority leaves it open to blackmail by opposition parties which might hold the balance of power and which might attempt to extort major concessions, even seats at the cabinet table, on this basis. Traditional Fianna Fáil strategy has therefore been based on the dictum that, if party leaders once give in to such demands, and particularly if they ever agree to share cabinet seats with other parties in order to get into office, then the party will not be credible when it attempts to take a tough line with its opponents on a future occasion when the party might well be better placed to govern alone. On this logic, it could be better for Fianna Fáil to go into opposition for a limited period, maintaining the credibility of its bargaining posture and in this way increasing its long-term chances of returning to power as a single party government, rather than to give in to demands for coalition,

If the logic of Fianna Fáil's traditional coalition veto has been based on the party's willingness and ability to face down a divided opposition, what changed in 1989? Was the opposition less divided? Was Fianna Fáil for some reason less willing to face them down? Or did party leaders simply make a tactical error? In this chapter, we set out to answer these questions in two ways. We analyse Fianna Fáil's bargaining position using techniques that are applied to the analysis of coalition bargaining in most of the rest of western Europe. We then assess how well this analysis fits with the events surrounding the historic formation of the Fianna Fáil-PD coalition in 1989.

COULD FIANNA FAIL HAVE GOVERNED ALONE? THE THEORY

The formation of government coalitions in Western Europe is a matter much analysed by political scientists, who have made considerable progress on this question over the past twenty years or so. One of the main things that they have been concerned with in recent times is the phenomenon of minority government. These governments are really rather common in Western Europe, comprising about 40 per cent of all administrations.[2] Many minority governments, furthermore, are quite stable, further evidence that minority government is not some weird deviation, a perversion of the democratic process, but a normal state of affairs.

One of the main ways to make sense of minority government is to take party policy seriously. If policy is what excites politicians, then a minority administration may be able to govern if it faces a divided opposition made up of parties whose policies differ more from each other than they do from the policies of the government. The opposition parties then cannot defeat the government, even if they have the votes to do so, because they cannot agree upon an alternative. Taking the legislature as a whole, this means that there is no alternative preferred by a majority of legislators to the minority government. Since there is nothing that the group of politicians as a whole would like better, the minority government can be seen in this sense as a "representative" government. On occasion, even parties well short of a majority can form a viable minority government, a situation that is particularly common in Scandinavia.

Given all of this, it becomes important to be clear about how the issues dividing the various parties are organised. One possibility is that these issues all relate to the same underlying ideological dimension. If only a single dimension is important in a particular party system, then the party at the centre, or median, of this dimension is effectively a policy dictator. This is because, once the "centre" party is in government, parties whose policies are to the left of it will not agree to a move to the right, while parties whose policies are to the right of it will not agree to a move to the left.

In every West European country, including Ireland, there can be no doubt that the most important ideological dimension is the traditional "left-right" dimension which has to do with fundamental economic strategy. When this is the only dimension that is important, the pivotal party need never leave office - a situation enjoyed in postwar years by Christian Democratic parties in Italy, Luxembourg and the Netherlands. This pivotal position is important even if the party is quite small - the most striking example of a small but pivotal party is that of the West German Free Democrats, rarely out of office in the postwar era, and exercising a high level of control over policy for the whole of that period.

Considering for the moment only a single left-right dimension in Irish politics, then it is conventional to portray Fianna Fáil as the type of pivotal party that we have just been describing, flanked on both left and right by a divided opposition. Several attempts have been made to be more systematic about this, and to chart the main dimensions of ideology in Irish party politics. The most recent of these uses a survey of political scientists writing on Ireland.[3] Based on the replies of about 40 of such "experts", the Irish parties can be located on the familiar left-right dimension of economic policy. Party positions can be estimated in terms of how much each party favours or opposes public ownership of business and industry. Fianna Fáil is located at the median of this dimension. It is flanked on the left by Labour, the Workers' Party and the Democratic Socialist Party (DSP) and on the right by Fine Gael and the PDs.

If only a single dimension of policy is important to the Irish parties, then coalition theorists would have been more or less unanimous in their advice to Haughey after the 1989 election. Their advice would have been to hang tough. They would have told him to keep proposing himself as Taoiseach, to keep throwing down the gauntlet to the opposition and to keep saying, quite simply, "beat me!". Since he was in office anyway as leader of a caretaker cabinet (even if this had a somewhat cloudy constitutional status), he would have remained as "acting" Taoiseach until someone had indeed beaten him. The opposition could keep defeating him on the vote for nomination as Taoiseach, but they wouldn't have been able to put anyone else in his place. Anticipating this, either they should have given up gracefully at an early stage or they should have given up after landing a few body blows and thereby confirming that they could not in fact knock their opponent down.

This appears to have been the logic of the 1987 Haughey government. Before the government was formed, various opponents suggested various concessions that might "reassure" them about a potential Haughey administration - but all they got for a reply was Haughey's unblinking stare. When push came to shove, despite all of the posturing, they voted in such a way as to allow a Fianna Fáil minority government to take office. Once the government had formed, the story was much the same. There were a few skirmishes and the odd government defeat on particular issues but, on anything big enough to bring down the government, the gauntlet was thrown down and the opposition backed off. The 1989 election was called, after all, not because the Haughey government had been defeated or even seriously threatened, but because it had got tired of throwing down the gauntlet over and over again and saw in the favourable opinion polls the chance to win itself a Dáil majority.

All of this makes sense if we see Fianna Fáil at the centre of a single dimensional policy system, with the opposition split hopelessly on what to replace it with. This cannot, however, be the full story, since Fianna Fáil has in the past been forced out of office by Fine Gael-Labour coalitions, something which is difficult to reconcile with a "one dimensional" analysis of Irish coalition bargaining. If more than one ideological dimension is important in Ireland, then it becomes much more likely that the opposition will be able to find some basis on which to agree to evict Fianna Fáil.

Economic policy always divided Fine Gael and Labour as coalition partners, which is why Fianna Fáil was always able to portray them as such an odd couple. Economic policy was at the root of most divisions within the coalition cabinets and it was fundamental disagreement over economic policy that brought the era of Fine Gael - Labour coalition irrevocably to a close in 1987. It must be the case, therefore, that some other dimension of policy in the Irish party system formed the basis of the Fine Gael - Labour coalitions that have succeeded, from time to time, in keeping Fianna Fáil out of office. This dimension is usually taken to have two interpretations. The first has to do with social policy, that is, policy on issues of public "morality" and constitutional reform, including matters such as divorce, contraception and sexual behaviour. The second, related, interpretation has to do with Northern Ireland and the extent to which Irish parties are prepared to take a hard line with the British on this vital issue.

Whichever interpretation is chosen, this dimension places Fianna Fáil, of the Dáil parties, at one end - as the most traditional on social policy and the most hardline with the British. The Workers' Party is at the other end of the scale; Fine Gael, Labour and the PDs are somewhere in the middle. This two dimensional view of Irish party politics, in which both economic and social policy are important, provides one account of the basis of the Fine Gael - Labour coalitions. It therefore places Fianna Fáil in a much weaker bargaining position since it suggests that there are conceivable alternative governments upon which the opposition might be able to agree. The advice that coalition theorists would have given Mr Haughey in such circumstances is rather more complicated, and depends upon more precise estimates of the policy positions of the parties.

The precise policy positions of the main Irish parties on both of the dimensions that we have been discussing were estimated immediately before the 1989 election using the expert survey mentioned above and are published for the first time in this chapter. Figure 10.1 shows these positions; the horizontal dimension relates to policies on public ownership, the vertical dimension to social policy. The black dots show party policy positions, the policies that could be expected from a single party government run by the party in question. The lattice of points shows the policies that could be expected from the various conceivable coalition governments. Thus, point "x", near the centre of the figure, shows what might be expected from a Fianna Fáil-PD coalition in which Fianna Fáil got its way on economic policy and the PDs got their way on social policy.[4]

Figure 10.1 thus gives us precisely the information we need in order to explore the extent to which those parties opposing Fianna Fáil were divided among themselves in policy terms. The large circles in Figure 10.1 (which are technically known as "indifference curves") show how each of the other parties feels about a single party Fianna Fáil government. The circle centred on Fine Gael shows how Fine Gael feels about this; each of the alternatives inside the circle is closer to Fine Gael and is thus preferred by Fine Gael to a single party Fianna Fáil government. Other circles show the alternatives preferred by Labour, the Workers' Party and the PDs. When two or more indifference curves overlap, then the alternatives inside the area of overlap are preferred to a single party Fianna Fáil government by each of the parties concerned. If a group of parties command a Dáil majority between them, the area of overlap of their respective circles shows the set of alternatives that can beat a single party Fianna Fáil government in a Dáil vote. (This is technically known as the "win set" of the Fianna Fáil government.)

Figure 10.1 Two dimensions of policy in Irish politics

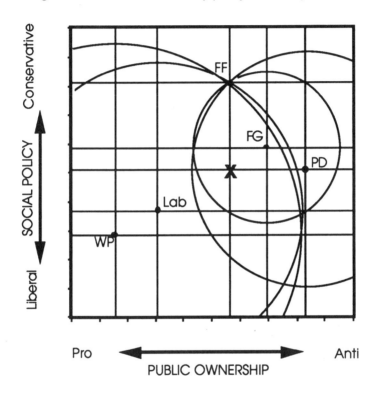

Working on the assumption that two dimensions of party ideology were important in 1989, this approach allows us to see that there was a clear distinction between the Dáil before, and the Dáil after, the election. Before the election, the four main opposition parties did not between them command a Dáil majority. After the election, they did. It becomes immediately relevant to ask whether they could agree, in purely policy terms, on an alternative to a single party Fianna Fáil government. Figure 10.1 suggests that there were indeed such alternatives and thus highlights the weakening of Fianna Fáil's bargaining position after the 1989 election. On the basis of the data at our disposal, the alternatives preferred by Fianna

Fáil's opponents include a Fine Gael minority government, a Fine Gael-PD coalition, a Fine Gael-Labour coalition and coalitions of Fianna Fáil with either Fine Gael, the PDs or Labour. Coalition theorists would have predicted that one of these six alternatives would replace a Fianna Fáil minority government after the 1989 election. In the language of coalition theory, the Fianna Fáil government was "vulnerable".

In addition to this, Figure 10.1 shows us that, in purely policy terms, Fine Gael moved into a stronger bargaining position than might seem to be the case at first sight as a result of the 1989 election. This is because the model suggests that it might have been potentially viable as a minority government in its own right, as we have just indicated. While a Fine Gael government could be beaten by Fianna Fáil in combination with any one of the opposition parties, it is possible, if two dimensions of policy were important, that no such combination would have been able to agree upon an alternative. Fianna Fáil and either the Workers' Party or the Labour Party might have agreed that they would have preferred a Fianna Fáil - Fine Gael coalition, but there is not much that they can do about this without the cooperation of Fine Gael. In other words, a Fine Gael minority government, had it formed, might have proved difficult to dislodge. This would have justified, in bargaining terms, some tough demands from Fine Gael, but it does not go far in itself towards explaining why the eventual government that formed was a Fianna Fáil-PD coalition. On the face of it, and considering only party policy, Fianna Fáil would have preferred a Fine Gael minority government to what actually happened! Given that Fine Gael was the basis of a potentially viable minority government, the real question, if two dimensions of ideology were important, was why Fine Gael was not able to force its way into government somehow or another.

To summarize, if policy was what excited Irish politicians bargaining over the formation of a government in 1989, then a one-dimensional view of party policy suggests that Fianna Fáil should have been able to hang on as a minority government, while a two dimensional view suggests that Fine Gael should have been able to force its way into office somehow. What happened? Did Fianna Fáil or Fine Gael make a mistake? Or was something else going on?

One way to answer these questions is to move beyond the assumption that Irish parties are concerned only with policy when they bargain over the formation of governments. If we assume that they are also trying to get into office for its own sake, regardless of the policies that they have to enact in order to do so, then the situation becomes much easier to interpret. Fianna Fáil and the PDs, in these terms, would not stand back and allow a Fine Gael minority government to form just because Fine Gael policies are close to their own. They would be concerned about all of the other perks that would be lost by staying out of office.

In practice, the assumption that parties are concerned only with policy is unrealistic. Across Western Europe, one of the main things that parties bargain about during government formation is the distribution of cabinet seats, seen as part of the spoils of office. In most countries, cabinet seats tend to be shared between coalition partners in close proportion to the number of seats won by each at election time. This makes it much more attractive, other things being equal, for a big party to go into coalition with a small party than with a large or medium sized one. A "fair" allocation of cabinet seats can then be agreed that still leaves the lion's share for the bigger party. In this account, Fianna Fáil should have dealt with the PDs simply because they were the smallest party with enough seats to tip the legislative balance. Their "legitimate" demand for seats at the cabinet table was thus less than that of Fine Gael. On this interpretation, Fianna Fáil wanted to stay in office for its own sake, and took on board the cheapest coalition partner.

Coalition theory, therefore, forces us to answer a series of hard questions about Irish politics in the aftermath of the 1989 election. If we think that only one dimension of ideology divides the Irish parties, then Fianna Fáil seems to have given in to demands for a coalition when it did not need to do so. If we think that two dimensions of ideology are important, then Fine Gael seems to have missed a chance to force its way into office. If we think that it is the spoils of office rather than the chance to affect public policy that puts a glint in an Irish politician's eye, then we can explain the Fianna Fáil-PD coalition quite nicely - Fianna Fáil wanted in at all costs and bought the cheapest ticket. But this is not the end of the story because we are then forced to answer another question. If getting into office is all that matters, how have Fianna Fáil minority governments survived in the past? In these terms, what has prevented the previous oppositions from combining, when they have certainly had the votes to do so, to evict Fianna Fáil minority governments from office?

As we can see, the existing panoply of theory gets us so far, but no further. It helps us to ask a series of intriguing questions about the politics of coalition in Ireland (and this is of course always the most important role for theory) but it comes up with no definite answers. In search of these, we now look at the events that surrounded the formation of the Fianna Fáil - PD coalition in 1989, to see whether we can reconcile these apparently inconsistent interpretations of what was going on.

COULD FIANNA FAIL HAVE GOVERNED ALONE? THE PRACTICE

How many dimensions of ideology?
The 1989 election campaign was fought largely on economic issues as Fianna Fáil, Fine Gael and the PDs spent most of their time arguing over who was best able to run the economy. Social policy, constitutional reform and Northern Ireland featured low on the debating agenda. Televised party confrontations were dominated by discussions of health cuts, tax reform, unemployment, emigration and the overall state of the economy. This emphasis reflected the importance attached to these issues by the electorate, at least as far as their views were reported by the opinion polls (which are analysed fully in chapter 5). In the first MRBI poll of the campaign, for example, respondents were asked "what do you feel are the main issues which the parties should be concerned about?" Without being offered any alternatives to choose from, 73 per cent named unemployment, 45 per cent named health cuts, 27 per cent named emigration, 21 per cent named taxation and 16 per cent named social welfare and poverty. Neither Northern Ireland nor social policy figured among the salient electoral issues. In the same poll, respondents were asked how they felt about certain named issues. While 93 per cent regarded unemployment as a "very important" issue, only 18 per cent regarded Northern Ireland as being very important.[5]

Just because voters were interested only in the state of the economy, we should not, of course, conclude that one dimension of ideology was all that divided the parties. Nonetheless, the Fianna Fáil government had operated within the framework of the Anglo-Irish Agreement; and contraception, divorce and abortion were issues that had been settled, for the foreseeable future, under the previous Fine Gael - Labour administration. All of this had taken much of the fizz out of the social policy agenda at elite level.

Thus neither politicians nor voters seemed to be much concerned with social issues in 1989, suggesting that a single left-right economic policy dimension was sufficient to describe the ideological basis of Irish party competition. This analysis was shared by many popular commentators who saw, in the election results, the emergence of a more "European" party system in Ireland, one more explicitly structured along class lines. On most constructions of the facts, therefore, the bargaining environment in which government formation took place was one dimensional.

Why coalition?
Given a single salient dimension of ideology, the theoretical analysis in the previous section poses one central question: why did Fianna Fáil give

in to demands for coalition in 1989, when there was patently no basis on which the opposition could agree to form an alternative government? A detailed account of the government formation process was provided in chapter 9 above. Here we confine ourselves to those aspects of the construction of the government which are highlighted by coalition theory.

The first thing to note is that Fianna Fáil initially accepted this analysis and attempted to bargain in these terms. The adverse legislative arithmetic of the 1989 election meant that Fianna Fáil could no longer rely on "outside" support from a few independents for its majority. Despite this, the party hoped to enlist Dáil support from somewhere or other on the basis of no more than "a constructive input into government".[6] Initially, it appeared that what Fianna Fáil had in mind was a modification of Fine Gael's "Tallaght strategy", whereby the opposition would be consulted on major political developments within some type of formal structure. But, apart from oblique references to select committees, Fianna Fáil never specified what shape this formal structure would assume. Twenty days into the government formation "crisis", after consultation with all of the parties, there was no obvious sign of progress towards forming a government. This is a strong indication that Fianna Fáil was at this stage still convinced that it could go it alone on much the same basis as had been done before. Why after all, did it need to consider the views of parties which had no hope of forming a government themselves?

Certainly the opposition, while strengthened in electoral terms, was no less divided on policy than it had been after the 1987 election. Indeed, the gains enjoyed by most of the opposition parties only hardened their individual policy positions. The left, in particular, were adamant in their refusal to bolster any right-wing administration, choosing instead to define their success as a modest step towards a left-right realignment of Irish politics. Ignoring all overtures and clearly planning for several elections down the line, they preferred to remain aloof and witness the "logical restructuring of the over-manned right wing sector", in the words of the leader of the Workers' Party.[7] Talks between Fianna Fáil and the the Labour Party were no more then a formality, after which Labour leader Dick Spring was able with a clear conscience to refuse to support Mr Haughey's nomination for Taoiseach.

This left Fianna Fáil with nowhere to turn but right. Here the prospects were more hopeful, since neither Fine Gael nor the Progressive Democrats seriously questioned Fianna Fáil's right to govern. Obviously, their combined seat total fell far short of the required majority, but the two right wing opposition parties made no serious attempt to form a cabinet and it was soon apparent that they had no intention of doing so.

In an RTE interview the day after the final results had been declared, the PDs' Mary Harney spoke as if there had been no electoral pact between her party and Fine Gael. The PDs, she said, would ensure that there was stability without any wheeling and dealing, even if this involved voting for a Taoiseach they didn't like. Later the same evening a PD spokesman, distancing the party from Ms Harney's opinion, emphasised that a price would be exacted for PD support. Far from reiterating their commitment to Fine Gael, the PDs were already talking in terms of "supporting" Fianna Fáil. This was not the language of prospective partners in cabinet.

On the Fine Gael side, Alan Dukes had met with Dick Spring to seek Labour Party support for his nomination for Taoiseach. A flat rebuff from Mr Spring ensured that no further talks on formal coalition between Fine Gael and the Labour Party took place.

Fine Gael offered concrete terms for a coalition deal with Fianna Fáil on June 22. These included an equal allocation of cabinet posts to each party and the rotating appointment of each party leader as Taoiseach for two years. Although Fine Gael had 55 seats to Fianna Fáil's 77, Alan Dukes argued that an effective coalition between them would require an equal distribution of government appointments, "given the size and long traditions of the two major parties".[8] Dukes also proposed changes in the committee system and other Dáil reforms to give the opposition a greater role. Both proposals were rejected as "totally unacceptable" to Fianna Fáil, who feared that they would lead to "a monolith in government with only minimal opposition".[9] After these rebuffs, Fine Gael does not appear to have played an active role in the process of forming a government.

With the left and Fine Gael out of the running and the PDs talking in terms of outside support, Haughey might seem to have been home free, able to exploit Fianna Fáil's pivotal position in the centre to form another stable minority government. Why, then, was he not able to do so?

As the man who had called the election in search of a Dáil majority and then led Fianna Fáil to the loss of four seats, Haughey had to go into coalition negotiations fielding virulent criticism for what the *Irish Times* termed his "grave misjudgement".[10] Thus he faced a dual task: not only that of keeping Fianna Fáil in government, but also that of ensuring his own political survival. During the weeks of negotiation, Mr Haughey came under inordinate pressure to produce a result as soon as possible. Most within Fianna Fáil had high hopes of what could be arranged. Even those who did take a more pragmatic view remained hostile to any talk of coalition.

The widely reported MRBI poll taken on July 4 put further pressure on Haughey. Presented with the choice between some sort of arrangement between the parties and another general election - the traditional threat of Irish parties when government formation proves tricky - only 17 per cent of voters favoured an election. Worse, no more than 26 per cent of Fianna Fáil's own election supporters favoured this. Worse still, the poll suggested that Fianna Fáil would lose two or more seats if an election were indeed held. And the worst was yet to come. MRBI asked voters how they would feel about alternative government arrangements. Only 24 per cent favoured a minority Fianna Fáil government led by Haughey. Almost as many, 17 per cent, favoured one led by Albert Reynolds, strongly tipped as a potential successor to the party leadership. And 40 per cent favoured some form of coalition between Fianna Fáil and Fine Gael.[11] Once this poll had been published, Fianna Fáil threats to go back to the country if they didn't get their own way lost most of their credibility.

To sum up, the clock was ticking for Charles J. Haughey as leader of Fianna Fáil, while his threat to call another election had lost all of its sting. Thus Haughey, sifting among an uncompromising opposition for support, knew that he could not just let matters drift. The left, as we have seen, had effectively ruled itself out of contention. Fine Gael, as by far the largest opposition party, would have found it very difficult electorally to settle for less than major concessions and had, as we have also seen, apparently lost interest in shaping the course of events. This left the PDs.

Mr Haughey opened negotiations with a tough no-coalition approach. This injected, initially at least, an air of unreasonableness to PD demands for cabinet seats. Careful to protect his leadership as talks proceeded, Haughey delegated negotiating responsibilities to Albert Reynolds and Bertie Ahern, two of those ultimately most likely to succeed him, retaining at the same time the right to hold direct talks between party leaders. Such talks not only enabled him to monitor progress, they allowed him to ensure that his leadership of Fianna Fáil would not be bargained away in exchange for PD support, as well as ensuring that his most likely successors were deeply implicated in the coalition formation process.

It was evident that members of the PD parliamentary party, especially Bobby Molloy, Máirín Quill and Pearse Wyse, were opposed to helping out Mr Haughey, whose style of leadership had influenced their original decision to quit Fianna Fáil for the PDs. One described Haughey's continuing leadership of Fianna Fáil as a "stumbling block" to a pact which could involve informal PD support for a Fianna Fáil minority government.[12] In fact Mr O'Malley's bargaining position, as leader of the PDs, was strengthened as a result of this well-publicised split. He needed to negotiate a substantial PD role in government in order to convince reluctant party colleagues. By nominating his leading anti-coalitionist, Bobby Molloy, as the party's chief negotiator in the talks on government formation, O'Malley increased the possibility of extracting major concessions from Fianna Fáil in exchange for PD support.

Policy differences between Fianna Fáil and the PDs were not great, at least on the economic policy dimension. By all accounts, the prospective coalition's policy package was agreed at an early stage in the negotiations. This left the allocation of the more tangible benefits of getting into office, which were considerable. For the PDs, seats at the cabinet table would give the party an unexpected lifeline after its disastrous electoral slump in 1989 - providing the chance to promote its senior parliamentarians as ministers and giving the party a secure spot in the political limelight. For Fianna Fáil in general, and for Charles Haughey in particular, staying in office, even as part of a coalition, meant the chance to preside over a rapidly growing economy. The main economic indicators had turned up more rapidly than expected and, after over a decade of recession, the party was unwilling to let anyone else take credit for the impending boom. And, as a piece of icing on the cake, whoever was Taoiseach on January 1 1990 would take over the Presidency of the European Commission, an increasingly coveted job among Europe's top politicians. Overall, the benefits of simply being in office were pretty much irresistible.

While it was clear from the outset that PD support for Fianna Fáil would be exacted only at a price, even those who favoured a deal seem to have been unsure about what that price ought to be. Immediately after the election, as we have seen, the PDs were talking about outside support rather than full participation in cabinet. However, the intensity of opposition to Haughey among sections of the PDs seems to have had inflationary effects on their eventual bottom line demands. The succession of uncompromising statements issued by leading members of Fianna Fáil, offering nothing concrete in exchange for PD support yet predicting confidently that "the PDs will come in - it's their only lifeline", seem to have hardened, rather than softened,the resolve of PD negotiators.

The bottom line in all of this, however, may well have had to do with the relative positions of the two leaders within their own parties. Both party leaders probably wanted to get into government equally badly and Fianna Fáil was by far the stronger party in terms of raw bargaining power. Yet, as the negotiations unfolded, it became clear that O'Malley had much less to lose by hanging on until he got the deal he really wanted. Haughey, in contrast, had everything to lose and faced steadily mounting pressure as a consequence. Every delay in forming a government further undermined his position and increased the possibility that a deal might emerge involving somebody else being leader of Fianna Fáil.

COULD FIANNA FAIL HAVE GOVERNED ALONE?
THE CONCLUSION

Everything we have seen when looking at the formation of the 1989 Fianna Fáil - PD coalition in Ireland suggests that only a single dimension of ideology, the familiar left-right dimension of economic strategy, was important. The politicians bargained just as coalition theory would predict as if there was no chance whatsoever to exclude Fianna Fáil on the basis of a policy agreement between right and left. Everyone, in short, behaved as if Fianna Fáil was sitting astride the most important dimension of contemporary Irish politics.

If this was the case, then Fianna Fáil's failure to form a viable minority government cannot be explained merely in terms of a concern by Irish politicians to get into office at all costs, rather than to influence public policy. Office payoffs were considerable in 1989, as we have seen, with added bonuses of an economic boom and the EC Presidency. But, if office was all the opposition cared about, they had not kicked Fianna Fáil out of office when they had previous chances to do so, and they made no serious attempt to do so this time. Everyone certainly behaved as if policy differences between the opposition parties precluded them forming a government, effectively acknowledging Fianna Fáil's dominant position.

Accepting that the left had credibly committed themselves to staying out of government this session, then Fine Gael's refusal to co-operate early in the negotiations forced Fianna Fáil into the arms of the PDs. For a party with only six legislators to win two cabinet portfolios and an appointment as minister of state was a major bargaining achievement, and the most plausible interpretation of how they were able to pull it off has to do with the internal politics of Fianna Fáil.

Purely theoretical accounts of coalition bargaining assume that the various actors look right down the line at the sequence of decisions that leads to the final outcome. They anticipate these and take account of them when formulating their current strategies. Such an approach, however, can easily miss the possibility that the very process of decision-making can have important political consequences. In this particular case, we see that anticipation of the possible course of decision-making may well have highlighted the conflict of interest between the Fianna Fáil party and its leader. In the short term, it was Charles Haughey, as party leader, not Fianna Fáil, as a party, who had to make the coalition deal. Given all of the information at his disposal, he could clearly anticipate a situation in which, if the negotiations went on too long, he would no longer be leader of Fianna Fáil. Our argument is that it was this hidden agenda that caused Haughey to abandon Fianna Fáil's powerful bargaining position and give up cabinet seats to the Progressive Democrats. A continuation of traditional Fianna Fáil strategy would have dictated facing down all opposition demands for cabinet participation - even if this had meant digging in for a long confrontation. Fianna Fáil's ability to pursue this traditional strategy and hang tough, however, depended upon having a leader who was prepared to pay the price of a stalemate. But a continuing stalemate would have put Haughey's leadership under severe threat, while the polls showed that there was no salvation in a snap election. Haughey just didn't have time to hang tough and the PDs, once Fine Gael had opted out, quickly sensed this.

In conclusion, we will never really know whether Fianna Fáil could have governed alone. What seems likely is that they could not have made a serious attempt to do so without jeopardising the political future of their leader.

FOOTNOTES

1   M. Laver and M. D. Higgins, "Coalition or Fianna Fáil? The politics of inter-party government in Ireland", in G. Pridham (ed.), *Coalitional Behaviour in Theory and Practice* (Cambridge: Cambridge University Press, 1986).

2   For a discussion of the role of minority governments see M. Laver and N. Schofield, *Multiparty Government: the Politics of Coalition in Western Europe* (Oxford: Oxford University Press, 1990); K. Strom, "Minority governments in parliamentary democracies: the rationality of non-winning cabinet solutions", *Comparative Political Studies* 17 (1984) pp. 199-227; K. Strom, *Minority government and majority rule* (Cambridge: Cambridge University Press, 1990).

3   M. Laver and W. B. Hunt, *Policy and Party Competition* (New York: Routledge, forthcoming 1991).

4   This approach is based on a model of coalition bargaining developed by M. Laver and K. Shepsle, "Government coalitions and intraparty politics" (*British Journal of Political Science*, forthcoming); M. Laver and K. Shepsle, "Coalitions and cabinet government", (Department of Government, Harvard University, 1989)

5   Market Research Bureau of Ireland, *Survey Report MRBI/3770/89* (Dun Laoghaire: MRBI, 1989).

6   *Irish Times* 20 June 1989.

7   *Irish Times* 13 July 1989.

8   *Irish Times* 23 June 1989.
9   *Irish Times* 23 June 1989.
10   *Irish Times* 1 July 1989.
11   Market Research Bureau of Ireland, *Survey Report MRBI/3780/89* (Dun Laoghaire: MRBI, 1989).
12   *Irish Times* 20 June 1989.

11. The Irish party system into the 1990s

Peter Mair

One of the more frequent reactions to the outcome of the 1989 Dáil election was that it reflected a further drift towards "European-style" politics in Ireland, whose political system has long been regarded by political scientists as one of the oddities of the European scene. Irish parties appeared to bear little or no relation to the mainstream political families which pervaded the neighbouring political systems; Irish political divides were inextricably bound up with the *sui generis* conflict deriving from the civil war. Of late, however, doubt has begun to be cast upon this traditional perspective and, to judge from the more immediate reactions, the 1989 election has been seen to confirm a new direction.

Signs of a new dynamic in Irish politics were not hard to find. The survival of the Progressive Democrats, who represented the most evident symptom of the challenge to civil war moulds, seemed to indicate the seriousness of the impetus for change. The marginal success of the Greens was also cited, as was the revival of Labour fortunes and the continued growth of the Workers' Party. Even the relatively lengthy and somewhat fraught process of government formation was seen as an indicator of a shift towards a European motif. One familiar adage states that government formation in European countries is determined not by the outcome of elections but rather by the results of negotiations between the political parties, and this now seems to apply to the Irish case as closely as it has done for some time in countries such as Belgium, Denmark and the Netherlands. Indeed, it is probably even more appropriate in the contemporary Irish case since, ironically, it was the two parties which suffered most at the hands of the electorate, Fianna Fáil and the Progressive Democrats, which emerged holding the spoils of office, while those which gained seats - Fine Gael, Labour and the Workers' Party - continued to languish in opposition.

Now that the dust has settled, however, and the initial excitement caused by the confounding of Fianna Fáil and the growth in support for the left has died down, it is worth looking more closely at the extent to which the 1989 outcome has resulted in a shift in the nature of the party system in general, and in a drift towards a more European-style politics in particular.

TOWARDS A EUROPEAN PARTY SYSTEM?

When dealing with any party system it is necessary to distinguish between the policy concerns of the various parties, on the one hand, and the actual configuration of the party system itself, on the other. To put it another way, it is necessary to distinguish *what parties do* from *what parties are*.

The first aspect deals with the issues which parties choose to emphasize, the policy appeals which they enunciate, and the positions which they adopt on a day-to-day basis. As such, it is likely to be strongly conditioned by the various social and economic problems confronting the society which is to be governed. The second aspect relates much more to the historical identity of the parties, reflecting the conflicts and divides which prevailed when the party system was consolidated, and the traditions and beliefs which still continue to inform the various party strategies. It is this which determines whether we continue to find Christian parties, Socialist or Communist parties, Nationalist or Liberal parties, or whatever. The different historical roots of party systems create the essential diversity among contemporary European party systems, whereas the broad policy concerns of the parties tend to produce a more uniform pattern.

Once this distinction is accepted then it is clear that, considering *what parties do,* Ireland is quite close to the European pattern. But this is far from a recent phenomenon. Indeed, for much of the postwar period, and in particular from the 1960s onwards, the policy concerns of the Irish parties have reflected a range of options which is effectively identical to that of their European neighbours. As with virtually every other European country in the postwar period, Irish parties and governments have been primarily concerned with the problems of economic growth, employment and social welfare. As elsewhere, debates on economic policy have revolved around the extent to which growth and employment should be fostered by active public sector involvement or by giving a free hand to the market. As elsewhere, debates on welfare have concerned the proportion of state spending which should be devoted to social expenditure and, more generally, the extent to which the quest for social justice should be balanced against the disincentives to initiative produced by high taxation. As elsewhere, albeit in a somewhat belated fashion, Ireland has also tended to follow a cycle which is now familiar to most of our European neighbours, which saw immediate postwar austerity replaced by major increases in government expenditure and then, more recently, by a withdrawal of the state and a greater reliance on weakly regulated private markets. In these terms at least, Ireland has never been particularly distinctive, and in this sense the policies adopted by Irish parties have tended to be couched within a commonplace set of terms of reference, within which 1989 placed us no nearer to, but also no further from, the European pattern.

Once we look at *what parties are*, on the other hand, considering the identity of parties and the configuration of the party system as a whole, the distinctiveness of Ireland relative to its European neighbours is readily apparent. Two related factors are of particular importance here. These are, first, the particular weakness of the class left in Ireland and, second, the presence of a single party of the centre-right which is capable of governing alone.

The Left

All West European party systems, of whatever type, share one particular characteristic: they incorporate a cleavage between a party or parties representing the class left (the historical socialist and communist left and its offshoots), on the one hand, and a party or parties representing bourgeois interests, on the other. The parties of the left tended to be mobilized in the early part of the century when voting rights were extended to the working class and the propertyless, while the bourgeois parties reflect a tradition which predates the universal franchise. This is the one and only feature of party systems which is common for all countries in Western Europe - including Ireland. This apart, the picture is one of diversity

Thus in some systems the class left has been united behind one party, while in others it has been traditionally divided between a Socialist party and a Communist party (although in recent years support for the latter has tended to wane across Western Europe as a whole). In all countries, without exception, the bourgeois "bloc" is divided, whether between Christian and secular parties, or between traditionally urban and traditionally rural parties, or whatever. In some cases, as in the UK or West Germany, this division is relatively minor and the centre right tends to be dominated by one major party. In other cases, most notably in Scandinavia, the division is quite pronounced and the bourgeois bloc is represented by several parties. In these terms alone, Ireland is not exceptional. The class left has always won representation in politics, though its vote is now divided between the Labour Party and the Workers' Party. The bourgeois bloc has also always been divided between two or more parties, albeit along lines which are quite unlike those in other European countries.

What is particularly distinctive about the Irish case, however, and what is arguably the single most important feature separating it from the mainstream of European politics, is the relative balance between the class left and bourgeois blocs, for in Ireland electoral support for the left has always remained remarkably low. Whereas support for the class left in most West European party systems exceeds 40 per cent, and in some averages around 30 per cent, electoral support for the left in Ireland has rarely reached even 20 per cent. The exceptional nature of the Irish case in this regard is amply illustrated by the data shown in Table 11.1, which record the average vote for the class left in thirteen European countries in the two twenty-year periods since 1945.

Table 11.1: Voting for the class left in Europe, 1945-85

	1945-65 %	1966-85 %
Austria	46.7	49.9
Belgium	38.6	29.4
Denmark	46.0	45.8
Finland	47.2	43.7
France	41.5	46.5
Germany	34.6	42.8
Ireland	**11.8**	**13.5**
Italy	41.2	46.1
Netherlands	34.9	34.6
Norway	50.4	46.7
Sweden	51.1	50.0
Switzerland	29.5	26.2
United Kingdom	46.0	40.8

As is evident from Table 11.1, the class left in many of the Western European countries tends to win sufficient electoral support to make forming a government on its own a realistic possibility. This is certainly the case in Austria, Denmark, Finland, France, West Germany, Italy, Norway, Sweden and the UK. And while it is not the case in Belgium, the Netherlands and Switzerland, nonetheless the class left in these countries is effectively united behind one substantial party which often enjoys a plurality over any other individual party in the system. To be sure, in some of those European countries in which the class left does exceed 40 per cent, notably in Finland, France and Italy, it is also badly divided, and partisan friction between Socialists and Communists is often more pronounced than that which exists between the more moderate Socialist parties and their bourgeois opponents. In these circumstances, a united government of the left is sometimes an unrealistic option. In Italy, for example, the Socialists shy away from the prospect of forming a left alternative in conjunction with the Communists, and are oriented towards an alliance with the Christian Democratic centre. In France, recent moves by the Socialist Party also indicate a preference for an alliance with elements of the centre rather than with their traditional Communist bedfellows. Nonetheless, despite these sometimes fraught relations, the left in these countries does win sufficient electoral support to allow it to govern alone should circumstances allow for compatible strategies.

In Ireland, on the other hand, the class left remains in a small electoral minority, and has never had any realistic hope of forming a government of its own. Indeed, the left in Ireland can have had little hope of even enjoying a plurality over either of the two bourgeois parties, Fianna Fáil or Fine Gael. Nor was this imbalance altered in 1989. The Workers' Party gained its highest vote since it began to contest elections, but still has only five per cent of the poll. Labour gained its highest vote since 1981, but remains below ten per cent, and actually polled a lower share of the vote than was the case at any election (with one exception) in the 1950s, 1960s or 1970s. (The single exception was in 1957, when it polled just nine per cent.) Therefore even if one adds the votes of the Democratic Socialist Party (largely Jim Kemmy) and Tony Gregory to those of Labour and the Workers' Party, the total for the class left in 1989 comes to only 15.5 per cent of all votes cast, a figure which is still well below even the weakest equivalent in the other European party systems. In this sense at least, 1989 has not represented a change, and Ireland is now no closer to a "European" configuration than before.

The Role of Fianna Fáil
The second and related feature which marks Ireland off from the pattern elsewhere in Western Europe, a feature which may well have changed since the outcome of the 1989 election, is that there is simply no other country which has had a party that was equivalent to Fianna Fáil. This is not so much because of the distinct nature of Fianna Fáil's appeal, which is indeed quite unusual but which does at least find echoes in French Gaullism, and, to a lesser extent, in Italian Christian Democracy; rather, it has to do with Fianna Fáil's traditional capacity to govern alone as a centre-right party in a multi-party system.

There are two elements which are important here. First, there is the fact that, despite having a multi-party system and a reasonably proportional electoral formula, single-party government has proved both remarkably frequent and remarkably durable in the Irish case. Multi-partism usually tends to lead to coalition government in Europe; apart from Ireland, it is only really in Norway and Sweden (and now, more recently, in the nascent Spanish party system) that one finds a regular coincidence of multi-partism and single-party governments. In both Norway and Sweden, as in Ireland, government alternation has taken the form of changes between single-party governments and coalitions. Elsewhere in Western Europe, government alternation tends to take the form of changes between different coalitions. In this case, as with the Liberals in West Germany, one particular party may end up playing a pivotal role in two competing alliances.

To be sure, the Irish party system is not highly fragmented, at least by European standards, and for much of the 1960s and 1970s, electoral support was concentrated almost wholly on the three traditional parties. Nonetheless, given the presence of three and sometimes more competing parties, the sheer fact that one of these parties, Fianna Fáil, has frequently won sufficient support to form single-party administrations (often majority ones), has been one of the more striking characteristics of the Irish party system. Across the postwar period as a whole, for example, Fianna Fáil's overall duration in office as a single-party government falls only slightly short of the record of the British Conservatives, where the simple two-party system and the first-past-the-post electoral system set that system off from the European pattern and regularly ensure single party majority governments.

What is even more striking in the Irish case, however, and this is the second important element, is that this degree of single party success in a multi-party system has been achieved by a party of the centre-right. Elsewhere in Western Europe, parties of the right or centre-right which enter government in multi-party systems do so as partners in coalitions of varying complexity. This is also true in Norway and Sweden; when these countries do produce single-party governments, they produce governments of the left rather than of the right, a phenomenon which, given the demographic strength of the working class, is not surprising. In contrast, Ireland is simply the only country in Western Europe in which a multi-party system has regularly produced a party of the centre-right capable of governing alone.

It is here that 1989 may have wrought a major change in Ireland. With the decision by Fianna Fáil to break with tradition and enter a formal coalition with the Progressive Democrats, this key distinguishing feature of the Irish party system may have become a matter of historical record rather than a feature of contemporary reality. To the extent that Fianna Fáil remains "coalitionable" in the future, the pattern of competition in the Irish party system may well begin to reflect that to be found elsewhere in Europe. Ironically, as we shall now see, far from weakening

Fianna Fáil, this may well have the effect of cementing its hold on office even more securely than before.

POLITICAL ALIGNMENTS, COALITION FORMATION AND THE CEMENTING OF FIANNA FÁIL IN OFFICE

Contemporary Irish party politics can be seen as being aligned along two distinct dimensions of conflict. The first is common to all West European systems, and pits left against right in terms of both economic and social policy, ranging from the more left wing commitment to welfarism, state intervention and social justice, to the more right wing emphasis on fiscal rectitude, private enterprise, and the need to give a free hand to market forces. As things currently stand in Irish politics, the parties can be aligned on this dimension as shown in Figure 11.1:

Figure 11.1: Alignment of parties on left-right dimension (percentage of Dáil seats)

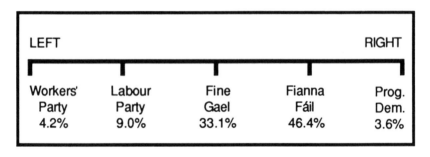

To a large extent, the party positions shown in Figure 11.1 seem uncontroversial. The leftist placement of the Workers' Party and the Labour Party is obvious, as is the rightist placement of the Progressive Democrats. The centrist positioning and ordering of Fianna Fáil and Fine Gael is somewhat more ambiguous. While Fianna Fáil has always enjoyed a position near the centre or centre-right of Irish politics (in its very early years, even near the centre-left), Fine Gael has traditionally acted as the voice of conservatism. In the 1960s and 1970s, however, not least as a result of its need to forge a common policy profile with the Labour Party, Fine Gael moved to the left of the political spectrum, and remained there until the late 1970s. Thereafter, wholly concerned with the need for fiscal austerity, the party again moved to the right, placing strains on its coalition arrangement with Labour which eventually forced a rupture between the two parties. Indeed, were this alignment to have been drawn in the early 1980s, a more rightward placement for Fine Gael would have been quite appropriate.

In the immediate future, however, and particularly as a result of the need both to distinguish itself from the Progressive Democrats and to forge an opposition to Fianna Fáil, it is likely that Fine Gael will revert to a more moderate social democratic position. This is certainly the approach which is being promoted by Alan Dukes, who has stated that Fine Gael "wanted to restore the dignity of every Irish man and woman and lead the way to a just society", and who has committed his party to "fight for the people who are represented by the Labour Party and the Workers' Party" (*Irish Times*, 13 July 1989). For this reason, Fine Gael can be considered as being likely to adopt a centrist position which is to the left of contemporary Fianna Fáil, criticized by Dukes as an "innately conservative" party. (Note that the expert survey on which the results of the previous chapter are based was conducted in the first half of 1989, before these developments had fully unfolded.)

The second dimension which divides the contemporary parties is more distinctively Irish, and involves the opposition between traditional religious and nationalist values, on the one hand, and a more secular, pluralist emphasis, on the other. Here, however, the alignment differs from that shown for the left-right dimension, since the Progressive Democrats are in a position closer to that of the small left parties. This second alignment is shown in Figure 11.2.

Figure 11.2: Alignment of parties on secular-traditional dimension (percentage of Dáil seats)

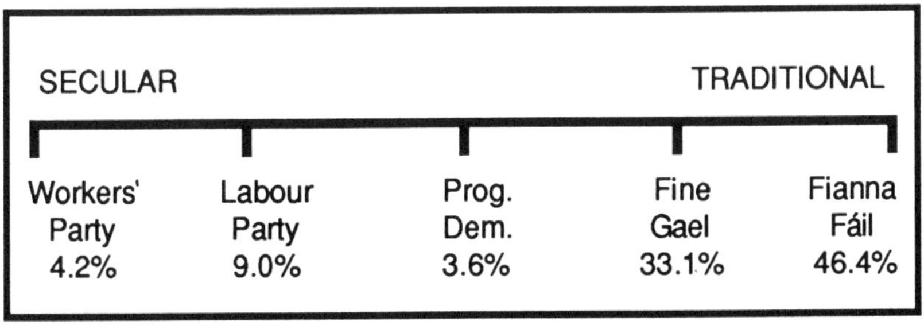

SECULAR				TRADITIONAL
Workers' Party 4.2%	Labour Party 9.0%	Prog. Dem. 3.6%	Fine Gael 33.1%	Fianna Fáil 46.4%

Here again, the relative placements of the parties are more or less self-evident. The secularist commitment of the Workers' Party is unequivocal, and despite its origins in Sinn Féin, it is also the most anti-nationalist and anti-irredentist of the present Dáil parties (with the exception of Jim

Kemmy's Democratic Socialist Party which, for present purposes, can be ignored). Labour, though less anti-nationalist than the Workers' Party, is also profoundly secularist. Both of these attributes are also clearly shared by many of the leaders - if not the supporters - of the Progressive Democrats, and are voiced more strongly than is the case in Fine Gael, which contains within its ranks many traditional nationalist politicians. The "extreme" position of Fianna Fáil is also uncontroversial; despite the party's recent endorsement of the Anglo-Irish Agreement, Fianna Fáil remains the most hardline irredentist party in the Dáil, and its traditionalist stance on the secularist/pluralist debate was made quite apparent during the recent referendums on divorce and abortion.

These, then, are the two principal dimensions of Irish political competition, and their relevance in this context derives from their implications for future patterns of coalition formation. Before looking at these potential patterns, however, it is necessary to spell out four crucial assumptions concerning the formation of coalition governments in general, and Irish coalition governments in particular.

The first assumption is that any coalition government is likely to require either an actual majority of Dáil seats or, at least, an effective majority over the other political parties. This latter qualification is necessary in that it has proved possible in the past for a minority government to survive in office with the support of non-aligned TDs. As the number of Independents has declined, however, and as those who do continue to win election are increasingly politicized, this type of external support is now not so easily secured. Moreover, while the majority requirement might be relaxed to the extent that divisions in the opposition can have the effect of ensuring that a minority government remains in office, it is also the case that potential Taoisigh do require a majority vote in the Dáil in order to take office in the first place. For this reason, a government which is to gain office and to endure is likely to require effective majority support if it is to be a *winning* coalition.

Second, any coalition which forms is not likely to include unnecessary parties. If two parties together can achieve a majority, they are not likely to try to persuade a third party to join the government; if three can form a majority, they are not likely to involve a fourth, and so on. In other words, and to adopt the terms used by students of coalition formation in Western European party systems, future coalitions are likely to be *minimal* winning.

Third, any coalition which forms is likely to have a policy rationale. In other words, those coalitions which are formed are likely to be minimal *connected* winning coalitions, in which the parties occupy contiguous positions along a relevant policy dimension. This is not to suggest that all the parties involved must have identical policies on all issues; rather, it is to say that there must be some shared basis of policy which will allow for a common programme of government. This was certainly the case for the first Fine Gael-Labour coalition in 1973, which formed in the wake of a convergence in the policies of both parties, and it is also the case for the present Fianna Fáil-PD alliance, in which the parties have forged a common programme on the basis of their shared commitment to reduce government spending.

Fourth, and perhaps most crucial of all, the shared policy concerns which will underline coalition formation are likely to be those which are relevant to the primary dimension of competition identified above, the left-right alignment. In other words, any coalitions which are formed are likely to be minimal connected winning coalitions *in terms of the left-right dimension*. Given the obvious centrality and importance of the issues involved in this dimension, it is safe to assume that these will be the issues which will occupy any government's day-to-day activities, and on which effective agreement must be reached. There is little point in having a common position on Northern Ireland and trying to live with conflicting positions on government spending, since it is the latter concern which will prove much more relevant to everyday policy-making. Rather, it would make much more sense to have a common position on government spending and to try to live with conflicting positions on Northern Ireland, since issues relating to the latter can be much more easily fudged. Hence the ability of Fianna Fáil and the Progressive Democrats to forge a common programme of government notwithstanding sharp divergences in their partisan views vis a vis both nationalist and secularist issues.

The importance of these assumptions must be underlined for, if they are valid, and if the balance of party forces in future Dála does not differ markedly from that in the 1989 Dáil, then they imply that the different theoretically possible minimal winning (if not always connected - see below) governments which can be formed in future Dála, assuming no drastic change in party strengths, are those which are listed below:

1. Fianna Fáil and Fine Gael (currently with 79.5 per cent of Dáil seats between them);
2. Fianna Fáil and Labour (54.4 per cent);
3. Fianna Fáil and the Workers' Party (50.6 per cent);
4. Fianna Fáil and the Progressive Democrats (50.0 per cent);
5. Fine Gael and Labour and the Workers' Party and the Progressive Democrats (50.0 per cent).

In addition, should Fine Gael gain further support, and/or should the left experience a continued increase, it might also be possible to conceive of one additional option:

6. Fine Gael and Labour and the Workers Party (currently 46.3 per cent).

Finally, should Fianna Fáil win back some of its lost support, or should it reabsorb the PDs, then a seventh option is also possible: a Fianna Fáil single-party majority government could again take office.

On the face of it, this range of options appears to represent a considerable expansion of the range of alternatives which prevailed prior to 1989. Then, and this was the case throughout the postwar period, the persistent refusal of Fianna Fáil to consider coalition had effectively reduced the options to just two - either Fianna Fáil would govern on its own (as in option 7), or a coalition of all other relevant Dáil parties would govern (as in option 5). Given that Fianna Fáil has now become coalitionable, however, and given that the Dáil itself has become more fragmented, it appears that there are at least seven logistically feasible options.

That said, the real question concerns the relative political feasibility of these options, for while all represent minimal winning governments, not all are likely to find a shared policy basis, and not all are likely to be connected in terms of the left-right space of competition.

The principal factor here is the Workers' Party, which is unashamedly on the left, and which proposes unequivocally radical policies. As things stand, it is virtually impossible to conceive of a coalition involving the Workers' Party and the right wing Progressive Democrats - or the Workers' Party and Fianna Fáil - which would have any degree of policy compatibility. For this reason, it is likely that options 3 and 5 can be ruled out. Moreover, regardless of how much Alan Dukes might attempt to compete to the left, it is also highly unlikely that a feasible and enduring coalition could emerge which would involve both Fine Gael and the Workers' Party.

Within this perspective it is clearly the presence of the Workers' Party in the Dáil which constitutes one of the most important new elements in Irish party politics in recent years. Previously, representation of the class left was monopolized by the relatively moderate Labour Party, whose willingness to come to terms with Fine Gael allowed a centre-left alternative to emerge with such effect in the 1970s. Now that the left is divided, however, even a renewed willingness by Labour to join with Fine Gael in some future coalition is unlikely to provide an adequate basis for a government. Other things being equal, and this would be true even if Fi-

218

anna Fáil does reabsorb the Progressive Democrats, any new non-Fianna Fáil coalition which might emerge is therefore likely to require the involvement of not only Fine Gael and Labour, as was the case in the 1970s, but also of the Workers' Party. And it goes almost without saying that such an option will clearly prove very difficult to realize. Hence, even if the left does gain in support, or if Fine Gael does experience an electoral resurgence, option 6 cannot really be considered to be politically feasible. To be sure, it might be possible to conceive of an alliance in which moderate Labour alone would be persuaded to join forces with Fine Gael and even with the Progressive Democrats, should the latter survive as an independent party and should the electoral balance be sufficient to give such an alliance a majority. But this would not only require a policy agreement between the Progressive Democrats and Labour, which would in itself be difficult, but would also demand that Labour ignore the possible damaging effect of such a decision on its continued capacity to compete with the Workers' Party for radical voters.

What must be emphasized here is that, in treating options 3, 5 and 6 as politically infeasible, I am assuming that the shared policy basis of future governments will relate only to the left-right dimension of competition. Should this not be the case, and should the secular-traditional dimension become heavily politicized, then a non-Fianna Fáil coalition involving not only Fine Gael, Labour and the Workers' Party, but also the Progressive Democrats, could not of course be ruled out. In and of itself, however, this is not likely to occur. The major issues involving church-state relations have already been fought out, and are unlikely to re-emerge unless there is some degree of all-party consensus. Nor is it likely that the Northern Ireland issue will emerge in the future with a sufficient degree of salience to force this dimension to the fore. Indeed, were it to do so, as might be the case in response to, say, a British declaration of intent to withdraw from Northern Ireland, the situation would be little short of dramatic, and the most probable southern response would be the creation of an all-party grand coalition, in which case the partisan considerations which are under discussion here would cease to be relevant.

In sum, if these options can be ruled out, then we are left with the following politically feasible choices: either single-party Fianna Fáil government; or a coalition between Fianna Fáil and Fine Gael, which was already mooted in the wake of the 1989 election; or a coalition of Fianna Fáil and Labour, which was talked about in the early 1980s; or a coalition of Fianna Fáil and the Progressive Democrats, which was the option actually chosen in the wake of 1989. And what is striking about all of these options is that *they each involve the participation of Fianna Fáil in government.*

Far from weakening the party's position - although this may be true at the electoral level - the shift in strategy of Fianna Fáil is therefore likely to secure its hold on office even more firmly than before. Given the fragmentation of the Dáil, and given in particular the extreme position of the Workers' Party, which more or less takes it out of contention as far as any government which is not of the left is concerned, Fianna Fáil *as a coalitionable party* now seems likely to remain in office indefinitely.

In terms of the logistics of government formation, therefore, Ireland can be seen to be moving away from a Scandinavian model, in which one dominant party competes with and alternates in government with a potential coalition of smaller parties. It appears to be moving towards an Italian model, in which the smaller partners in government shift in and out, but in which the core of all government coalitions - represented in Italy by the very powerful Christian Democrats - remains continually in office. This pattern is also increasingly evident in the Netherlands, where the powerful centre-right party, the Christian Democratic Appeal, has the option of coalescing to the right with the Liberals, or to the left, with the Labour Party, but now does not really seem to face the prospect of losing office itself.

Fianna Fáil has always enjoyed a unique status in West European politics as a party of the centre-right in a multi-party system which more often than not has held government on its own. This has also proved a key element in sustaining its own electoral support, for Fianna Fáil has always sold itself as the only party which could ensure single-party, and hence stable government. Now, in the wake of 1989, it has abandoned that unique position and has reluctantly accepted its role as just another political party. Ironically, however, it is the abandonment of this shibboleth which, in hindsight, may well prove to be its guarantor of office.

Given Fianna Fáil's electoral strength; given its key position in the centre of the political spectrum; given the internal divisions in the opposition; and now, most recently, given its coalitionable status, it is difficult to conceive of a situation in which it will be forced out of government. Fianna Fáil may now be just another party, but the other party it may now come to resemble most closely is the Italian Christian Democrats, whose own record in office is unmatched in postwar Western Europe. Fianna Fáil could hardly hope to find a better model.

APPENDIX
TABLES AND MAPS

Electorate, valid votes and first preferences at general election, 15 June 1989

Const	Elect-orate	Valid votes	Fianna Fáil	Fine Gael	Lab	PDs	WP	Grn Party	Sinn Féin	Oths
Carl-Kilk	79073	54531	23909	16796	9599	3068	1159			
Cav-Mon	75712	53107	26824	19505					4849	1929
Clare	63065	44308	24450	16114		3744				
Cork E	56251	40998	16247	14731	1377	1098	7414			131
Cork NC	63395	41247	13588	10789	7058	4203	3395		766	1448
Cork NW	41098	32427	14476	17691						260
Cork SC	78385	53617	21814	13690	6300	7206	4457			150
Cork SW	43548	32403	14361	16386		1259				397
Don NE	44450	27789	10916	8397					1091	7385
Don SW	47027	28866	15924	9653			2768			521
Dub C	65971	41332	18539	5296	2561	1418	1827	1529	2670	7492
Dub N	50765	33817	15719	8058	6076	1011		2953		
Dub NC	55827	38274	19765	9954	3326	690	2595			1944
Dub NE	53043	35216	16626	6708	2866	817	5968	1332		899
Dub NW	48492	29926	10592	4434	2462		8829	1327	1255	1027
Dub S	82936	54162	23472	15738	4134	4607	1440	4771		
Dub SC	72389	45092	17825	12013	3464	1314	6849	2264	1241	122
Dub SE	58063	32897	11450	9100	4014	2853	1816	3329		335
Dub SW	64995	39013	13083	3346	8734	4323	7166	1259	1018	84
Dub W	77766	48026	19177	11806	2063	2572	8218	1915	1398	877
Dun Lg	81169	52443	17107	17174	2987	4710	6729	2686	940	110
Gal E	42016	29129	17324	11393						412
Gal W	77178	49339	19645	11284	7727	8917	1555			211
Kerry N	46715	34087	15277	8692	10118					
Kerry S	43159	31318	16773	6477	6408	1458				202
Kildare	78724	50921	18498	15858	8767	2126	1520	1462		2690
Laois-Of	75120	52374	28452	16087	3030	4411				394
Lim E	66471	46341	15029	8520	1006	12618				9168
Lim W	43690	31411	18967	8484		3960				
Long-W	60786	42295	22942	15252		733				3368
Louth	63151	43612	18868	11773	8375	2146			2291	159
Mayo E	39470	27113	13892	13221						
Mayo W	39505	29301	15157	8957						5187
Meath	77127	50535	26404	15101	4625	1128	890		1002	1385
Roscmn	40447	30893	11705	12258						6930
Sligo-L	58358	42778	19720	15374		1255			1482	4947
Tipp N	41382	31634	16076	8264	7215					79
Tipp S	54734	39170	16857	11110	7080	1171				2952
Waterfd	60504	41320	14368	10911	7823	3489	4570			159
Wexford	70424	51312	23493	16918	9253	599	1049			
Wicklow	66429	42439	16161	11994	8541	2109	2049			1585
Dublin	711416	450198	183355	103627	42687	24315	51437	23365	8522	12890
Leinster	570834	388019	178727	119779	52190	16320	6667	1462	3293	9581
Munster	702397	500281	218283	151859	54385	40206	19836	0	766	14946
Con-Ul	464163	318315	151107	110042	7727	10172	4323	0	7422	27522
Ireland	2448810	1656813	731472	485307	156989	91013	82263	24827	20003	64939

Turnout and percentage votes at general election, 15 June 1989

Constituency	Turnout	Fianna Fáil	Fine Gael	Lab	PDs	WP	Grn Party	Sinn Féin	Oths
Carlow-Kilk	69.0	43.8	30.8	17.6	5.6	2.1			
Cavan-Mon	70.1	50.5	36.7					9.1	3.6
Clare	70.3	55.2	36.4		8.4				
Cork E	72.9	39.6	35.9	3.4	2.7	18.1			0.3
Cork NC	65.1	32.9	26.2	17.1	10.2	8.2		1.9	3.5
Cork NW	78.9	44.6	54.6						0.8
Cork SC	68.4	40.7	25.5	11.8	13.4	8.3			0.3
Cork SW	74.4	44.3	50.6		3.9				1.2
Donegal NE	62.5	39.3	30.2					3.9	26.6
Donegal SW	61.4	55.2	33.4			9.6			1.8
Dublin Central	62.7	44.9	12.8	6.2	3.4	4.4	3.7	6.5	18.1
Dublin N	66.6	46.5	23.8	18.0	3.0		8.7		
Dublin NC	68.6	51.6	26.0	8.7	1.8	6.8			5.1
Dublin NE	66.4	47.2	19.0	8.1	2.3	16.9	3.8		2.6
Dublin NW	61.7	35.4	14.8	8.2		29.5	4.4	4.2	3.4
Dublin S	65.3	43.3	29.1	7.6	8.5	2.7	8.8		
Dublin SC	62.3	39.5	26.6	7.7	2.9	15.2	5.0	2.8	0.3
Dublin SE	56.7	34.8	27.7	12.2	8.7	5.5	10.1		1.0
Dublin SW	60.0	33.5	8.6	22.4	11.1	18.4	3.2	2.6	0.2
Dublin W	61.8	39.9	24.6	4.3	5.4	17.1	4.0	2.9	1.8
Dun Laoghaire	64.6	32.6	32.7	5.7	9.0	12.8	5.1	1.8	0.2
Galway E	69.3	59.5	39.1						1.4
Galway W	63.9	39.8	22.9	15.7	18.1	3.2			0.4
Kerry N	73.0	44.8	25.5	29.7					
Kerry S	72.6	53.6	20.7	20.5	4.7				0.6
Kildare	64.7	36.3	31.1	17.2	4.2	3.0	2.9		5.3
Laois-Offaly	69.7	54.3	30.7	5.8	8.4				0.8
Limerick E	69.7	32.4	18.4	2.2	27.2				19.8
Limerick W	71.9	60.4	27.0		12.6				
Longford-Wm	69.6	54.2	36.1		1.7				8.0
Louth	69.1	43.3	27.0	19.2	4.9			5.3	0.4
Mayo E	68.7	51.2	48.8						
Mayo W	74.2	51.7	30.6						17.7
Meath	65.5	52.2	29.9	9.2	2.2	1.8		2.0	2.7
Roscommon	76.4	37.9	39.7						22.4
Sligo-Leitrim	73.3	46.1	35.9		2.9			3.5	11.6
Tipperary N	76.4	50.8	26.1	22.8					0.2
Tipperary S	71.6	43.0	28.4	18.1	3.0				7.5
Waterford	68.3	34.8	26.4	18.9	8.4	11.1			0.4
Wexford	72.9	45.8	33.0	18.0	1.2	2.0			
Wicklow	63.9	38.1	28.3	20.1	5.0	4.8			3.7
Dublin	63.3	40.7	23.0	9.5	5.4	11.4	5.2	1.9	2.9
Leinster	68.0	46.1	30.9	13.5	4.2	1.7	0.4	0.8	2.5
Munster	71.2	43.6	30.4	10.9	8.0	4.0		0.2	3.0
Conn-Ulster	68.6	47.5	34.6	2.4	3.2	1.4		2.3	8.6
Ireland	67.7	44.1	29.3	9.5	5.5	5.0	1.5	1.2	3.9

Seats and candidates at general election, 15 June 1989

	Total	FF	FG	Lab	PD	WP	Grns	SF	Oth	LDs
Carlow-Kilk	5- 9	2-3	2-3	1-1	1	1				1
Cavan-Mon	5-10	3-3	2-3					1	3	3
Clare	4- 9	2-4	2-2		3					2
Cork E	4- 8	2-2	1-2	1	1	1-1			1	3
Cork NC	5-14	2-4	1-2	1-1	1-1	1		1	4	6
Cork NW	3- 5	1-2	2-2						1	1
Cork SC	5-11	2-4	1-2	1-1	1-2	1			1	2
Cork SW	3- 7	1-2	2-2		1				2	3
Donegal NE	3- 7	1-2	1-2					1	1-2	3
Donegal SW	3- 6	2-2	1-2			1			1	1
Dublin Cen	5-13	3-3	1-1	2	1	1	1	2	1-2	5
Dublin N	3- 8	1-3	1-2	1-1	1			1		2
Dublin NC	4-12	3-3	1-2	2	1		1		3	5
Dublin NE	4-12	2-3	1-2	2	1	1-1	1		2	5
Dublin NW	4-11	2-2	1-2	1		1-2	1	1	2	4
Dublin S	5-10	2-3	2-3	1	1	1	1-1			2
Dublin SC	5-12	2-3	2-2	2	1	1-1	1	1	1	4
Dublin SE	4-11	1-3	2-2	1-1	1	1	1		2	3
Dublin SW	4-10	1-2	2	1-1	1-1	1-1	1	1	1	4
Dublin W	5-13	2-3	2-2	1	1	1-1	1	2	2	5
Dun Laog	5-13	2-3	2-3	2	1	1-1	1	1	1	4
Galway E	3- 6	2-3	1-2						1	1
Galway W	5-10	2-3	1-2	1-1	1-1	1			2	3
Kerry N	3- 5	1-3	1-1	1-1						0
Kerry S	3- 6	2-2	1	1-1	1				1	2
Kildare	5-10	2-3	2-2	1-1	1	1	1		1	3
Laois-Offaly	5-10	3-4	2-3	1	1				1	2
Limerick E	5- 9	1-3	1-2	1	2-2				1-1	1
Limerick W	3- 4	2-2	1-1		1					0
Longford-Wm	4- 9	2-3	2-3		1				2	2
Louth	4-10	2-3	1-3	1-1	1			1	1	4
Mayo E	3- 4	2-2	1-2							0
Mayo W	3- 6	2-3	1-2						1	0
Meath	5-14	3-4	2-2	1	2	2		1	2	7
Roscommon	3- 6	1-2	1-2						1-2	1
Sligo-Leitrim	4- 8	2-3	2-2		1			1	2	2
Tipperary N	3- 6	2-2	1-2	1					1	2
Tipperary S	4- 9*	1-2	1-2	1-1	1				1-3*	3
Waterford	4- 9	2-3	1-2	1-1	1	1			1	2
Wexford	5-10	2-4	2-3	1-1	1	1				2
Wicklow	4- 9	2-2	1-2	1-1	1	1			2	4
Dublin	48-125	21-31	15-23	3-16	1-10	6-11	1-10	8	1-16	43
Leinster	37- 81	18-26	14-21	5- 7	9	6	1	2	9	25
Munster	49-102	21-35	15-23	6- 9	4-14	1- 4		1	2-16	27
Conn-Ulster	32- 63	17-23	11-19	1- 1	1- 2	2		3	2-13	14
Ireland	166-371	77-115	55-86	15-33	6-35	7-23	1-11	14	5-54	109

The left-hand figure in each column is the number of seats, the right-hand figure the number of candidates. (* denotes Ceann Comhairle, independent Seán Treacy returned automatically in Tipperary South.)

The right-hand column of the table shows lost deposits. The breakdown by party was: Fianna Fáil 3; Fine Gael 7; Labour 8; PDs 20; Workers' Party 9; Greens 5; Sinn Féin 12; Others 45; total 109.

Appendix

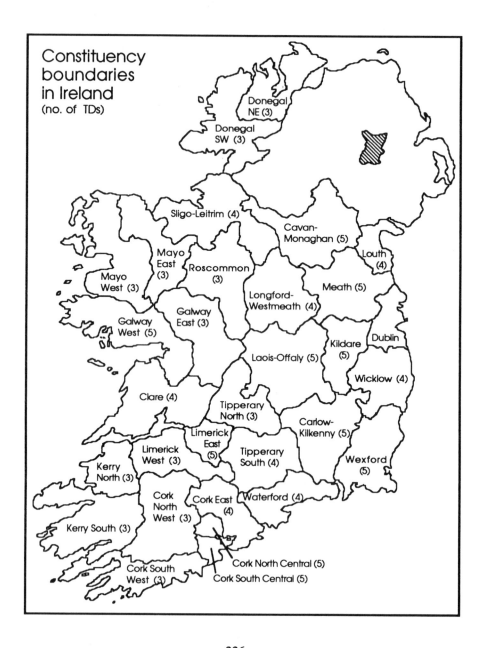

Constituency
boundaries
in Ireland
(no. of TDs)

226

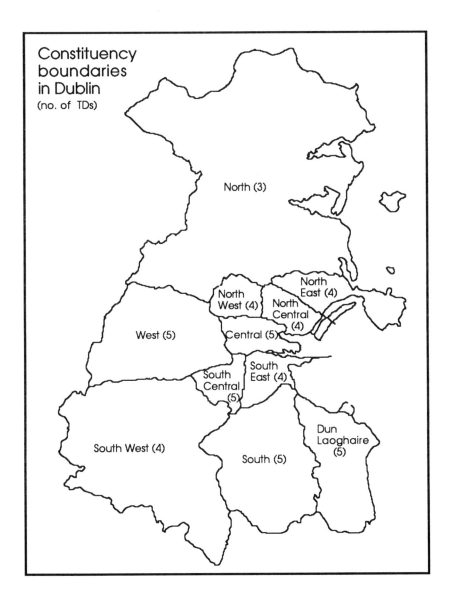

Constituency
boundaries
in Dublin
(no. of TDs)

North (3)

North
West (4)

North
East (4)

North
Central
(4)

West (5)

Central (5)

South
East (4)

South
Central
(5)

South West (4)

South (5)

Dun
Laoghaire
(5)

NOTES ON CONTRIBUTORS

Audrey Arkins is a lecturer in the Department of Political Science and Sociology, University College, Galway. Her research interests include parliamentary reform, political communications and the mass media. She has published on Irish parliamentary select committees and legislative-executive relations in Ireland.

John Coakley, Lecturer in Politics at the University of Limerick, is the author of a number of articles and chapters in books in the area of Irish and European politics and on the comparative study of nationalist movements.

Brian Farrell is Professor of Politics in University College Dublin, and is the author of *Chairman or Chief? The Role of the Taoiseach in Irish Government* (Gill and Macmillan, 1971) and *Seán Lemass* (Gill and Macmillan, 1984).

David M. Farrell lectures on the institutions of the European Community at the School of European Studies, University of Wales College of Cardiff. He is currently researching on the socioeconomic background and work patterns of MEPs.

Michael Gallagher is a lecturer in the Department of Political Science at Trinity College Dublin. He is author of *The Irish Labour Party in Transition* (1982) and *Political Parties in the Republic of Ireland* (1985), and co-editor of *Candidate Selection in Comparative Perspective: the secret garden of politics* (1988). His current research interests include comparative electoral systems.

Brian Girvin is lecturer in history in the Department of Modern History, University College, Cork. His current research interests include political culture in comparative context, conservative politics since 1890, and the politics of industrial development. Recent publications include the edited volume *The Transformation of Contemporary Conservatism* (Sage, 1988) and *Between Two Worlds: Politics and Economy in Independent Ireland.*

Patrick Keatinge is an Associate Professor in Political Science in Trinity College Dublin. His publications include *A Singular Stance: Irish neutrality in the 1980s,* and articles on Ireland's involvement in European Political Cooperation and on other aspects of Irish foreign policy.

Michael Laver, Professor of Political Science and Sociology at University College Galway, has taught at a range of universities in Europe and America. He is author of several books on various aspects of politics, the most recent of which are *Social Choice and Public Policy* (Oxford, Blackwell) and *Multiparty Government* (forthcoming, Oxford University Press).

Peter Mair is a Senior Lecturer in the Department of Government at the University of Manchester. He is author of *The Changing Irish Party System* (1987), and co-author of *Identity, Competition and Electoral Availability* (1990). He is editor of a number of volumes including, most recently, *Understanding Party System Change* (1989) and *The West European Party System* (1990). He is currently engaged in a cross-national project gathering data on party organisational change.

Michael Marsh is a Senior Lecturer in Political Science at Trinity College, Dublin and was coeditor of *Candidate Selection in Comparative Perspective: the secret garden of politics* (1988). He is the author of a number of articles and book chapters on electoral behaviour and contributed to the Irish Independent during the last two general elections.

Tony Parker is lecturer in Geography and Director of the Centre for Retail Studies in University College Dublin. He is joint editor of *Ireland: a Contemporary Geographical Perspective* (Routledge, 1989), and author of a number of articles on electoral geography and ecological analyses.

Richard Sinnott is Lecturer in Politics in University College Dublin, where he is also Director of the Centre for European Economic and Public Affairs. He has written extensively on Irish elections and Irish public affairs.

For information on the authors of Chapter 3, see the respective contributions.

How Ireland Voted 1987
edited by
Michael Laver, Peter Mair and Richard Sinnott

The previous volume in this series, *How Ireland Voted 1987* is the definitive account of the 1987 election

CONTENTS

1. The road to 1987 — *Tom Garvin*
2. The campaign — *Brian Girvin*
3. Policy competition — *Peter Mair*
4. Campaign strategies: the selling of the parties — *David Farrell*
5. The outcome — *Michael Gallagher*
6. Patterns of party support — *Michael Laver*, *Michael Marsh*, *Richard Sinnott*

7. The road from 1987; government formation and institutional inertia — *Brian Farrell*
8. The election in context; historical and European perspectives — *John Coakley*

Appendix: Results and maps

How Ireland Voted 1987 is available at a post-paid rate of £7.50 (outside Europe, £8.50 surface, £10 airmail). Orders should be sent to:

**How Ireland Voted 1987
Social Sciences Research Centre,
University College Galway, Ireland.**